William I. Paulding

A Book of Vagaries

Comprising the New mirror for travellers and other whim-whams

William I. Paulding

A Book of Vagaries
Comprising the New mirror for travellers and other whim-whams

ISBN/EAN: 9783743355149

Manufactured in Europe, USA, Canada, Australia, Japa

Cover: Foto ©Andreas Hilbeck / pixelio.de

Manufactured and distributed by brebook publishing software (www.brebook.com)

William I. Paulding

A Book of Vagaries

A BOOK OF VAGARIES.

A

BOOK OF VAGARIES;

COMPRISING

THE NEW MIRROR FOR TRAVELLERS

AND OTHER

WHIM-WHAMS:

BEING SELECTIONS FROM THE PAPERS OF

A RETIRED COMMON-COUNCILMAN,

EREWHILE KNOWN AS

LAUNCELOT LANGSTAFF,

AND, IN THE PUBLIC RECORDS,

AS

JAMES K. PAULDING.

EDITED BY WILLIAM I. PAULDING.

NEW YORK:
CHARLES SCRIBNER AND COMPANY.
1868.

Entered, according to Act of Congress, in the year 1867, by

WILLIAM I. PAULDING,

In the Clerk's Office of the District Court of the United States for the Southern District of New York.

CAMBRIDGE:
STEREOTYPED AND PRINTED BY JOHN WILSON AND SON.

INTRODUCTION.

THE title which I have given to this volume of the works of James K. Paulding was not devised for the sake of any bizarre effect it might be supposed to have, but because it seemed to me really to suggest the character of the contents. Even "The New Mirror for Travellers", which occupies so much space in it, is rather a series of satirical observations varied with brief essays or stories than a connected work.

Mr. Paulding, even when he started out with some special object in view, was apt to follow the lead of his fancy as it warmed, and to set down just what popped into his head. If this rambling and discursive habit has its great disadvantages, it is not without a certain compensation, in the assurance which it gives to the reader that he is not entrapped into a piece of sentiment, or led up, like a partridge by cautiously-strewed grains of buckwheat, into a hair-noose of a jest.

Old birds of readers, familiar with the arts of writing men, will call to mind many a seed that they have seen dropped on the way, to be harvested by and by with as much certainty as a rye crop. Why, some men dibble 'em in, like cabbage-plants; and one knows that they will, in due time, weather and worms permitting, blow out into full head.

A skittish man abhors these studied surprises. But he

may plunge unsuspiciously into Mr. Paulding's fields and pastures. If a flower springs in his path, Nature put it there; and if he pricks his finger with a bramble while he stretches forth his hand to gather a blossom, *à la bonne heure!*, he must not complain, for, be sure, it will turn out a black-cap or a wild raspberry, and it was in the very constitution of things that they should be associated.

It certainly is a charm, if it be not a merit, in Mr. Paulding's writings, that they are absolutely unvarnished. If an exquisite thought came from him, "*totus, teres, atque rotundus*", we may be assured that it had not been rolled about and polished assiduously, like a jeweller's work: — rather it was the natural gem of the mine. Indeed, as he prattles away in his careless fashion, we are sometimes reminded of the girl in the fairy-tale, who dropped pearls from her mouth in her ordinary talk.

Above all, he was not of the men that say to themselves: — Go to; now let us be funny, — and who fetch up their tears with a rotary pump, that one can hear creak as they work at it. No: his humor flitted about, like the bobolink athwart the breeze, now on this tack now on that as the fancy took him, but with no more calculation about its effect upon men than the bird makes when he gushes blithely into song; while there was an ever-living spring of sentiment within him, stealing away, for the most part, unseen, like the natural overflow amid the grass, and only once in a while gleaming in the sunlight, because it happened to cross the sunlight's path.

The notion of attributing the papers to "a retired Common-councilman" was suggested by the title-page of "Chronicles of the City of Gotham": and, as it seemed to me not inappropriate, I have transferred the dedication of that volume to this. "The whim-whams and opinions of Launcelot Langstaff, Esq., and others", of the first series of "Salmagundi", were reduced in the second to those of Launcelot **Langstaff**, Esq., alone. As we have in this volume more of the idiosyncrasies of that gentleman, I thought that his name might fairly appear upon the title-page.

The engraving of Mr. Paulding in this volume is after a medallion executed by J. G. Chapman, about the year 1843. He was then sixty-five years of age; and his appearance did not materially change till within two or three years of his death, when he ceased to shave.

Mr. Paulding had a detestation for watering-places, and a good deal of "The New Mirror for Travellers", published in 1828., is devoted to gibes against Saratoga and Ballston. In "Letters from the South", he has a shy at such resorts. "In all the constituents of a fashionable watering-place, Berkeley maintains a most respectable rank, inasmuch as it affords as great a variety of character, as many gay equipages and gay people, and almost as great a lack of amusement, as Ballston or Long Branch." Again, in "A Sketch of Old England", referring to Barmouth in Wales, frequented for the purpose of bathing, he grimly says:—"The town is mean, incommodious, and difficult of access, presenting, on the whole, nearly all the inconveniences which form the principal attraction of watering-places."

Any one in possession of a print of a street scene of about this period will be amused with Mr. Paulding's comments on the costume of the day, and especially on the head-gear of the ladies. In "The New-York Mirror" for January 15th, 1831., there is an engraving of The Battery, "done in a style that cannot fail, we think, of giving universal satisfaction." There are front, rear, and profile, views of bonnets in it, that are amazing.

I set down here, as matter of antiquarian interest, what little I have been able to gather about the taverns and eating-houses of New York and Albany, incidentally alluded to in the production. For this information, (and some other), I am under obligation to Mr. James H. Hackett and Mr. Gulian C. Verplanck.

From the first-mentioned gentleman I have the following, in reference to matters on page 21:—

"The Bank Coffee House locality was South-East corner of Pine and William streets. It was kept by William Niblo, as I can remember distinctly, from 1816 to 1820; when I departed New York City, and went to and settled in Utica as a merchant. In 1825, when I had returned as such and resumed a residence in New York, (23 Broadway), and first became personally known to your late father, who was a neighbor, Niblo — tho' still keeping the Bank Coffee House — had been measurably surpassed in popularity, as a public caterer for nice palates, by one Sykes, (an Englishman and an adventurer), who had become more famous for his gastronomic preparations, and kept a public house, also in William street, — but, nearly opposite the front of the present Delmonico Building, corner of Beaver street.

"Niblo soon thereafter partially withdrew from competition with Sykes, and, refitting some old family-mansion, not far from where is now the intersection of 61st street by the Third Avenue, and ornamenting its few surrounding acres, called the premises, 'Kensington House'; and also got up and ran, at certain hours of summer days, between that and the Bank Coffee House, an omnibus, — the first vehicle of the kind which had then been seen in New York.

"Sykes eventually became a bankrupt, and was notorious for his profligacy, and for his large and many debts and defalcations; and, finally, 'twas said of him, as of the poor old Frenchman in the tale of *Monsieur Tonson*, after having been so long teased by the wag, Tom King, —

'Away he ran and ne'er was heard of more.'"

The Turtle Club, mentioned on page 22, met at Hoboken,

and included most of the wealthy gourmands of **New York**. It was more notorious for its high feeding than for its wit.

I get, from Mr. Verplanck, the ensuing particulars in reference to two houses of entertainment specified on page 167.

"Cruttenden's and Rockwell's, at Albany, are of an historical record and connected with the political history of the State.

"Rockwell's was a large double house of yellow brick, built for the residence of some of the old dignitaries of Albany, but raised some stories and enlarged. It stood, and I think still stands, though converted into shops, &c., in Pearl street, something North of State street, on the East side of the way. It was for years the winter resort of many of the chief men of the old Democratic party. There was always to be found the eloquent Peter R. Livingston, Walter Bowne, afterwards Mayor, long in the State Senate, and others of name.

"Cruttenden's was of still more note, though not of so marked a political character. It is still standing, though destined to be soon removed, as it is on the ground ceded for the new capitol. It stands, originally one only, subsequently the *two* last houses on the N. corner facing the present park in front of the Capitol, being on the East side.

"It was long famous for its landlord and its guests. *He* was a man of infinite jest, and besides kept the best table in Albany or indeed in the country. The house was resorted to by Elisha Williams and all the great lawyers, Rudolph Bunner, and other men of pleasantry. It was the scene of sundry droll incidents which told on public opinion through the State."

Mr. Verplanck remarks, further :— "A full note on these two houses, especially Cruttenden's, would be of much interest." This I regret that I am unable to furnish.

A few foot-notes, included in brackets, have been added to this edition of The New Mirror for Travellers.

The compositions which form the residue of the volume are, (with the exception of the last two), selected from a number of the same whimsical cast contributed by Mr. Paulding to The New-York Mirror during the years 1831 and 1832. They may be called representative papers; for he wrote a great variety of the sort, which he strewed about at random everywhere during his life. They are representative also in the fact that, odd as may be the superstructure, the foundation is always laid in that strong and manly common-sense which was one of his principal characteristics.

"Jonathan's Visit to the Celestial Empire" had a certain basis in fact — what, I have been unable to ascertain, definitively. It is not unlikely that he heard the story when Secretary of the Navy Board, at Washington. The ginseng was a traditional part of the yarn. He has, probably through inadvertence, antedated it a little. Some very small vessels undoubtedly made the voyage to the East Indies, late in the eighteenth century. For example: — The brig Rose, of 82 tons, belonging to E. H. Derby, Nathaniel Silsbee commander, arrived at Salem from the East Indies in 1788. — The sloop Union, of 96 tons, John Boit master, sailed from Newport, August 29. 1794, for Canton, and arrived in Boston, July 11. 1796.

"The History of Uncle Sam and his Boys", published February 19. 1831, has in view the various schemes agitated from time to time in Congress for a distribution among the States, sometimes of the public lands, sometimes of the surplus public revenue. In a modified form, the measure was eventually carried through, in 1836. As early as January 30, 1830, Mr. Paulding had written to Mr. Irving, then Secretary to the American legation at the Court of St. James : —

"If you read the American papers, you will see that Congress is reckoning its chickens before they are hatched, and dividing a surplus revenue before they are out of debt. I am in hopes something will turn up to oblige them to borrow money and run in debt again, for I had rather see this, than quarreling about the division of Uncle Sam's estate before he is dead. How all this wretched squabbling about the spoils of the General Government will end I know not, but it is evident to me that parties no longer involve principles;" &c.

"The History of Uncle Sam and his Womankind", published July 7. 1832 — (as nearly on the National Anniversary as was possible in a weekly paper) — in like manner refers to the agitation which resulted, November 24, 1832, in the notorious nullification "ordinance" of South Carolina.

It were well could these two papers pass into the popular mind. Mayhap, they are worthy the study of them that claim the standing of American statesmen. On the surface mere jokes of the day, they play over most of our sectional characteristics with an acuteness, and lay finger on certain all-important national questions with a strength, that give them historical and daily value. They are imbued throughout with that broad spirit of nationality which was the very life of his mind, but which is as yet so rare among our leading men.

Mr. Paulding was fond of writing apologues and fables, after the fashion of the East. In "Haschbasch, the Pearl-diver", he has effected a very ludicrous combination of Oriental scenery with thoroughly American idea.

"Killing, No Murder" is one of the many protests he uttered against that almost universal American failing, the desire of making as much show on one thousand dollars a year as can be made upon an income of fifty.

"Six Weeks in the Moon" is Swiftian for vigor. Not so frightful and ghastly as the account of "the grand academy of Lagado", which it in a measure recalls, it is perhaps equally searching. Of the same essential spirit, the work of the later author is rendered more agreeable by the more genial character of the man. The idea is not a new one, nor was it for the first time worked by him in this paper. "Selections from the Journal of a late Traveller to the Moon" appeared in The New-York Mirror for June 7, 1834. As often happened with him, he seems to have forgotten this entirely. In the United States Review for June, 1853, he repeated the same general course of thought in a somewhat different shape. I give the article as an illustration — (one, among many that might be produced) — of how little his "natural force" was "abated" by reason of lengthened years. He was then close on to seventy-five.

As an example of his sadder vagaries, I have closed the volume with a little essay, which formed originally one of the "Letters from the South", and to which I have given the title — "A Mood of Nature and of Man." It is redolent of that old English "humour" which the literature of no other race has approached; and authorizes me, as I think, to make the remark, (which at least appears to me impartial), that he has done many things well, and some in a manner that has scarcely been surpassed.

W. I. P.

CONTENTS.

	PAGE
Epistle Dedicatory, and Petition	3
Preface to The New Mirror for Travellers	11
The New Mirror for Travellers	17
The Nymph of the Mountain	287
Jonathan's Visit to the Celestial Empire	303
The History of Uncle Sam and his Boys	325
The History of Uncle Sam and his Womankind	341
Haschbasch, the Pearl-diver	363
Killing, no Murder	381
Six Weeks in the Moon	395
A Mood of Nature and of Man	413

EPISTLE DEDICATORY

AND

PETITION.

TO THE RIGHT WORSHIPFUL THE

MAYOR, ALDERMEN, AND COMMON COUNCIL

OF THE

ANCIENT CITY OF GOTHAM.

RIGHT WORSHIPFUL:

It hath been from time immemorial a subject of contention among the learned, whether Osiris, Confucius, Zoroaster, Solon, Lycurgus, Draco, Numa Pompilius, Mahomet, Peter the Great, Napoleon Bonaparte, Jeremy Bentham, or the author of the New Charter of Gotham, was, or is, the greatest law-giver. Without diving into the abstruse profundity of this knotty question, I myself am of opinion that it may be easily settled, by putting them all out of sight at once, as bearing no sort of comparison, in the art of concocting numerous laws and multifarious enactments, with your Honours of the Common Council. What constitutes greatness, but bulk, numbers, and dimensions? And who, of all legislators in every age, can compare with, or, as the vulgar say, hold a candle to, your Honours, in the length, breadth, profundity, and multiplicity of your laws? I am credibly informed, and do believe,—(nay, hath not my former participation in your counsels taught me?) — that, provided all the enactments of your Honourable Body (which, like the king, never dieth) were carefully collected in good substantial volumes, bound in calf, they would build another tower of Babel, and cause a second confusion of tongues, to the utter discomfiture and dispersion of the worthy citizens of Gotham.

Another question, moreover, hath from time to time sorely puzzled the learned, to wit, whether offences do not increase in number exactly in proportion to the multiplication of the laws. I myself, with due submission, am inclined to believe that such is actually the case; seeing all experience teaches us that there is a pestilent itching in the blood towards the practice of disobedience. To forbid children to go out of their bounds is, peradventure, the most powerful incitement to wandering; and to caution them against dangers is the infallible way of making them run their heads into them. Even so with men and women, who are morally certain to be put in mind of the pleasure of transgressing, by the anticipation of punishment. They actually persuade themselves there must be something vastly delectable in the offence, to make it necessary to denounce such severe penalties against it. I do modestly assure your Honours that, no longer ago than yesterday, I saw a child burn its fingers with paper, for no other reason, that I could perceive, than because the mother had threatened to punish it if it did so. As a further illustration, I will, with your Honours' permission, instance the example of a decent, well-behaved, and indeed exemplary horse I once knew, who had been for years accustomed to pasture at will, in a common appertaining to our township, open on all sides to his excursions. Beyond this he was never known to stray one step. But, in process of time, our little corporation, impelled by the ever-busy spirit of improvement, unluckily passed a law for enclosing this common; and, from that fatal era, this horse seemed possessed with an invincible and wicked propensity to trespass and go astray. From being an example to all the animals of the town, he degenerated into all sorts of irregularities; was pounded three or four times a week; thrashed out of enclosures; and cudgelled from barn-yards. Finally, as I believe, he wilfully drowned himself in a swamp, where he never before dreamed of going. Having thus illustrated my position by the example of both reason and instinct, I will proceed to the prime objects of this, my humble Epistle Dedicatory and Petition.

And firstly, my request is, that although, as I cannot deny, there is a great plenty, not to say superabundance of most valuable works, such as tracts, tales, romances, improved grammars, spelling-books, class-books, and all that sort of thing, coming out every hour of the day; yet is there a certain class of works, to wit, those that nobody buys or reads, that lack legislative encouragement and protection. Besides, your Honours, even if this were not the case, your Honours must be fully aware that there are certain good things of which the world cannot have too many, such as laws, colleges, paper dollars and paper books. If one law is not sufficient, the spirit of the age requires another exactly opposite in its provisions, so that, approaching as they do both before and behind, it is next to impossible for a criminal to escape. So, if there is not sufficient liberality in the public, or sufficient love of learned lore, to afford encouragement to one university, the only remedy for such sore evils is to establish another. Between two stools we must certainly fall to the earth, which every body knows is the most solid foundation after all for learning. In respect to paper-money, it is quite a sufficient indication of the necessity of having plenty of that invaluable commodity, to instance the avidity of every body for more. Besides, if it were not for the establishment of new banks, in a little while we should have no paper-money at all, seeing the number of old ones that become bankrupt every day. The wear and tear of these useful manufactories of paper is such as to require perpetual repairs. So with books: being, for the most part, forgot in a few weeks, in consequence of the perpetual supplies of novelty, it necessarily becomes proper to apply new stimulants to the spirit of the age and development of the human mind. The May-flies, that live but for a day, are as the sands of the sea in number, and are succeeded, hour after hour, by new generations of insects, who glitter in the noontide sun, and perish in the first dews of the evening.

Now, forasmuch as this multiplication and quick succession of new books is calculated to interfere with, and circumscribe the circulation of, this my work, which I now lay at the feet of your Honours' munificence, I humbly beseech your Honours to afford it your special protection, in the manner and form following, to wit:

First. That you will cause your Finance-Committee to subscribe for a thousand, or (not to be particular) two thousand, copies, and direct a warrant to be issued in favour of your petitioner for the amount. Professing himself a reasonable man, he hereby relinquishes all right of demanding that your Honours shall read them.

Secondly. That your Honours will refer the historical piece, entitled and called, "Jonathan's Visit to the Celestial Empire," in this my book, to the Water-Committee, with directions to report definitively a favourable criticism on its merits, sometime in the course of the present century, or as soon thereafter as practicable.

Thirdly. That your Honours will be pleased to refer the memoir of Haschbash, the pearl-diver, unto the Committee on Applications for office, with peremptory directions to nominate your petitioner to some good fat place, with a liberal salary and nothing to do. Your humble petitioner, being by profession an anti-busybody, will engage to neglect his duties equally with any man living, except, perhaps, certain of the Street-Inspectors.

Fourthly. That your munificent, patriotic, and law-giving Honours, will in like manner refer the elaborate itinerary, styled, "THE NEW MIRROR FOR TRAVELLERS.", to a special Committee of Silence, with instructions to say nothing on the subject. If a sufficient number of silent members cannot be detected in your Honourable Body, your Honours will find plenty in Congress.

Fifthly. That your Honourable Body will graciously instruct the Committee of Arrangements for the fourth of July and other masticatory celebrations, not to forget to invite your petitioner to the aforesaid jolly anniversaries, as hath been the case ever since he had the misfortune to empty a bottle of champagne into the right worshipful pocket of the late worthy and lamented Alderman Quackenbush, of immortal memory.

Sixthly. That your munificent Honours, being the patrons of literature, the fine arts, and the like, will, as an honourable testimony to the benefits this his work is likely to shower on the present age and on posterity, confer immortality on your humble petitioner, by voting him the freedom of the city in a gold box, taking especial care that it be not too large to be converted into a convenient snuffbox.

Lastly. That your munificent Honours will take compassion on all idle and useless citizens and strangers, who, having (like your petitioner) nothing to do, are very apt to get tired; and, in due time, cause to be constructed a suitable number of cosy seats on the Battery, well lined and stuffed, with seemly high backs, for our special and exclusive accommodation. If your illustrious and industrious Honours only knew how idle your petitioner is, and what a horror he hath of a hard bench without a back, you would shed tears at beholding him luxuriating in agony on the Battery in the beautiful summer twilight. Many a worthy citizen, as he verily believes, hath been driven to the most enormous excesses of tippling and debauchery, by the utter impossibility of obtaining a moment's ease and relaxation upon those instruments of torture, miscalled benches, and, in a paroxysm of impatience, cast himself utterly away upon the quicksands of Castle Garden or the Battery Hotel.

And your petitioner shall ever vote, &c.

THE
NEW MIRROR FOR TRAVELLERS;

AND

GUIDE TO THE SPRINGS.

"ADIEU LA BOUTIQUE!"

PREFACE

TO

THE NEW MIRROR FOR TRAVELLERS.

EVER since the invention of steam-engines, steamboats, steam-carriages, Liverpool packets, railroads, and other delightful facilities for travelling, the march of the human body has kept pace with the march of the human mind, so that it is now a moot point which gets on the faster. If the body moves at the rate of fifteen miles an hour, the mind advances in an equal pace, and children of sixteen are in a fair way to become wiser than their grandfathers. While the grown-up gentleman goes to Albany in twelve hours, and comes back in forty-eight with a charter in his pocket, the aspiring school-boy smatters a language, or conquers a science, by the aid of those vast improvements in the "*machinery*" of the mind, which have immortalized the age. In fact, there seems to be a race between matter and mind, and there is no telling which will come out first in the end.

Legislators and philosophers may flatter themselves as they will, but they have little influence in shaping this world. The inventors of paper-money, cotton-machinery, steam-engines, and steam-boats, have caused a greater revolution in the habits, opinions and morals of mankind, than all the systems of philosophy, aided by all the efforts of legislation. Machinery and steam-engines have had more influence on the Christian world than Locke's metaphysics, Napoleon's code, or Jeremy Bentham's codification; and we have heard a great advocate for domestic manufactures predict, that the time was not far distant when men and women and children would be of no use but to construct and attend upon machinery — when spinning-jennies would become members of Congress, and the United States be governed by a steam-engine of a hundred and twenty horse power. We confess ourselves not quite so sanguine, but will go so far as to say, that we believe the time may come when a long speech will be spun out of a bale of cotton by a spinning-jenny; a president of the United States be made by a combination of machinery; and Mynheer Maelzel be beaten at chess by his own automaton.

Without diving deeper into such speculations, or tracing the effects of these vast improvements in the condition of mankind, who will soon have nothing to do but tend upon machinery, we shall content ourselves with observing that the wonderful facilities for locomotion furnished by modern ingenuity have increased the number of travellers to such a degree, that they now constitute a large portion of the human family. All ages and sexes are to be found on the wing, in perpetual motion from place to place. Little babies are seen crying their way in steam-boats, whose cabins are like so many nurseries — people who are the most comfortable at home, are now most fond of going abroad — the spruce shopman exclaims, " Adieu La Boutique," and leaves the shop-boy to cheat the town for him — the young belle, tired of seeing and being seen in Broadway, breaks forth in all her glories in a new place at five hundred miles distance — bed-rid age musters its last energies for an expedition to West Point, or the Grand Canal — and even the thrifty housewife of the villages on the banks of the Hudson, who heretofore was "all one as a piece of the house," thinks nothing of risking a blow-up, or a break-down, in making a voyage to New York to sell a pair of mittens, or buy a paper of pins. We have heard a great political economist assert, that the money spent in travelling between New York and Albany, in the last fifteen years, would go near to maintain all the paupers of the United States, in that, the purest possible, state of independence — to wit, a freedom from an ignominious dependence on labour and economy. It is high time, therefore, that the wandering Arabs of the West should have a code of laws and regulations for their especial government; and the principal design of the present work is to supply this desideratum.

We have accordingly prepared a system of jurisprudence, which, we flatter ourselves, will not suffer in comparison, either with the code Napoleon, the code Bentham, or any other code which the march of mind hath begotten on the progress of public improvement in the present age. The traveller, if we mistake not, will find in it ample instructions, as to his outfit in setting forth for unknown parts — the places and things most worthy of attention in his route — the deportment proper in divers new and untried situations — and, above all, critical and minute instructions concerning those exquisite delights of the palate which constitute the principal object of all travellers of taste.

In addition to this, we have omitted no opportunity of inculcating a passion for travelling, which, from long and laborious experience, we pronounce the most exquisite mode of killing time and spending money ever yet devised by lazy ingenuity. It would occupy our whole book, (which is restricted to a certain bulk, so as not to interfere with the ladies' bandboxes and the gentlemen's trunks), were we to indulge in a summary of all the delights and advantages of seeing new and distant parts. Unfortunately for us, we write solely for the benefit of the world, holding our own especial emolument in sovereign contempt; and, still more unfortunately, if this were not the case, we belong not to that favoured class of writers who can take the liberty of publishing in six royal octavos matter which might be compressed into one. We have only space to observe, that a man who has travelled to good purpose, and made a proper use of his opportunities, may commit as many blunders and tell as many good stories as he pleases, provided he confines himself to places where *he* has been and his hearers have not. Books are of no authority in opposition to an eye-witness; who is, as it were, like so many of our great politicians, *ex officio*, a judge of every thing.

Two persons were once disputing, in a large company, about the Venus de Medici. One maintained that her head inclined a little forward to the right, the other that it inclined to the left. One had read

Winkelmann, and a hundred other descriptions of the statue. The other had never read a book in his life; but he had been at Florence, and had looked at the Venus for at least five minutes.

"My dear sir, *I ought to know;* for I have read all the books that ever were written on the Venus de Medici."

"My dear sir, *I must know;* for I have been at Florence, and seen her."

Here was an end of the argument. All the company was perfectly satisfied that the man who had seen with his own eyes was right — and yet he was wrong. But seeing is believing, and being believed too. You may doubt what a man affirms on the authority of another; but, if he says he has seen the sea-serpent, to question his veracity is to provoke a quarrel. Such are the advantages of seeing with our own eyes! Let us therefore set out without delay on the GRAND NORTHERN TOUR.

THE

NEW MIRROR FOR TRAVELLERS, &c.

In compiling and excogitating this work, we have considered ourselves as having no manner of concern with travellers until they arrive in the city of New York, where we intend to take them under our especial protection. Doubtless, in proceeding from the south, there are various objects worth the attention of the traveller, who may take the opportunity of stopping to change horses or to dine, to look round him a little, and see what is to be seen. But, generally speaking, all is lost time until he arrives at New York, of which it may justly be said, that as Paris is France, so New York is — New York. It is here then that we take the fashionable tourist by the hand and assume the rôle of cicerone.

The city of New York, to which all travellers of taste resort from the remotest corners of the earth, and from whence they set out on what is emphatically called the GREAT NORTHERN TOUR, is situated at the confluence of two noble waters, and about eighteen miles from the Atlantic Ocean. But we have always thought it a singular piece of impertinence in the compilers of road-books, itineraries, and guides, to take up the traveller's time in describing things he came expressly to see, and shall therefore confine ourselves to matters more occult, and inaccessible to transient sojourners. New York, though a very honest and well-intentioned city as times go, (with the exception of Wall Street, which labours under a sort of a shadow of suspicion), has changed its name almost as often as some graceless rogues, though doubtless not for the same reasons. The Indian name was Manhadoes; the Dutch called it New Amsterdam and New Orange; the English, New York, which name all the world knows it still retains. In 1673, it was a small village, and the richest man in it was Frederick Philipse, or *Flypse*, who was rated at eighty thousand guilders. Now it is the greatest city of the new world; the third, if not the second, in commerce, of all the world, old and new; and there are men in it, who were yesterday worth millions of guilders — in paper-money: what they may be worth to-morrow, we can't say, as that will depend on a speculation. In 1660, the salaries of ministers and public officers were paid in beaver skins: now they are paid in bank-notes. The beaver skins were always worth the money, which is more than can be said of the bank-notes. New York contains one university, and two medical colleges; the latter always struggling with each other in a noble spirit of generous, scientific emulation. There are twenty-two banks — good, bad, and indifferent; forty-three insurance companies — solvent and insolvent; and one public library: from whence it may be reasonably inferred, that money is plenty as dirt — insurance-bonds still more so — and that both are held in greater estimation than learning. There are also one hundred churches, and about as many lottery-offices, which accounts for the people of New York being so much better than their neighbours.

In addition to all these, there is an academy of arts, an athenæum, and several other institutions for the discouragement of literature, the arts, and sciences. The academy languishes under the patronage of— names. The athenæum is a place where one may always meet with La Belle Assemble, Ackerman's Magazine, and the last number of Blackwood. In addition to these places of popular amusement and recreation, New York supports six theatres, of various kinds: from whence it may be inferred, that the people are almost as fond of theatres as churches. There *was* an Italian opera last year. But, *Eheu fugaces, Posthume!,* the birds are flown to other climes.

Besides these attractions and ten thousand more, New York abounds beyond all other places in the universe, not excepting Paris, in consummate institutions for cultivating the noble science of gastronomy. The soul of Heliogabalus presides in the kitchens of our hotels and boarding-houses, and inspires the genius of a thousand cooks—not sent by the devil, as the old proverb infamously asserts, but by some special dispensation. There too will be found canvas-backs from the Susquehanna; venison from Jersey, Long Island, and Catskill; grouse from Hempstead Plains; snipe from the Newark meadows; and partridges from Bull Hill; which last, if the gourmand hath never eaten, let him despair. Then, as for fish!—O for a mouth to eat, or to utter the names of, the fish that flutter in the markets of New York, silently awaiting their customers like so many pupils of Pythagoras. It is a pleasure to keep Lent here. It is impossible to enumerate them all: but we should consider ourselves the most ungrateful of mankind, were we to omit making honourable mention of the inimitable trout from the Fireplace, whose pure waters are alone worthy the gambols of these sportive Undinæ; or of the amiable sheep's-head, whose teeth project out of his mouth as if to indicate that he longs to be eating up himself;* or of the blackfish, which offers a convincing proof that nature knows no distinction of colours, and has made the black skin equal to the white — at least among fishes; or of the delicious bass — the toothsome shad — and the majestic cod, from the banks of Newfoundland, doubly remarkable, as being almost the only good that ever came of banks. All these, together with countless varieties of smaller fry, offer themselves spontaneously to the experienced connoisseur, a new delicacy for every day in the year. We invoke them all! — thee, sea-green lobster of the Sound, best-beloved of southern invalids, a supper of whom is a sovereign cure for dyspepsia; thee luscious soft-crab, the discovery of whose unequalled excellence has made the city of Baltimore immortal; catfish and flounder, slippery eel and rough-shelled mussel; elephant-clam, which the mischievous boys of the Sound call by a more inglorious name; — we invoke ye all! And if we forget thee, O most puissant and imperial oyster, whether of Blue Point, York

---

* The unlearned traveller will be careful not to confound the sheep's-head, with the head of a sheep, as did the honest Irishman at Norfolk.

River, Chingoteague, or Chingarora, may our palate forget its cunning, and lose the best gift of heaven — the faculty of distinguishing between six different Madeira wines, with our eyes shut! All these and more may be seen of a morning at Fulton and Washington Markets; and the traveller who shall go away without visiting them has travelled in vain.

Then, for cooking these various and transcendent excellencies, these precious bounties — Thee we invoke — thee of the *Bank Coffee House,* who excellest equally in the sublime sciences of procuring and serving up these immortal dishes, and hast no equal among men, but the great SYKES, with whom thou didst erewhile divide the empire of the world. But, *Eheu fugaces, Posthume,* too! the smoke of his kitchen, which bore up incense worthy of the gods, is now gone out — he himself is like a shadow long departed, and nothing is left of him but the recollection of his suppers and his debts. Neither must we commit the crying sin of passing unnoticed and unhonoured the utterly famous gastronomium of the great DROZÉ, master of the twelve sciences that go to the composition of a consummate cook; nor the flagrant injustice of omitting to point the nose of the curious traveller to *Him of the New Masonic Hall,*[*] great in terrapin soup — greater in fricassees and fricandeaux — greatest of all in a calf's head! Neither would we pass over the modest merits of HIM OF THE GOOSE AND GRIDIRON, who, like the skilful logician, can make the worse appear the better reason, and convert, by

---

[* This building stood on the East side of Broadway, a little South of Pearl street. It is figured and described in the New-York Mirror of September 26, 1829.]

the magic of his art, material no more than so-so into dishes worthy the palates of the most erudite members of the Turtle Club, whose soup and whose jests are the delight of the universe. But we should never have done, were we to pass in review an hundred, yea, a thousand illustrious worthies, to be found in every street and lane of this eating city, who tickle the cunning palate in all the varieties of purse and taste, from a slice of roast beef and a glass of beer, at a shilling, to grouse and canvas-backs, and Bingham wine, at just as much as the landlord pleases. Suffice it to say, that if, as the best practical philosophers do maintain, the business of man's life is eating, there is no place in the universe where he can live to such exquisite purpose as in the renowned city of NEW YORK. We have heard it confessed by divers morose Englishmen, who had eaten and grumbled their way through all parts of Europe where there was any thing to eat, that they nowhere found such glorious content of the palate as at this happy emporium of all good things. If any corroboration of this testimony should be thought necessary, we will add the experience of twenty-five years of travel in various countries, during which we have tasted, by actual computation, upwards of five thousand different dishes. Still further, to establish the glories of our favourite city, we will adduce the authority of a young gentleman, who travelled several years on the continent, and approved himself a competent gourmand, by bringing home a confirmed dyspepsia. He has permitted us to insert a letter written originally to a friend at the south, which, besides setting forth the excellent attractions of NEW YORK, exemplifies in a most striking manner the benefits derived from travel, which improving divertisement it is the design of our work to encourage and provoke by all manner of means. Truly did the great philosopher and moralist, Dr. Johnson, who passed all his life in the fear of death, truly did he inculcate the superiority of the knowledge derived from *seeing*, to all other knowledge. Who that hath visited the grand opera at Paris, but will have, all his life after, a more vivid impression of legs! Who that hath expatiated in the vast eating-houses of New York and Paris, but will cherish an increasing faith in the primary importance of the noble science of gastronomy! And who, that has once beheld the magnificent contrast between the king and his beggarly subjects in some parts of the old world, but must feel ennobled by the example of what human nature is capable of, if properly cultivated! But to our purpose. The letter alluded to is one of a series written by the members of a most respectable family from the south, to which we have politely been permitted access, and from which we shall occasionally borrow some others.

STEPHEN GRIFFEN, ESQ. TO FRANK LATHAM.

NEW YORK, ———.

Verily, Frank, this same New York is a place that may be tolerated for a few weeks, with the assistance of the Signorina, the unequalled cookery, and above all the divine Madame ———. Only think of a real, genuine opera-dancer in these parts! Five years ago, I should as soon have expected to see an Indian war-dance at the *Théâtre Français*. It is really a vast comfort to have something one can relish after Paris. I think it bad policy for a young fellow to go abroad, unless he can afford to spend the rest of his life in New York. Coming home to a country life is like going from high-seasoned dishes to ham and chickens. Such polite people as one meets with abroad! they never contradict you as long as you pay them what they ask for every thing;—such a variety of dishes to eat! why, Frank, a bill of fare at a Parisian hotel is as long as a list of the passengers in Noah's ark or a Liverpool packet, and comprehends as great a diversity of animals. Nothing can equal it, except New York. And then, such a succession of amusements! Nobody ever yawned in Paris, except one of the real John Bulls, some of whom have their mouths always open, either to eat or yawn. To see a fat fellow gaping in the Louvre, you would think he came there to catch flies, as the alligators do, by lying with their jaws extended half a yard. How I love to recall the dear delights of the grand tour!—and, as I write at thee, not to thee, Frank, I will incontinently please myself at this present, by recapitulating, if it be only to refresh my memory and make thee miserable at thy utter ignorance of the world.

I staid abroad six years; just long enough to cast my skin, or shed my shell, as the snakes and crabs do every now and then. In France, I threw away my clod-hopping shoes, and learned to dance. I got a new stomach too, for I took vastly to Messrs. the restaurateurs. In Italy, I was drawn up the Apennines by six horses and two pair of oxen, and went to sleep every day for three weeks, at the feet of the Venus de Medici. There were other Venuses at whose feet I did *not* go to sleep. I was, moreover, deeply inoculated, or rather, as the real genuine phrase is, vaccinated, with a raving taste for music, and opera-dancing, which last, in countries where refinement is got to such a pitch that nobody thinks of blushing, is worth, as Mr. Jefferson says of Harper's Ferry, "a voyage across the Atlantic." By the way, they have an excellent custom in Europe, which puts all the women on a par. They paint their faces so that one can't tell whether they blush or not. Impudence and modesty are thus on a level, and all is as it should be.

Italy is indeed a fine place. The women are so *sociable*, and the men so polite. France does pretty well; but even there they sometimes — particularly since the *brutifying* revolution — they sometimes so far forget themselves as to feel dishonour and resent insult. All this is owing to the bad example of that upstart Napoleon, and his upstart officers. Now, in Italy, when a gentleman of substance takes an affront, he does not dirty his fingers with the affair; he hires me a fellow whose trade is killing, and there is an end of the matter. Then it is such a cheap country. Every thing is cheap, and women the cheapest of all. Everything there, except pagan antiques, is for sale; and you can buy heaven of his holiness, for a hundred times less money than it costs to purchase the torso of a heathen god without legs or arms.

In Germany, and especially at Vienna, they are excessively devout, and — what I assure you is, in very refined countries, not in the least incompatible — exceedingly profligate at the same time. I mean among the higher ranks. This is one of the great secrets a young fellow learns by going abroad. If he makes good use of his time, his talents, and, above all, his money, he will discover the secret of reconciling a breach of the whole decalogue with the most exemplary piety. When I was first in Vienna, they had the Mozart fever, and half the city was dying of it. On my second visit, Beethoven was all the vogue. He was as deaf as a post — yet played and composed divinely; a proof — you, being of the pure *Gothic*, will say — that music can be no great science, since it requires neither ears nor understanding. Beethoven had a long beard, and a most ferocious countenance; there was no more music in it than in a lion's. He was moreover excessively rude and disobliging, and would not play for the emperor unless he was in the humour. These peculiarities made him irresistible. The Beethoven fever was worse than the Mozart fever, a great deal. I ventured a third time to Vienna — and Beethoven was starving. They were all running after a great preacher, who, from being the editor of a liberal paper, had turned monk, and preached in favour of the divine right of the emperor, notwithstanding the diet and all that sort of trumpery. But music is their passion: it is the source of their national pride.

I once said to a worthy banker who had charge of my purse-strings — "Really, monsieur, you are very loose in your morals, here." "Yes, but we are the most musical people in the world", replied he triumphantly. "Your married ladies of fashion have such crowds of lovers." "Yes, but then they are so musical." "And then, from the prime minister Prince Metternich downwards, every man of the least fashion is an intriguer among women." "True, my dear sir; but then Prince Metternich has a private opera-house, and you hear the divinest music there." "And then the peasantry are in such a poor condition — so ignorant." "Ignorant, sir — you mistake — there is hardly one of them but can read music!" Music covers a multitude of sins at Vienna. It is worth while to go to Vienna only to see the peasantry — the female peasantry from the country, with bags, picking up manure, and singing perhaps an air of Mozart or Beethoven.

In England I got the last polish — that is to say, I learned to box enough to get a black eye now and then, in a set-to with a hackney-coachman, or an insolent child of the night — videlicet, a watchman. Moreover, I learned to give an uncivil answer to a civil question; to contradict without ceremony; to believe that an American mammoth was not half so big as a Teeswater bull; that one canal was worth a dozen rivers; that a railroad was still better than a canal, and a tunnel better than either; that M'Adam was a greater man than the Colossus of Rhodes; that liberty was upon the whole rather a vulgar, ill-bred minx; and that a nation without a king and nobility was no better than a human body wanting that absolute requisite, the seat of honour. Finally, I brought home a great number of clever improvements — to wit, a head enlightened with a hundred conflicting notions of religion, government, morals, music, painting, and what not; and a heart divested of all those vulgarisms concerning love of country, with which young Americans are apt to be impestered at home. Thus, I may say I got rid of all my home-bred prejudices; for a man can only truly be said to be without prejudices when he has no decided opinions on any subject whatever. Lastly, I had contracted a habit of liberal curiosity which impelled me to run about and see all the fine sights in the world. I would at any time travel a hundred miles to visit an old castle, or ogle a Canova or a Raphael. In short, I was a gentleman to all intents and purposes, for I could neither read, work, walk, ride, sit still, nor devote myself to any one object, for an hour at a time.

This was my motive for coming hither. I came in search of sensation: whether derived from eating lobsters, or seeing opera-dancers, is all one to me. But, alas!, what is there here to see, always excepting the dinners and suppers, worth the trouble of opening one of one's eyes, by a man who has seen the Opera Français, the Palais Royal, the inside of a French cook-shop, the Pantheon, St. Peter's, the carnival, the coronation, and the punch of all puppet-shows, a legitimate king; besides rowing in a Venitian gondola, and crossing Mont St. Bernard on a donkey! Last of all, friend Frank, I brought home with me the genuine patent of modern gentility — a dyspepsy, which I caught at a famous restaurateur's, and helped to mature at the Palais Royal, where they sit up at nights, eat late suppers, and lie abed till five o'clock in the afternoon.

But this dyspepsy, though excessively high-bred at that time, is now becoming vulgar. Since my arrival here, I have actually heard brokers and lottery-office-keepers complain of it. Besides, it spoils the pleasure of eating; and a man must have made the grand tour to little purpose, not to know that eating is one of the chief ends of man. I vegetated about for a year or two, sans employment, sans amusement, sans every thing—except dyspepsia. The doctor advised hard work and abstinence, remedies ten times worse than the disease—to a man who has made the grand tour. "Get a wife, and go and live on a farm in the upper country." "Marry, and live in the country!—not if it would give me the digestion of an ostrich," exclaimed Signior Stephen Griffen. By the way, this same Christian name of mine is a bore. Griffen will do— it smacks of heraldry; but Stephen puts one in mind of that degenerate potentate whose breeches cost him only half a crown, a circumstance in itself sufficient to stamp him with ignominy unutterable. Be this as it may, it pleased my doughty god-father, (whom I shall never forgive for not giving me a better name), to accede to the wishes of that exceedingly sensible rice-fed damsel, his pet niece, and my predestined rib, alias better half, to visit the springs at Ballston and Saratoga—the great canal—the great falls—and other great lions of these parts. So here we are established for ten days or a fortnight, for the purpose of taking a preparatory course of lobsters, singers, dancers, dust, and ashes. Broadway is a perfect cloud of dust. It has been M'Adamized—for which may dust confound all concerned.

Thine, S. G.

The approach to New York, either through the Narrows or the Kills, as they are called, is conspicuously beautiful, and worthy of the excellent fare to which the fortunate traveller who visits the city at a proper season is destined. And here we must caution our readers to beware of all those unlucky months that are without the fortunate letter, R, which may be called the tutelary genius of oysters, inasmuch as no oyster can enjoy the pleasure of being eaten in New York during any of the barren months, which are without this delightful consonant. It is against the law, experience having demonstrated the ill effects of indulging in these delicious dainties in hot weather — witness the sudden deaths of divers common-councilmen after supper. For this reason most of the fashionable people go out of town during those infamous months that begin with May and end with August, not one of which contains the fortunate R, there being nothing left worth staying for. This period may justly be called the season of Lent. No canvas-backs — no venison — no grouse — no lobsters — no oysters; — nothing but lamb, and chicken, and green peas! No wonder all people of taste go out of town; for, as a famous prize-poet writes,—

> "Without all these, the town's a very curse,
> Broadway a bore, the Battery still worse;
> Wall Street the very focus of all evil,
> Cook-shops a hell, and every cook the devil." *

New York is not only beautiful in its approach, beautiful in itself, and consummate in eating: its liquors are inimitable — divine. Who has not tasted the "Bingham" — the "Marston" — the "Nabob" — and the "Billy Ludlow!" Above all, who has not tasted of the unparalleled "Resurrection" wine — so called from its having once actually brought a man to

---

* See a prize-poem on the opening of the Goose and Gridiron, for which the fortunate author received a collation and twelve oyster suppers, besides having his mouth stuffed full of sugar-candy, after the manner of the Persian poets.

life, after he was stone-dead under the table. Nobody that ever had any of this wine ever died until he had no more of it left; and a famous physician once affirmed in our presence, that every drop was as good as a drop of buoyant, frisky, youthful blood, added to the body corporate. No wonder then that eating and drinking is the great business of life in New York, among people that can or cannot afford these exquisite dainties, and that they talk of nothing else at dinner; for, as the same illustrious prize-poet has it,—

> "Five senses were, by ever-bounteous heaven,
> To the thrice-lucky son of Adam given.
> Seeing, that he might drink e'en with his eyes,
> And catch the promise that taste ratifies;
> Hearing, that he might list the jingling glass,
> That, were he blind, might unsuspected pass;
> Smelling, that, when the rest, mayhap, are gone,
> Will for their traitorous absence half-atone;
> And feeling, which, when the dim, shadowy sight,
> No longer guides the pious pilgrim right,
> Gropes its slow way unerring to the shop,
> Where Dolly tosses up her mutton-chop,
> And sacred steams of roasted oysters rise,
> Like incense, to the lean and hungry skies."

Of the manner in which the various manœuvres of gastronomy are got through with in New York, at dinners and evening parties, the following, which we have politely been permitted to copy from the unpublished letters we spoke of, will sufficiently apprise the courteous reader. It is high *ton* throughout, we assure him, though there are at present some symptomatic indications of a change for the better—(better at least according to the notions of Colonel Culpeper)—in the evening parties, from whence it is, we understand, contemplated to banish late hours, oysters, and champagne. Against this last innovation we protest, in the name of posterity and the immortal gods. Banish beauty — banish grace — banish music, dancing, flirtation, ogling, and making love — but spare, O spare us the oysters and champagne! What will become of the brisk gallantry of the beaux, the elegant vivacity of the belles, the pleasures of anticipation, and the ineffable delights of fruition, if you banish oysters and champagne?

The fashionable reader will be tempted to smile at the colonel's antediluvian notions of style and good-breeding; but what can you expect from a man born and brought up among the high hills of Santee? His strictures on waltzing are especially laughable. What do women — we mean fashionable women — dress and undress, wear *bishops,* and wind themselves into the elegantly-lascivious motions of the waltz, for? — but to excite sensation in the gentlemen, who ought to be eternally grateful for the pains they take.

COLONEL CULPEPER TO MAJOR BRANDE.

NEW YORK, May 6, 1827.

DEAR MAJOR, — I have been so occupied of late in seeing sights, eating huge dinners, and going to evening parties to matronize Lucia, that I had no time to write to you. The people here are very hospitable, though not exactly after the manner of the high hills of Santee. They give you a great dinner or evening party, and then, as the sage Master Stephen Griffen is pleased to observe, "let you run." These dinners seem to be in the nature of a spasmodic effort, which exhausts the purse or the hospitality of the entertainer, and is followed by a collapse of retrenchment. You recollect ———, who staid at my house during a fit of illness, for six weeks, the year before last. He has a fine house, the inside of which looks like an upholsterer's shop, and lives in style. He gave me an invitation to dinner, at a fortnight's notice. I ate out of a set of china, which, my lady assured me, cost seven hundred dollars, and drank out of glasses that cost a guinea a piece. In short, there was nothing on the table of which I did not learn the value, most especially the wine, some of which, mine entertainer gave the company his word of honour, stood him in eight dollars a bottle, besides the interest, and was half a century old. I observed, very gravely, that it bore its age so remarkably well that I really took it to be in the full vigour of youth. Upon which all the company set me down as a bore.

In place of the pleasant chit-chat and honest jollity of better times, there was nothing talked of but the quality of the gentlemen's wines, which, I observed, were estimated entirely by their age and prices. One boasted of his Bingham; another, of his Marston; a third, of his Nabob; and a fourth, of his Billy Ludlow. All this was Greek to me, who was obliged to sit stupidly silent, having neither Bingham, nor Marston, nor Nabob, nor Billy Ludlow; nor indeed any other wine of name or pedigree: for, the fact is, as you very well know, my wine goes so fast, it has no time to grow old.

But there was one pursy, pompous little man at table, a foreigner I think, who (my lady whispered me) was worth a million and a half of dollars, and who beat the others all hollow. He actually had in his garret a dozen of wine seventy years old, last grass, that had been in his family fifty years — which, by the way, as a sly neighbour on my right assured me, was farther back than he could carry his own pedigree. This seemed to raise him high above all competition, and gave great effect to several of the very worst jokes I ever heard. It occurred to me, however, that his friends had been little the better for the wine thus hoarded to brag about. For my part, I never yet met a real honest, liberal, hospitable fellow that had much old wine. Occasionally the conversation varied into discussions as to who was the best judge of wine, and there was a serious contest about a bottle of Bingham and a bottle of Marston, which I was afraid would end in a duel. All, however, bowed to the supremacy of one particular old gentleman, who made a bet that he would shut his eyes, hold his nose, and distinguish between six different kinds of Madeira. I did not think much of this, as a man don't drink wine either with his eyes or nose; but politely expressed my wonder, and smacked my lips, and cried, "Ah!" in unison with this Winkelmann of wine-bibbers, like a veritable connoisseur.

There can be no doubt that these dinners are genteel and splendid, because every body here says so. But, between ourselves, major, I was wearied in spite of Bingham and Marston, and the Nabob. There wanted the zest, the ease, the loose gown and slippers, the elbow-room for the buoyant, frisky spirits to curvet and gambol in a little; without which your Bingham and canvas-backs are naught. In the midst of all this display, I sighed for bacon and greens and merry faces.* As I am a Christian gentleman, there was not the tithe of a good thing said at the table; and, to my mind, eating and drinking good things is nothing without a little accompanying wit and humour as sauce. The little pursy, important man of a million, it is true, succeeded several times in raising a laugh, by the weight of his purse rather than the point of his joke. The dinner lasted six hours, at the end of which the company was more silent than at the beginning, a sure sign of something being wanting. For my part, I may truly affirm, I never was at a more splendid dinner, or one more mortally dull. However, my friend paid his debt of hospitality by it, for I have not seen the inside of his house since. He apologizes for not paying me any more attention, by saying his house is all topsy-turvy with new papering and painting, but assures me that by the time we return in autumn madam will be in a condition to give us a little party. I believe he holds me cheap, because I have no *dear* wine that stands me in eight dollars a bottle.

'Tis the fashion of the times, so let it pass. But, fashion or not, nothing in the range of common-sense can rescue this habit of cumbrous display and clumsy ostentation from the reproach of bad taste and vulgarity. This loading of the table with costly finery, and challenging our admiration by giving us the price of each article; this boasting of the age, the goodness, and, above all, the cost, of the wine, is little better than telling the guests, they are neither judges of what is valuable in furniture, nor commendable in

* It is plain the colonel knows nothing of Tournure. Bacon and greens — stuff!

wines. Why not let them find these things out, themselves; or remain in most happy ignorance of the price of a set of china, and the age of a bottle of wine. It is for the tradesman to brag of his wares, and the wine-merchant of his wines, because they wish to sell them; but the giver of good things should never overwhelm the receiver with the weight of gratitude, by telling him their value.

From the dinner-party, which broke up at nine, I accompanied the young people to a tea-party, being desirous of shaking off the heaviness of that modern merry-making. We arrived about a quarter before ten, and found the servant just lighting the lamps. There was not another soul in the room. He assured me the lady would be down to receive us in half an hour, being then under the hands of Monsieur Manuel, the hair-dresser, who was engaged till nine o'clock with other ladies. You must know this Manuel is the fashionable hair-dresser of the city, and it is not uncommon for ladies to get their heads dressed the day before they are wanted, and to sit up all night to preserve them in their proper buckram rigidity. Monsieur Manuel, as I hear, has two dollars per head, besides a dollar for coach-hire, it being utterly impossible for monsieur to walk. His time is too precious.

We had plenty of leisure to admire the rooms and decorations, for Monsieur Manuel was in no hurry. I took a nap on the sofa, under a superb lustre which shed a quantity of its honours upon my best merino coat, sprinkling it handsomely with spermaceti. About half past ten, the lady entered in all the colours of the rainbow and all the extravagance of vulgar finery. I took particular notice of her head, which, beyond doubt, was the masterpiece of Monsieur Manuel. It was divested of all its natural features, which I suppose is the perfection of art. There was nothing about it which looked like hair, except it might be petrified hair. All the graceful waving lightness of this most beautiful gift of woman was lost in curls, stiff and ungraceful as deformity could make them, and hair plastered to the head till it glistened like an overheated "gentleman of colour." She made something like an apology for not being ready to receive us, which turned, however, pretty much on not expecting any company at such an early hour. Between ten and eleven, the company began to drop in; but the real fashionables did not arrive till about half past eleven, by which time the room was pretty well filled. It was what they call a conversation party, one at which neither cards nor dancing made up any part of the amusement; of course therefore I expected to enjoy some agreeable chit-chat. Old bachelor as I am, and for ladies' love unfit, still I delight in the smiles of beauty; and the music of a sweet voice speaking intelligence is to me sweeter than the harmony of the spheres, or the Italian opera.

Accordingly, I made interest for introductions to two or three of the most promising faces, and attempted a little small-talk. The first of these ladies commenced by asking me in a voice that almost made me jump out of my seat, if I had been at Mrs. Somebody's party, last week? To the which I replied in the negative. After a moment's pause, she asked me if I was going to Mrs. Somebody's party, the next evening? To the which, in like manner, I replied in the negative. Another pause, and another question, whether I was acquainted with another Mrs. Somebody, who was going to give a party? To this I was obliged to give another negation; when the young lady, espying a vacant seat in a corner on the opposite side, took flight without ceremony, and, by a puss-in-the-corner movement, seated herself beside another young lady, with whom she entered into conversation with a most interesting volubility.

Though somewhat discouraged, I tried my fortune a second time, with a pale, delicate, and interesting-looking little girl, who I had fancied to myself was of ethereal race and lived upon air, she looked so light and graceful. By way of entering-wedge, I asked her the name of a lady, who, by the bye, had nothing very particular about her, except her dress, which was extravagantly fine. My imaginary sylph began to expatiate upon its beauty and taste in a most eloquent manner, and concluded by saying: "But it's a pity she wears it so often." Why so? " O, why — because." Is it the worse for wear? " O dear, no; but then one sees it so often." But, if 'tis handsome, the oftener the better, I should think; beauty cannot be too often contemplated, said I, looking in her face rather significantly. What effect this might have had upon her I can't say, for, just then, I observed a mysterious agitation among the company, which was immediately followed by the appearance of a number of little tables, wheeled into the room by servants in great force, and covered with splendid services of china, filled with pickled oysters, oyster soup, celery, dressed lobsters, ducks, turkeys, pastry, confectionery, and the Lord knows what besides. My little ethereal upon this started up, seated herself at a little round marble table which was placed in the middle of the room, and commenced her supper, by the aid of two obsequious swains who waited on her with the spoils of the grand table. I never could bear to see a young woman eat when I was a young man, and I have never seen above half a dozen ladies who knew how to manage the work with pure sentimental indifference. It is at the best but a vulgar, earthly, matter-of-fact business, and brings all people on a level, belles and beaux, refined and not refined. It is, in truth, a sheer animal gratification, and a young lady should never, if possible, let her lover see her eat, until after marriage.

Now, major, let me premise, that I am not going to romance one tittle when I tell you I was astounded at the trencher-feats of my little sylph. It was not in the spirit of ill-natured espionage, I assure you, that I happened to look at her as she took her seat at the little round table; but, having once looked, I was fascinated to the spot. Here follows a bill of fare which she discussed, and I am willing to swear to every item.

   Imprimis — Pickled oysters.
   Item — Oyster soup.
   Item — Dressed lobster and celery.
   Item — Two jellies.
   Item — Macaroons.
   Item — Kisses.
   Item — Whip-syllabub.
   Item — Blanc-mange.
   Item — Ice-creams.
   Item — Floating-island.

Item — Alamode beef.
Item — Cold turkey.
Item — A partridge wing.
Item — Roast duck and onions.
Item — Three glasses of brown stout, &c. &c.

Do you remember the fairy-tale, where a man eats as much bread in a quarter **of** an hour as served **a** whole city? I **never** believed a word of it till now. But all this **is** vulgar, you will say. Even so; but the vulgarity consists in eating so horrifically, not in noticing **it.** The thing **is** essentially ill-bred, and, should this **practice** continue to gain ground, there is not the least doubt that the number of old bachelors and maidens will continue to increase and multiply, **in a** manner quite contrary to Scripture. To conclude this heart-rending subject, **I** venture to affirm that assemblages of this kind ought to be called eating, instead of tea-drinking, or conversation, parties. Their relative excellence and attraction is always estimated, among the really fashionable, refined people, **by the** quality and quantity of the eatables and drinkables. One great **requisite** is plenty of oysters; **but** the *sine qua non* **is oceans** of champagne. Master Stephen, who **is high** authority in a case of this sort, pronounced this party quite unexceptionable, for there was little conversation, a great deal of eating, and the champagne **so plenty,** that nine first-rate dandies (including himself) got so merry that they fell fast asleep **on** the lounges of the supper-room up stairs. I can answer **for** king Stephen, who was discovered in this situation **at three in** the morning when the fashionables **began to think of** going **home.**

For my part, major, I honestly confess, I was again wearied, even unto yawning desperately in the very teeth of beauty. But I don't lay it altogether to the charge of the party, being somewhat inclined to suspect that the jokes of the little man of a million, and the Bingham wine, were partly at the bottom of the business. I wonder how it came into the heads of people of a moderate common-sense, that old wine could ever make people feel young, and, consequently, merry. There is gout, past, present and future—gout personal, real, and hereditary—lurking at the bottom of old wine; and nothing can possibly prevent this universal consequence of drinking it, but a natural and incurable vulgarity of constitution, which cannot assimilate itself to a disease of such genteel origin.

I have since been at several of these first-rate fashionable conversaziones, where there was almost the same company, the same eatables and drinkables, and the same lack of pleasing and vivacious chat. I sidled up to several little groups, whose loud laugh and promising gestures induced me to believe there was something pleasant going on. But I assure you nothing could equal the vapid insignificance of their talk. There was nothing in it, but, "La, were you at the ball last night?"—and then an obstreperous roar of ill-bred, noisy laughter. There is no harm in people talking in this way, but it is a cruel deceit upon the unwary, to allure a man into listening. In making my observations, it struck me that many of the young ladies looked sleepy, and the elderly ones did certainly yawn most unmercifully. There was, at one of these polite stuffings, an elderly lady, between whose jaws and mine a desperate sympathy grew up and flourished. Our mouths, if not our eyes, may truly be said to have met in this accord of inanity, and twenty times in the course of the evening did we involuntarily exchange these tokens of mutual good-understanding. The next party we happened to meet at, I determined to practise the most resolute self-denial. But it would not do; there was an awful and irresistible attraction about the maelstrom of her mouth, that drew me toward its vortex, and we have continued to yawn at each other whenever we have met since. Wherever I turn my eyes, the cavern opes before me, and my old habit of yawning has become ten times more despotic than ever.

But, seriously speaking, it is not to be wondered at that the indefatigable votaries of fashion should look sleepy at these parties. Some of them have sat up all the night before, perhaps, in order not to discompose the awful curls of Monsieur Manuel. Others, (and, I am told, the major part of them), have been at parties five nights in the week, for two or three months past. You will recollect that, owing to the absurd and ridiculous aping of foreign whims and fashions, these evening parties do not commence till the evening is past, nor end till the morning is come. Hence it is impossible to go to one of them without losing a whole night's rest, which is to be made up by lying in bed the greater part of the next day. Such a course, for a whole season, must prostrate the physical and moral strength, and convert a young woman into a mere machine, to be wound up for a few hours by the artificial excitements of the splendours of wealth, the vain gratification of temporary admiration, or the more substantial stimulus of the bill of fare of the sylph ethereal aforesaid. It is no wonder that their persons are jaded, their eyes sunk, their chests flattened, their sprightliness repressed by midnight revels, and that they supply the absence of all these by artificial allurements of dress, and artificial pulmonic vivacity. You will wonder to hear a chivalrous old bachelor rail at this ill-natured rate. But, the truth is, I admire the last best work so fervently, that I can't endure to see it spoiled and sophisticated by a preposterous imitation of what is called the fashion; and so love the native charms of our native beauties, that it grieves my heart and rouses my ire to see them thus blighted and destroyed, in the midnight chase of a phantom miscalled pleasure.

Not three years ago, I am told, it was the custom to go to a party at eight, and come away at twelve, or sooner. By this sober and rational arrangement, a young lady might indulge in the very excess of fashionable dissipation, without absolutely withering the roses of her cheeks, and dying at thirty of premature old age. But, in an evil hour, some puppy, who, like my Master Stephen, had seen the world, or some silly woman that had been three months abroad, came home, and turned up the nose at these early vulgarities — telling how the fashionable parties began at midnight and ended at sunrise, and how the foreigners all laughed at the vulgar hours of the vulgar parties of the vulgar republicans. This was enough. Mistress Somebody, the wife of Mr. Such-a-one, who had a fine house in a certain street, "with folding doors and marble mantel-pieces," and all that sort of thing, set the fashion, and now the gentility of a party is estimated in no small degree by the hour. If you want to be tolerably genteel, you must not go till half past nine — if very genteel, at ten — if exceedingly genteel, at eleven; — but if you want to be superlatively genteel, you must not make your appearance till twelve.

The crying absurdity of this disposition, in a society where almost every person at these parties has business or duties of some kind to attend to by nine o'clock the next day, must be apparent. The whole thing is at war with the state of society here, and incompatible with the system of domestic arrangements and out-door business. It is a pitiful aping of people abroad, whose sole pursuit is pleasure, and who can turn-day into night, and night into day, without paying any other penalty than the loss of health and the abandonment of all pretensions to usefulness. If our travelled gentry cannot bring home something more valuable than these mischievous absurdities, they had better stay at home. They remind me of our good friend Sloper, who spent seven years, travelling in the east, and brought nothing home with him but an excellent mode of spoiling rice and chickens, by cooking them after the Arabian fashion.

Among the most disgusting of these importations is the fashion of waltzing, which is becoming common here of late. It was introduced, as I understand, by a party of would-be fashionables, that saw it practised at the operas with such enchanting languor, grace, and lasciviousness, that they fell in love with it, and determined to bless their country by transplanting the precious exotic. I would not be understood as censuring those nations among whom the waltz is, as it were, indigenous — a national dance. Habit, example, and practice from their earliest youth, accustom the women of these countries to the exhibition, and excuse it. But for an American woman, with all her habits and opinions already formed, accustomed to certain restraints, and reared in certain notions of propriety, to rush at once into a waltz, and to brave the just sentiment of the delicate of her own and the other sex with whom she has been brought up and continues to associate, is little creditable to her good sense, her delicacy, or her morals. Every woman does, or ought to, know, that she cannot exhibit herself in the whirling and voluptuous windings of a waltz, without calling up in the minds of men feelings and associations unworthy the dignity and purity of a delicate female. The free motions — the upturned eyes — the die-away languors — the dizzy circlings — the twining arms — the projecting front — all combine to waken in the bosom of the spectator analogies, associations, and passions, which no woman, who values the respect of the world, ought ever willfully to challenge or excite.

I must not forget one thing that amused me, amid all this aping and ostentation. I was at first struck with the profusion of servants, lamps, china, and silver forks at these parties; and could not help admiring the magnificence of the entertainer, as well as his wealth. But by degrees it began to strike me, that I had seen these things before; and at last I fairly detected a splendid tureen, together with divers elegant chandeliers and lamps, which I had actually admired the night before at a party in another part of the town. As to my old friend Simon, and his squires of the body, he and I are hand and glove. I see him and his people, and the tureen, and the china, and the lamps, everywhere. They are all hired, in imitation of the fashionable people abroad. They undertake for every thing here, from furnishing a party to burying a Christian. I can't help thinking it is a paltry attempt at style. But adieu, for the present. I am tired — are not you?

If ever the pure and perfect system of equality was completely exemplified upon earth, it will be found in New York, where it is the fashion to dress without any regard to time, purse, station. There is no place where the absurd, antiquated maxim, about cutting your coat according to your cloth, is so properly and consummately *cut*, as here, where a full dress is indispensable on all occasions, particularly in walking Broadway or going to church. Whoever wishes to see beauty in all its glory must walk Broadway of a morning, or visit a fashionable church — for there is a fashion in churches — on a fine Sunday. On these occasions it is delightfully refreshing to see a fashionable, looking like a ship on a gala-day, dressed in the flags of all nations. Many cynical blockheads, who are at least a hundred years behind the march of mind and the progress of public improvements, affect to say that this beautiful and florid style of dressing in the streets or at church is vulgar; but we denounce such flagrant fopperies of opinion, maintaining that, so far from being reprehensible, it is perfectly natural, and therefore perfectly proper. The love of finery is inherent in our nature; it is an inborn appetite: and all experience indicates that the more ignorant and unsophisticated people are, the more fond are they of gewgaws. The negro, (meaning no offence, as it is an illustration, not a comparison), the African negro adores a painted gourd, decked with feathers of all colours; the Nooheevans affect the splendours of a great whale's-tooth; the Esquimaux will starve themselves, to purchase a clam-shell of red paint; the Indians sell their lands for red leggins and tin medals; and the whites run in debt for birds-of-paradise, French hats, travelling-chains, and Cashmere shawls. All this is as it should be, and, so far from betokening effeminacy or undue refinement, is a sure indication of an approach to the primitive simplicity of nature.

This barbarous, or, more properly, natural, taste or passion for finery pervades all classes of people in this delightful city, and if there is any superiority of dress observable, it is among the most vulgar and ignorant; in other words, those who are nearest to a state of nature. The maid is, if possible, finer than the mistress; displays as many feathers and flowers, and exhibits the same rigidity of baked curls, so that, in walking the streets, were it not for that infallible private mark of a gentlewoman, the foot and ankle, nobody but their friends could tell the difference. There are, as we have been credibly informed, Lombard and Banking Companies incorporated by the legislature, on purpose to maintain this beautiful equality in dress, every article of which, from a worked muslin to a lace veil, may be hired, "at prices to accommodate customers," so that a fine lady can be fitted out for a cruise, at a minute's warning.

This beautiful exemplification of a perfect equality extends to the male sex also. He that brushes his master's coat often wears a better coat than his master; and Cuffee himself, the free gentleman of colour, struts up and **down** Broadway, arm-in-arm, four-abreast, elbowing the fine ladies, clothed from head to foot in regent's-cloth of fourteen dollars the yard. All this redounds unutterably to the renown of the city, and causes it to **be** the delight **of** sojourners and travellers, **who,** instead **of** having their eyes offended and their feelings outraged by exhibitions of inglorious linsey-woolsey and vulgar calico, **see** nothing all around them but a universal diffusion of happiness. What is **it** to **us** tourists where the money comes from, or who pays for all this? The records of bankruptcy and the annals of the police are not the polite studies of us men of pleasure, nor have we any concern with the insides of houses or the secrets **of** domestic life, so long as the streets look gay, and every body in them *seems* happy. What is it to us, if the husband **or** the father of the gay butterfly we admire **as she** flutters along, clothed in the spoils of the four quarters of the globe, is at that very moment shivering in the jaws of bankruptcy, perspiring out his harassed soul in inward anxieties to weather another day of miserable splendours, and resorting to all the mean, degrading expedients of the times, to deceive the world a little longer. The city is charming — the theatres and churches **are** full of splendours; the hotels **and** boarding-houses abound in all that can pamper the appetite; the habitations are all showily furnished; all that we see is delightful; and as to what we don't see, it exists not to us. We travellers belong to the world, and the world, with the exception of its cares and troubles, belongs to us.

Now, as there is a highly meritorious class of travellers, who are almost continually in motion and never stay long in one place if they can help it, to whom it may be important to know the secrets of the art of living, as the butterflies live, without toiling or spinning, and tasting all the fruits of the field without having any fields themselves, we commend them to the records of bankruptcy, the police, and the Quarter-Sessions. It is there they will become adepts in this most important of all branches of human knowledge. Any fool may live by working and saving: but to live, and live well too, by idleness and unthrift — to enjoy the luxuries of taverns, fine clothes, canvas-backs, turtle-soup, and Bingham wine, without money, and without credit — is the *summum bonum*, and can only be attained by long experience, and a close attendance upon the police-courts. If High-Constable Hays would only give to the world, agreeably to the fashion of the times, his " Reminiscences," what a treasure they would be to the class of tourists we are addressing! There they might behold the grand drama of life behind the scenes, and under the stage; there they might learn how to dress elegantly at the expense of those stupid blockheads who prefer living by the sweat of their own brows to living by the sweat of those of other people;. there they would be taught by a thousand examples, not how to cut their coats according to their own cloth, but that of their neighbours, and learn how easy it is to be a fine gentleman — that is to say, to live at a hotel, get credit with a tailor, diddle the landlord and the doctor, and pick a few pockets and a few locks, by way of furnishing one's self with a watch and a diamond breast-pin. There, too, they would learn how a little staining of the whiskers, a new wig, and an *alias*, enable a man to come forth from the state-prison, "redeemed, regenerated, and disenthralled," by the irresistible genius of universal philanthropy. Seriously therefore do we hope the high-constable will employ his *otium cum dignitate* in a work of this kind, for the benefit of the inexperienced in the art of raising the wind.

But to return from this digression, which we have indulged in from motives of pure philanthropy. By the way, we shall frequently, in the course of this work, encourage these little excursive irregularities of the pen, being firmly of opinion that no person ought to make the Grand Northern Tour who has any better use for his money than in buying, or for his time than in reading, this book.

In New York there is an unfailing round of amusements, for every hour of the day as well as the night. There is the Academy of Arts, where the amateur of painting may see pictures which *cost* more than Domenichino received for his communion of St. Jerome, or Raphael for his masterpiece; and which, strange to say, are not worth above half as much. Nothing is more easy than to kill an hour or two of a dull morning at the Academy, from whence we would advise the intelligent tourist, if of the male sex, to adjourn to the far famed gastronomium, (in the vernacular, oyster-stand), of Jerry Duncan, who certainly opens an oyster with more grace and tournure than any man living. But alas! how few — how very few, in this degenerate age, understand the glorious mysteries of eating! Some fry their oysters in batter — infamous custom! Some sophisticate them with pepper and salt — (that ought to be a state-prison offence!) — some with vinegar and butter — (away with them to the tread-mill!) Others stew, broil, roast, or make them into villanous pies — hard labour for life, or solitary imprisonment, ought to be the lot of these. And others, O murder most foul!, cut them in two before they eat them; a practice held in utter abhorrence by all persons of common humanity — this ought to be death by the law. As our reader loves oysters — as he aspires to become an adept in the great science — as he hopes to be saved — let him never cut his oyster in two pieces, or eat it otherwise than raw. If his mouth is not large enough to swallow it whole, let him leave it with a sigh to the lips of some more fortunate being, to whom nature has been more bountiful. A reasonable sojourn at Jerry's will bring round the hour to one o'clock, when it is proper to take the field in Broadway, or at least to go home and prepare for that solemn duty. From this till dinner, the intelligent tourist can employ his time to great advantage, in walking back and forth from the Battery to the south corner of Chambers Street. Beyond this he must not stir a step, as all besides is *terra incognita* to the fashionable world. People will think you are going to Cheapside, or Bond Street, or Hudson Square, or some other haberdashery place, to buy bargains, if you are found beyond the north corner of the Park. At three, return to your lodgings to dress for dinner. This must positively be celebrated in Broadway, in one of those majestic old houses which the piety of young heirs consecrates to the god of eating, in honour of their ancestors. We are not ignorant that some ill-natured people affirm this is not their motive, but that they are actuated by the filthy lucre of gain, in thus turning their fathers' homes into dens of tourists; but we ourselves are fully convinced they are impelled by sheer public spirit, warmed by the irresistible effervescence of universal philanthropy, the warmth of which pervades this whole city, insomuch that there is scarcely a place extant where people are more cordially taken in. Let no one blame these pious young heirs, since, in the east, nobody but kings and saints built caravanseras for the accommodation of travellers; and, in the west, none but people of a devout and royal spirit erect taverns. The only difference is, and it is not very material, the caravanseras charge nothing for lodging travellers, and the taverns make them pay double.

And now comes the hour — the most important hour of every day between the cradle and the grave — THE DINNER HOUR! On this point it is necessary to be particular. Look out for the sheep's-head, the venison, the canvas-backs. Don't let your eyes, any more than your mouth, be idle a moment; but be careful not to waste your energies on common-place dishes. First, eat your soup as quick as possible without burning your mouth. Then your fish — then your venison — then your miscellaneous delights — and conclude with game. At the climax comes the immortal canvas-back, whose peculiar location to the south,* in our opinion gives a decided superiority to that favoured portion of the universe; and entitles it to furnish the less favoured parts of the United States with presidents, so long as it furnishes us with this incomparable water-fowl. From our souls, which according to

---

* We have heard that canvas-backs have been seen in Rhode Island. If the natives can prove this, we think they ought to furnish the next president.

some good authorities are seated in the palate — from our souls, we pity the wretched inhabitants of the old world — wretched in the absence of even tolerable oysters, and wretched beyond all wretchedness in the utter destitution of canvas-backs and Newtown pippins.

Respecting wines, there is some diversity of opinion. Some prefer French wines, such as Burgundy, Chateau-Margaux, Lafitte, Latour, Sauterne, and Sillery. Others affect the purple and amber juices of the Rhine, affirming that the real Johannisberg is inimitable. Others again prefer the more substantial product of Spain, Portugal, and the veritable Hesperides — the group of the Madeiras — maintaining that the existence of the people of this world, before the discovery of these last, is one of those miracles not to be accounted for, like that of a toad in a block of marble. As there is no such thing as accounting for tastes, or reconciling them, we would propose an amicable medium, that of sipping a little of each in the course of the afternoon, thus reconciling the conflicting claims of these most exquisite competitors. A bottle of each would be rather too much for the head or pocket of a single amateur, wherefore we would recommend some half a dozen to club their wines, by which means this objection would be obviated. By the time these ceremonies are got through, the company will be in a condition to adjourn to the theatres, with a proper zest for the Flying Dutchman, Peter Wilkins, and "I've been roaming." After sitting or sleeping out these elegant spectacles, it is reasonable to suppose our traveller will be hungry, and, being hungry, it is reasonable that he should eat.

Wherefore it is our serious advice that he adjourn forthwith to the Goose and Gridiron. After partaking of a good supper there he may go anywhere he pleases, except home, it being proper that a rational and enlightened traveller should make the most of his time.

To the young female tourist, encumbered with time and papa's money, New York affords inexhaustible resources. The mere amusement of dressing for breakfast, for Broadway, and for dinner, and undressing for evening parties, is a never-failing refuge from ennui. In the intervals between dressing, shopping, visiting, and receiving visits, it is advisable for her, if she is fond of retirement and literary pursuits, to seat herself at one of the front windows, on the ground-floor of the hotel, with a Waverley or a Cooper, where she can comport herself after the fashion of people in divers old-fashioned pictures which I have seen; that is to say, hold her book open, and at the same time complacently contemplate the spectators. The following list of " Resources" is confidently recommended to our female travelling readers.

Lying in bed till ten.

Dressing for breakfast. N. B. If there is nobody in the hotel worth dressing for, any thing will do: or, better, take breakfast in bed, and another nap.

Breakfast till eleven. N. B. It is not advisable to eat canvas-backs, oysters, or lobsters, at breakfast. A little smoked salmon, a modicum of frizzled beef, or a bit of chicken about as big as a bee's wing, is all that can safely be indulged. N. B. Beefsteaks and mutton-chops are wholly inadmissible, except for married ladies.

Twelve to one. Dress for shopping. N. B. The

female tourist must put on her best, it being the fashion in New York for ladies and their maids to dress for walking as if they were going to church or a ball. Care must be taken to guard against damp pavements, by putting on prunello shoes. If the weather is dry, white satin is preferable.

One till three. Sauntering up and down Broadway, and diversifying the pleasure by a little miscellaneous shopping — looking in at the milliners, the jewellers, &c. N. B. No lady should hesitate to buy any thing because she does not want it, since this dealing in superfluities is the very essence of everything genteel. Above all, never return home but with an empty purse.

At three, the brokers, who set the fashion in New York, go home to their canvas-backs and Bingham wine, and it becomes vulgar to be seen in Broadway.

Dinner at four, the earliest hour permitted among people of pretensions. Owing to the barbarous practice of banishing ladies from all participation in the learned discussions of wines, the period between dinner and dressing for the evening party is the most trying portion of female existence. If they walk in Broadway, they will see nobody worth seeing; of course, there is no use in walking. A nap, or a Waverley, or perhaps both, is the only resource.

It will be expedient to wake up at eight, for the purpose of dressing for a party; else there is no earthly reason why you may not sleep till half-past-ten or eleven, when it is time to think of going, or you may possibly miss some of the refreshments. N. B. A lady may eat as much as she pleases at a ball, or a conversazione.

Should there be no party for the evening, the theatres are a never-failing resource of intellectual enjoyment. The sublime actions of The Flying Dutchman and Peter Wilkins,* and the sublime displays in " I've been roaming," † cannot fail to enlighten the understanding, refine the taste, and improve the morals of the rising generation, as well as, if not better than, bridewell or the penitentiary. N. B. The bashful ladies generally shut both their eyes at, " I've been roaming." Those who retain a fragment of the faculty of blushing, open only one eye; but such as are afraid of nothing, use a quizzing-glass, that nothing may escape them.

After all, there is nobody that can do full justice to the ever-changing shadows and lights of fashionable dress, manners, and amusements, but a sprightly girl, just come out with all her soaring anticipations unclipped by experience, and all her capacities of enjoyment fresh and unsoiled. We will therefore take occasion to insert in this place two letters, written by a young lady of the party from whose correspondence we have already made such liberal selections.

LUCIA CULPEPER TO MARIA MEYNELL.

New York, ———.

My dear Maria,— I could live here forever. We have a charming suite of rooms fronting on Broadway, that would be a perfect paradise, were it not

---

[* " Peter Wilkins, or The Flying Islanders," and " The Flying Dutchman", were spectacular dramas of the day — the first-named, fairy, the second, nautical.]

[† This was a song arranged by Charles E. Horn for Madame Vestris, in London.]

for the noise, which prevents one's hearing one's self speak, and the dust, which prevents one's seeing. But still it *is* delightful to sit at the window with a Waverley, and see the moving world forever passing to and fro, with unceasing footsteps. Everybody, as well as everything, appears to be in motion. The carriages rattle through the streets; the carts dance as if they were running races with them; the ladies trip along in all the colours of the rainbow; and the gentlemen look as though they actually had something to do. They all walk as if they were in a hurry. On my remarking this to my uncle, he replied, in his usual sarcastic manner: " Yes, they all seem as if they were running away from an indictment." I did not comprehend what he meant. Every thing is so different, that it does not seem to me possible that I should be in the same world, or that I am the same person I was a month ago.

Sitting at my window on the high hills of Santee, I saw nothing but the repose, the stillness, and the majesty of nature. At a distance, and all around, the world was no more than a faint outline of blue mountains that seemed almost incorporated with the skies. Nothing moved around me, but the mists of morning, rising at the beck of the sun; the passing clouds; the waving foliage of the trees; the little river winding through the valley; and the sun riding athwart the heavens. The silence was only interrupted at intervals by the voice or the whistle of the blacks, about the house or in the fields; the lowing of the cattle wandering in the recesses of the hills; the echo of the hunter's gun, or the crash of the falling tree; the soft murmurings of the river under the window; and, sometimes, the roaring of the whirlwind through the forest, or the reverberation of the thunder among the distant rocks. My uncle was master of all that could be seen without — I, mistress of all within. There all was nature — here all is art. Every thing is made with hands, except the living things; and, of these, the ladies and gentlemen may fairly be set down as the work of the milliners and tailors. Even the horses are sophisticated, as my uncle will have it; and, instead of having long, flowing tails and manes, amble about with ears, tail, and mane cropt, as if they had been under the hands of the barber.

But when I look in the glass, it seems that not all the changes of animate and inanimate nature equal those I exhibit in my own person. The morning after I came here, I received a circular; don't let your eyes start out of your head, Maria — yes, a circular: and from whom do you suppose? Why, a milliner! Only think what a person of consequence I must be, all at once! It informed me, in the politest terms, that Madame ———— had just received an assortment of the latest Paris fashions, which would be opened for inspection the next day. I was determined to have the first choice of a hat; so I got up early, and proceeded with *Henney* to the milliner's rooms, which, to my great surprise, I found full of fine ladies, who, as I afterwards understood, had not been up at such an hour since the last fashionable exhibition of Parisian finery. You never saw such a crowd; such tumbling of silks and gauzes; such perplexity of choice; such profound doubts; such hesitating decision; such asking of everybody's opinions, and following none; and such lingering, endless examinations. There was one lady that tried on every hat in the place, and went away at last in despair. I don't wonder, for it was the choice of Hercules, not between two, but between hundreds. For my part, I did nothing but wonder. You never saw such curiosities as these Parisian hats. It is quite impossible to describe them: I can only give you an idea of the size, by saying that mine, which is very moderate, measures three feet across, and has a suit of embellishments, bows, puffs, points, feathers, flowers, and wheat-sheaves, that make it look almost twice as large. The rule is, here, for the smallest ladies to wear the largest hats, so that my uncle insists upon it they look like toad-stools, with a vast head and a little stem. Mine was the cheapest thing ever offered for sale in New York, as madame assured me; it cost only twenty-eight dollars. It would not go into the bandbox, so Henney paraded it in her hand. A man on horseback met her just as she was turning a corner, and the horse was so frightened that he reared backwards and came very near throwing his rider. One of our horses is lame, and my uncle has advertised for one that can stand the encounter of a full-dressed fine lady. If he can do that, the old gentleman says, he can stand any thing.

The next thing I did was to bespeak a couple of walking-dresses — one of batiste, the other of silk plaid. They cost me only fifty-six dollars, which was quite moderate, seeing they had, or were said to have, in the bill, ninety odd yards of one thing or another in them. I believe I must drop my money in the street, for I am almost ashamed to apply to my uncle so often. He takes it all good-humouredly, for he is a generous old soul — only he has his revenge, in laughing at me, and comparing me to all sorts of queer things. I was surprised, when I first went out, to see what beautiful curling hair they all had — ladies, ladies' maids, and little babies, all had the most charming profusion you ever saw. This struck me very much, as you know very few have curling hair to the south, except the negroes. And such curls, too! Dear me, Maria, it would make your hair stand on end to see them. They look more like sausages than any thing else — and I thought, to be sure, they must be starched. On expressing my admiration to Stephen, he laughed outrageously, and assured me most solemnly, that every one of these sausages was purchased — not at the sausage-makers, but at the curl-shops, where you could buy them either of horse-hair, mohair, or human hair, and of any size and colour you pleased. He assured me it was impossible to live five minutes in New York without them, and advised me to procure a set without delay. You'd laugh to see mine. They are as stiff as the powder and pomatum of Doctor Brady's wig could make them: they are hollow in the middle, which my uncle assures me is very convenient, now that the ladies wear no pockets. One can put a variety of small matters in them as we did in our muffs, formerly. Do you know, they bake them in the oven to make them stiff. My uncle gives another reason for it, which I won't tell you.

My bonnet and curls seem to have almost conquered Stephen, who declares he has seen nothing equal to my "costume," as he calls it, since he left

Paris. He has actually offered to walk with me in Broadway, and did us the honour to go with us to the theatre, one stormy night. To be sure, Madame —— danced. You never saw such droll capers, Maria: I declare I hardly knew which way to look. But all the ladies applauded; so I suppose I don't know what is proper, not having seen much of the world. Stephen was in ecstacies, and bravoed and encored, till my uncle bade him be quiet, and not make a jackanapes of himself. I was delighted with the theatre. It is lighted with gas; and the play was one of the finest shows I ever beheld;— processions — thunder and lightning, and dancing — fighting — rich dresses — a great deal of fiddling, and very little poetry, wit, or sense. I was a little disappointed at this: but Stephen says, nothing is considered so vulgar as a sensible, well-written play. Music and dancing are all in all — and, as it is much easier to cut capers, and produce sounds without sense than with it, this is an excellent taste — for it saves a great deal of useless labour in writing plays, as well as acting them properly. I sometimes think Stephen's notions are a little strange; and my heart, as well as my understanding, revolts at some of his decisions. But he has been abroad, and ought to know. Sometimes I think I should like to know Graves' opinion: but he hardly ever speaks unless spoken to; and ever since I got such a great bonnet, and such great curls, he scarcely seems to know me. As for my uncle, he don't make any secret of his opinions. But then he is out of fashion; and, as I don't find any body agree with him, I think he must be wrong.

Next week, we think of setting out for the Springs.

My uncle has forsworn the steam-boats, ever since our voyage from Charleston. So we are to go by land up the right bank of the Hudson, and return on the other side, unless we should visit Boston, as my uncle sometimes threatens. Good bye, my dear Maria; I long to see you:— don't you long to see me, in my incomprehensible, indescribable hat, and my baked curls? I must not omit my travelling-chain, which is a gold cable of awful dimensions, without which no lady of any pretensions can visit the Springs. Alas! poor woman! born to be the slave of a hundred task-masters;— first, of the boarding-school, where she is put to the torture of the dancing-master and the school-mistress; next, of fashion, when she is obliged to appear a fool, rather than be singular; and last and worst, of her husband, the very Nero of tyrants. Pray, sometimes stop in, and see how my old nurse, Hannah, gets on. Adieu.

P. S. I wish you could only hear that good-natured, pragmatical old soul, my kind, generous uncle, rail at almost every thing he hears and sees. He calls himself an old fool fifty times a day, and says that old people are like old trunks, which will do very well while they are let alone in a corner, but never fail to tumble to pieces if you move them. He pronounced the steam-boat a composition of horrors, such as modern ingenuity, stimulated by paper-money, stock-companies, and I know not what, could alone produce; and congratulates himself continually upon living in a remote part of the country, where there are neither banks nor incorporations, and where, as he says, indulgent nature, by means of high mountains and other benevolent precautions, has made it actually impossible to intrude either a canal or a railroad. Every time I come to him for money, which indeed is pretty often, for I have found out a hundred new wants since I came here, he affects to scold me, and declares that unless the price of cotton and rice rises, he shall be a pauper before the end of our journey. But what annoys him most of all, and indeed appears strange to me, is to see white men performing the offices of negroes in the south — waiting at table, cleaning boots, brushing clothes, driving carriages, and standing up behind them. He says this is degrading the race of white men in the scale of nature, and has had several hot discussions with an old Quaker, with whom he somewhere scraped acquaintance. Our black man Juba, or gentleman of colour, (for that is the style here), is grown so vain at being sometimes waited on by white men, that he is good for nothing but to parade up and down Broadway. Henney says he is keeping a journal, and talks of making up to the old Quaker's daughter; I suppose on the strength of the good gentleman's arguments about equality. To conclude, my good uncle calls me a baggage and Stephen a puppy, twenty times a day. L. C.

LUCIA CULPEPER TO MARIA MEYNELL.

NEW YORK, ———.

MY DEAR MARIA, — How I wish you were here to help me enjoy all the fine things I see from morning till night. You know I have no friends in this place, and among all our party I can find no confidante but Henney, who wonders ten times more than I do. My uncle, though a most indulgent old soul, you know has a habit of finding fault with every thing, and of always exalting the past at the expense of the present, which to young people, to whom the present time is every thing, is quite odd. Graves is as grave as his name, and is all the time taken up with state-prisons, alms-houses, houses of refuge, and all sorts of institutions for making people wiser and better; or, as my uncle will have it, idle and profligate. As for Stephen, he won't let me admire any thing in peace. The moment I begin, he discharges upon me a comparison with something in Paris, Rome or London, which goes near to accuse me of a total want of taste. If you believe him, there is nothing worth seeing here but what comes from abroad. I am sure he'll never like me well enough to fulfil my uncle's wishes, and that is my great comfort. For alas! Maria, I fear he has no heart; and, judging from what comes out of it, but little head. I don't want a man to be always crying or talking sentiment, or forever acting the sage; but a heartless fool is the bane of womankind. You know Stephen's father saved my uncle's life at the battle of the Eutaw Springs, and that my uncle has long made up his mind to make him my lord and master, and leave us his whole fortune, with the exception of a legacy to poor Graves. The older I grow, the more I dislike this plan. But I would not thwart my dear, kind, generous uncle — father — if any thing less than my future happiness is at stake. He calls Stephen, puppy, jackanapes, and dandy, ten times a day. But I can see his heart is still set upon the match. So true is it, that it is almost impossible for old people to give up a long-cherished and favourite plan. But

I have made up my mind in the solitude of the mountains to meet what may come — come what will.

My head is now full of finery, and all my senses in a whirl. I wish you could see me. My hat is so large that there is no bandbox on the face of the earth big enough to accommodate it; and yet you will be surprised to hear that it is fit neither for summer nor winter, rain nor sunshine. It will not keep off either one or the other, and so plagues me when I go into the street, that I hardly know which way to turn myself. Every puff of wind nearly oversets me. There are forty-two yards of trimmings, and sixty feathers to it. My dress is a full match for my hat. It took twenty-three yards of silk, five yards of satin, besides, "bobbin, ben-bobbin," and ben-bobbinet, — I don't know what else to call it — beyond all counting. You must think I have grown very much. I am so beflounced, that my uncle laughs at me whenever I come where he is, and declares, that a fine lady costs more to fit her out nowadays than a ship of the line. What between hat and flounces, &c., a lady has a time of it when the wind blows and the dust is flying in clouds, as it does in Broadway all day long. I encountered a puff at the corner of one of the streets, and there I stood, holding my hat with one hand, and my cardinal-cloak (which has fifty-six yards of various commodities in it) with the other. I thought I should have gone up like a balloon; and stood stark still until I came near being run over by a great hog, which was scampering away from some mischievous boys. At last a sailor took compassion on me, and set me down at the door of a store. As he went away, I heard him say to his companion: "My eyes,

Bill, what a press of canvass the girls carry nowadays!"

O, it's delightful to travel, Maria! We had such a delightful sail in the steam-boat, though we were all sick; and such a delightful party, if they only had been well. Only think of sailing without sails, and not caring which way the wind blows; and going eight miles an hour, happen what would. It was quite charming; but, for all this, I was glad when it was over, and we came into still water. Coming into the Narrows, as they are called, was like entering a paradise. On one side is Long Island, with its low shores, studded with pretty houses, and with foliage of various kinds mixed up with the dark cedars; on the other, Staten Island, with its high bluff, crowned by the telegraph and signal poles; and beyond, the great fort that put me in mind of the old castles which Stephen talks about. We kept close to the Long Island shore, along which we glided, before wind and tide, with the swiftness of wings. Every moment some new beauty opened to our view. The little islands of the bay, crowned with castles; the river, bounded by the lofty ledge of perpendicular rocks called The Palisades; and, then, the queen of the West, the beautiful city, with its Battery and hundred spires; coming one after the other, and at last combined in one beautiful whole — threw me almost into raptures, and entirely cured my sea-sickness. Add to this, the ships, vessels, and boats, of all sizes, from the seventy-four to the little thing darting about like a feather, with a single person in it; and the grand opening of the East River, with Brooklyn and the charming scenery beyond, — and you can form some little idea of my surprise and delight. Signior Maccaroni, as my uncle calls him, looked at it with perfect nonchalance. The bay was nothing to the bay of Naples; and the castle, less than nothing, compared with Castel Nuovo. Thank heaven, I had not been abroad to spoil my relish. Even my uncle enjoyed it, and spoke more kindly to me than during the whole passage. He was very sick, and called himself an old fool fifty times a day. I believe half the time he meant "young fool," that is me, for persuading him to the voyage. Graves' eyes sparkled, but as usual he said nothing. He only gave me a look, which said as plainly as a thousand words, "how beautiful!" But whether he meant me or Dame Nature is more than I can tell.

The moment we touched the wharf, there was an irruption of the Goths and Vandals, as my uncle called the hackney-coachmen, and the porters, who risked their necks in jumping aboard. "Carriage, sir," — "Baggage, sir," — "City Hotel, sir," — "Mansion House," — "Mrs. Mann's," — were reiterated a thousand times; and I thought half a dozen of them would have fought for our trunks, they disputed and swore so terribly. Stephen declared it was worse than London; and Graves said it put him in mind of the contest between the Greeks and Trojans for the body of poor Patroclus. My uncle called them hard names, and flourished his stick, but it would not do. When we got to the hotel, I thought we had mistaken some palace for a public-house. Such mirrors — such curtains — such carpets — such sofas — such chairs! I was almost afraid to sit down upon them. Even Stephen evinced his approbation, and repeated over and over again: " Upon my soul, clever — quite clever — *very* clever indeed, upon my soul." My uncle says, all this finery comes out of the cotton-plantations and rice-swamps; and that the negroes of the south work like horses, that their masters may spend their money like asses in the north.

Poor *Henney* does nothing but stand stock-still with her mouth and eyes wide open, and is of no more use to me than a statue. She is in every body's way — and in her own way too, I believe. I took her with me the other day to a milliner's, to bring home some of my finery. She stopped at every window, with such evident tokens of delight, that she attracted the attention of the boys, and came very near being mobbed. Missing her, I was obliged to turn back, and found her in ecstasies with a picture of Madame Hutin dancing before a droll figure in a fur cap and spectacles. Juba is keeping a journal, I believe, for you know that my uncle, while he abuses the practice with his tongue, assents to it in his heart, and humours his slaves more, perhaps, than a professed philanthropist in his situation would do. I should like to see Juba's lucubrations.

I begin to be weary — so, good night, my dear Maria. I will write again soon.   Your Lucia.

P. S. What do you think, Maria? — whisper it not to the telltale echoes of the high hills of Santee — they say bishops and pads are coming into fashion. I have seen several ladies that looked very suspicious.

Besides eating, and the various other resources of sense for passing the time in New York, there are sundry intellectual delights of most rare diversity —

exhibitions of fat oxen, to charm the liberal-minded amateur — Lord Byron's helmet — and Grecian dogs, whose wonderful capacity fully attests to the astonished world that the march of mind has extended even to the brute creation, insomuch that the difference between instinct and reason is now scarcely perceptible to the nicest observer, and it is the opinion of many of our learned men, that a dog of the nineteenth century is considerably wiser than a man of the sixteenth. There are also highly amusing methods of drawing teeth, and teaching grammar and tachygraphy, as well as all sorts of sciences and languages, by systems and machinery, which are pretended to be original, but which may be found in the famous Captain Lemuel Gulliver's voyage to Laputa. There are moreover an infinite number of highly diverting inventions for improving the condition of lazy loons, and teaching them economy and industry, by enabling them to live without either at the expense of other men. There are taverns, where amateurs may drink and smoke all the morning, without offence to man or beast. There is a famous musician, who can imitate the barking of dogs on his instrument, so as to deceive a dog himself, and whose "lady" screams exactly like a cat; so that they make the divinest harmony that ever was heard. There are the ladies' bonnets and curls, which are worth travelling a hundred miles to see; and their — what shall we call them? — bishops or pads, which are worth a voyage to the moon, to behold in all their majestic rotundity. There is also — no, there will be, as we are enabled to state positively on the best authority — there will be an exhibition, which is better worth the attention of people of real refined taste, than all those just enumerated put together. The gentleman has politely favoured us with a programme of his evening's exhibition, with permission to publish it, and to announce to the world of fashion, that he will be here on or about the first of June.

"You shall either laugh or cry."

THEATRICAL, DESCRIPTIVE, PHILOSOPHICAL, &c.

Mr. Hart, the preacher of natural religion, the play-actor, the tin-pedler, the attorney and counsellor-at-law, a lover of music, and an admirer of the fair sex, respectfully informs the ladies and gentlemen of New York, that on or about the first day of June next, at evening candle-light, he will go through an act of his own composition, at some place of fashionable resort, to consist of the following parts, viz.:

First. Music and dancing, and whirling round part of the time on one leg, and part of the time on two legs, like a top, fifty times, without showing the least giddiness.

Second. An address to Hope, in blank verse.

Third. The difference pointed out between happiness above and happiness below.

Fourth. Music.

Fifth. Orlando, an imaginary character, to his sweetheart.

Sixth. Music, dancing, and whirling round fifty times.

Seventh. An address to the departed spirit of George Washington.

Eighth. Music.

Ninth. The lover, **solus**.

Tenth. Music, dancing, and whirling round fifty times.

Eleventh. Orlando in despair marries one he does not love, runs mad, and whirls round fifty times to music.

Twelfth. Description of his contriving to get a divorce by means unprecedented in modern times.

Thirteenth. Music, dancing, and whirling round fifty times.

To conclude with Mr. Hart's acting the natural fool, talking to the departed spirits of General Washington and Thomas Paine, and making crooked mouths and wry faces at the audience.

We are much mistaken in the taste of the town, if this exhibition of Mr. Hart will not prove one of the most attractive ever presented to the patronage of the fashionable world, and go near to ruin all the theatres. The bill presents a variety of attraction perfectly irresistible to all refined palates. First, there is music, and dancing, and playing the teetotum, for the lovers of the Italian opera and gymnastics; then, an address to Hope, for the lovers of poetry; then, a philosophical disquisition, for the lovers of philosophy; then, music, to put us in a proper frame to listen to Orlando's love-letter; then, dancing and whirling, for the amateurs of the grand ballet; then, an address to a shade, for the devourers of witch and ghost stories; then, a lover talking to himself, for inamoratos; then, running mad, for the amusement of despairing young gentlemen; then, the contrivance for getting a divorce, which we prophesy will be received with great applause. But the cream of all will be the playing of the fool and making wry faces at the audience, which cannot do otherwise than please our theatrical amateurs, unless they should happen to have been surfeited with it already. In short, we think Mr. Hart's bill of fare fairly distances all play-bills, not excepting Peter Wilkins, and that Mr. Hart himself must possess a greater versatility of talent than the gentlemen and ladies who play six characters at a time, or even than the prince of buffoons and imitators, Mr. Mathews himself. We have no doubt the whole town will flock to see him, and that we shall observe, soon after his arrival, a great improvement in the taste of the people, as well as in our theatrical exhibitions, which may borrow a few hints from him with great advantage.

There are various branches of domestic industry cultivated by the young ladies of New York, the principal of which is the spinning of street-yarn, which they generally practise about four hours a day. Hence they are technically termed spinsters. But the great branch of domestic industry among the men is the trade in politics, in which vast numbers are engaged, some at stated seasons, others all the year round. Of the arts and mysteries of this business we profess to know nothing; but we believe, from the best information, that the whole secret consists in a certain opportune turning of the coat, which ought always to have two sides, one the exact contrast to the other in colour and texture. By the aid of this sort of harlequin jacket, a dexterous trader in politics can, if he possesses the ordinary instinct of a rat, always keep a strong house over his head, a tight vessel under him, and be always in the right, that is to say, upon the strongest side, which, according to fundamental principles, must be ever in the right. Some intolerant persons take upon themselves to denounce such manœuvring of the outward garment as unprincipled and disgraceful; but for our parts we hold that, *necessitas non habet legem* — and it is within the sphere of our knowledge, that no inconsiderable portion of this abused class of people, if they did not turn their coats pretty often, would very soon have no coats to turn.

On the other occupations or mysteries, such as spending a great deal of money without having any, and running in debt without possessing any credit, our limits will not allow us to dilate so copiously as we could wish. Suffice it to say, that New York is in this respect by no means behindhand with its neighbours, inasmuch as it is not uncommon to see people riding in splendid carriages, living in splendid houses, and owning a whole street, who, when they come to settle with death and their other creditors, pay the former and that is all. For the benefit of all fashionable tourists, we would wish to enter upon a full development of this the most valuable secret of the whole art of living, which may possibly one day stand them in stead. But it would require volumes of illustrations, and a minuteness of detail irreconcilable with the plan of this work. And even then it is doubtful whether the tourist would be able to put the system in practice, since many are of opinion that nothing but a regular apprenticeship in the arts of stock-jobbing, stock-companies, hypothecation, and blowing bubbles and bursting them, as practised *par excellence* in the *beau monde* of New York, will qualify a person for living upon nothing, unless indeed he have an uncommon natural genius.

Among the many modes of raising the wind in New York, that of buying lottery-tickets is one of the most effective. It is amazing what a number of prizes every lottery-office-keeper has sold either in whole or in shares, and, what is yet more extraordinary as well as altogether out of fashion, paid them too, if you will take his word for it. The whole insides and a large portion of the outsides of many houses in Broadway are covered with statements of the vast sums thus liberally dispensed to the public; and, what is very remarkable, among all those who have made their fortunes in this pursuit, we never heard of a single person who was brought to ruin by it! People need have no scruples of conscience about trying their luck in this way, since, if it were really gambling, the legislature of New York state, which is a great enemy to horse-racing, (save in one consecrated spot),* and all other kinds of gambling, would certainly never have authorized a series of lotteries, of which some people may recollect the beginning, but nobody can predict the end. Nothing can exceed the philanthropic earnestness with which the dispensers of fortune's favours, in the lotteries, strive to allure the ignorant and obtuse, who are not awake to the certainty of making a fortune after this fashion, into a habit of depending on the blind goddess, instead of always stupidly relying upon the labour of their hands and the sweat of their brows. Nor ought the unwearied pains of these liberal-hearted persons, to coax them into parting with all they have, in the

[* The Union Course, Long Island.]

moral certainty of getting back a hundred, yea a thousand, fold, pass without due commendation; for certain it is, that if any body in New York is poor, it must be owing to his own obstinate stupidity in refusing these disinterested invitations. N. B. There are very severe laws against gambling in New York.

There are many other ways of living and getting money here, and spending it too, which it is not necessary to enumerate. We have premised sufficient to enable the enlightened tourist, (who, peradventure, may have been left destitute in a strange place by a run at cards, a failure of remittances, or any other untoward accident), to retrieve his fortune, if he possesses an ordinary degree of intrepidity and enterprise. A complete knowledge of the world is the first requisite for living in the world, and the first step to the attainment of this is to know the difference between catching and being caught, as aptly exemplified in the fable of the fox and the oyster.

Once upon a time — it was long before the foxes had their speech taken from them lest they should get the better of man — as Reynard was fishing for oysters with his tail, he had the good-luck to put the end of it into the jaws of a fine *Blue-Pointer* that lay gaping with his mouth wide open, by reason of his having drank too much salt-water at dinner. " Ah ha!" cried the oyster, shutting his mouth as quickly as his corpulent belly would permit — " Ah ha!, have I caught you at last!" Reynard, tickled to death at this wise exclamation, forthwith set off full-tilt for his hole, the oyster holding on with all his might, though he got most bitterly bethumped against the rocks, and exclaiming all the while, " Ah ha! my honest friend, don't think to escape me — I've got you safe enough — ah ha!" All which he uttered without opening his mouth, as was the manner of speaking in those days. Reynard, who had wellnigh killed himself with laughing, at length came safe to his lodging with the clumsy oyster still fast to his tail. After taking a little breath, he addressed it thus: "Why, thou aquatic snail — thou nondescript among animals, that art neither fish, flesh, nor fowl — hadst thou but one single particle of brains in all that fat carcass of thine, I would argue the matter with thee. As it is, I will soon teach thee the difference between catching and being caught." So saying, he broke the shell of the honest oyster with a stone, and swallowed the contents with great satisfaction.

Having seen everything worth seeing, and eaten of everything worth eating, in New York, the traveller may begin to prepare for the ineffable delights of the Springs. After the month of April, oysters become unlawful; and canvas-backs are out of season. There is then nothing to detain the inquisitive tourist, and there are many things that render his speedy departure highly expedient. As Cæsar was cautioned by the seer, to beware the Ides of March, so do we, in like manner, seriously and vehemently caution the tourist to beware of the first of May, in other countries and places the season of May-poles, rural dances, and rustic loves; but, in New York, the period in which a great portion of the inhabitants seem to be enjoying a game at puss-in-a-corner. Woe be to the traveller who happens to sojourn in a house where this game is going on, for he will find no rest to the soles of his feet. His chair and his bed, his carpet and his joint-stool, will be taken from under him, and he will be left alone as it were like a hermit in the desert. People, as well as their establishments, seem to be actually deranged, insomuch that the prize-poet whom we have quoted before, not long since produced the following impromptu on the first of May:

> " Sing, heavenly muse! which is the greatest day,
> The first of April, or the first of May;
> Or, ye who moot nice points in learned schools,
> Tell us which breeds the greatest crop of fools!"

For a more particular account of this festival, which especially distinguishes the city of New York from all others in the known world, we refer our readers to the following letter. There is, however, some reason to surmise that it prevailed in Herculaneum and Pompeii, and was one of the causes which brought the vengeance of the gods on those unfortunate cities.

COLONEL CULPEPER TO MAJOR BRANDE.

NEW YORK, May 2, 1827.

MY DEAR MAJOR,—I am sorry to inform you that yesterday morning at daylight, or a little before, a large portion of the inhabitants of this city ran mad, in a most singular, I might say, original, manner; for I don't remember to have seen this particular form of insanity described in any work on the subject. This infirmity is peculiar to this precise season of the year, and generally manifests itself, a day or two previous to the crisis, in a perpetual fidgeting about the house, rummaging up of every thing, putting every thing out of place, and making a most ostentatious display of crockery and tin-ware. In proof of its not having any affinity to hydrophobia, it is sufficient to observe that the disease invariably manifests itself in a vehement disposition to scrubbing floors, washing windows, and dabbling in water in all possible ways. The great and decisive phenomenon, and one which is always followed by an almost instantaneous remission of the disorder, is scrambling out of one house as fast as you can, and getting into another as soon as possible. But, as I consider this as one of the most curious cases that ever came under my observation, I will give you a particular account of every prominent symptom accompanying it, with a request you will communicate the whole to Dr. Brady, for his decision on the matter.

It being a fine, bright, mild morning, I got up early, to take a walk on the Battery, the most glorious place for a morning or evening stroll to be found in the world. It is almost worth coming here, to inhale the exquisite coolness of the saline air, and watch the ever-moving scenery of little white sails, majestic displays of snowy canvas that look like fleecy clouds against the hills of Jersey and Staten Island, and all the life of nature, connected with her beautiful repose on the bosom of the expansive bay. Coming down into the entry, I found it cluttered up with a specimen of almost every thing that goes to the composition of house-keeping, and three or four sturdy fellows with hand-barrows, on which they were piling everything they could lay hold of. I asked what the matter was, but all I could get out of them was, "First of May, sir — please to stand out of the way — first of May, sir." So I passed on into the street, where I ran the gauntlet, among looking-glasses, old pictures, baskets of crockery, and things in general. The sidewalks were infested with processions of this sort, and in the middle of the streets were innumerable carts loaded with a general jail-delivery of all the trumpery that the carelessness of servants had broken, or the economy of the housewives preserved. If I stopped to contemplate this inexplicable scene, some male monster was sure to bounce against me out of a street-door, with a feather-bed, or assault me in the breach with the corner of a looking-glass, or some projection still more belligerent; while all the apology I got was, " First of May — take care, sir — first of May." At one time I was beleaguered between two hand-barrows, coming different ways, and giving each other just enough room to squeeze me half to death: at another, I was run foul of by a basket of crockery or cut glass, with a woman under it, to the imminent risk of demolishing these precious articles so dear to the heart of the sex, and got not only sour looks but hard words, while my bones were aching with bumps and bruises.

Finding there was no peace in Israel, I determined to get home without further delay, and ensconce myself snugly, until this fearful commotion of the household gods and their paraphernalia had died away. But I forgot that, " returning were as tedious as go o'er." There was not an old chair, or a looking-glass, or a picture, or any article cursed with sharp angles, that did not appear to have an irresistible attraction towards some part of my body, especially that portion which oftenest comes in contact with other bodies. In attempting to steer clear of a hand-barrow, I encountered a looking-glass, which the lady owner was following with pious care, and shattered it into a thousand pieces. The lady fainted, and, in my zeal to apologize to and assist her, I unfortunately grazed a glass lustre, which caught in my button-hole, and drew after it a little French woman, who luckily lighted on a feather-bed which an Irishman had set down, to rest himself. "Mon Dieu!" cried the little woman; "Jasus!" exclaimed the Irishman; the lady of the looking-glass wept; the little demoiselle laughed; the Irishman stole a kiss of her; and the valiant Colonel Culpeper made a masterly retreat into the entry of his domicile, where by the same token he ran full against my landlady, (who, in a paroxysm of the disorder, was sallying forth with both hands full), and demolished her spectacles irretrievably.

Finding myself thus environed with perils on all sides, I retreated to my bedchamber, but here I found the madness raging with equal violence. A serving-maid was pulling up the carpet, and pulling down the curtains, and making the dust fly in all directions, with a feverish activity that could only have been produced by a degree of excitement altogether unnatural. There was no living here, so I retreated to the dining-room, where every thing was out of its place, and the dust thicker than in the bedroom. Mops were going in one corner, brooms flourishing in another, side-boards standing in the middle of the room, and dining-tables flapping their wings, as if partaking in that irresistible propensity to motion which seemed to pervade everything animate and inanimate.

"Pray, sir," said I to a grave old gentleman who sat reading a newspaper, apparently unmoved amid the general confusion,—"Pray, sir, can you tell me what all this confusion means?" "O, it's only the first of May," he replied, without taking his eyes off the newspaper. Alas! he, too, is mad, thought I. But I'll try him again.

"The first of May — what of the first of May?"

"'Tis moving-time."

"Moving-time! what is that?"

"The time when every body moves."

"But, why does every body move just at this time?"

"I can't tell, except it be because it is the first of May. But," added he, looking up at last with a droll smile, "you seem to be a stranger, and perhaps don't know that the first of May is the day, the bane of the year, on which the good people of this town have, one and all, agreed to play at the game of move-all. They are now at it, hammer and tongs. To-morrow, things will be quiet, and we shall be settled in a different part of the street."

"O, then the people are not mad," said I.

"By no means: they are only complying with an old custom."

"'Tis an odd custom."

"It is so, but not more odd than many others in all parts of the world."

"Will you be so obliging as to tell me its origin, and the reason for it?"

"Why, as to the reason, half the old customs we blindly follow are just as difficult to account for, and apparently as little founded in design as this. It would be too much to make people give reasons for every thing they do. This custom of moving in a body on May-day is said, however, to have originated at a very early period in the history of New York, when there were but two houses in it. The tenants of these, taking it into their heads to change their domiciles, and having no others to remove to, agreed to start fair at one and the same time with bag and baggage, and thus step into each other's shoes. They did so, and the arrangement was found so convenient that it has passed into general practice ever since."

"And so the good people take it for granted, that a custom which necessity forced upon them when there were but two houses in the city is calculated for a city with thirty thousand. A capital pedigree for an old custom."

"'Tis as good as one half the usages of the world can boast of," replied the philosopher, and resumed his studies. "But," said I, "how can you possibly read in all this hubbub?" "O," replied he, "I've moved every May-day for the last forty years."

Having ascertained the location of the house into which the family was moving, I made for it with all convenient speed, hoping to find at least an asylum for my wearied and bruised body. But I fell out of the frying-pan into the fire. The spirit of moving was here more rampant than at my other home, and, between moving in and moving out, there was no chance of escaping a jostle or a jog from some moving movable, on its arrival or departure. Despairing of a resting-place here, I determined to drop in upon an old friend; and proceeded to his house. But he, too, was moving. From thence I went to a hotel, in hopes of a quiet hour in the reading-room; but the hotel was moving too. I jumped into a hack, bidding the man drive out of town as fast as possible. "I'm moving a family, sir, and can't serve you," cried he; and just then somebody thrust the corner of a looking-glass into my side, and almost broke one of my ribs. At this critical moment, seeing the door of a church invitingly open, I sought refuge in its peaceful aisles. But alas! major, every thing was in confusion here; the floors in a puddle, the pews wet, the prayer-books piled in heaps, and women splashing the windows furiously with dippers of water. "Zounds!" said I to one of them, "are *you* moving too?", and, without waiting for an answer, walked into the church-yard, in hopes I should find the tenants quiet there. Here I sauntered about, reading the records of mortality, and moralizing on the contrast between the ever-moving scene without and the undisturbed repose within. There was but a wooden fence to mark the separation between the region of life and that of death. In a few minutes my perturbation subsided, and the little rubs and vexations I had undergone during the day faded into insignificance before the solemn meditations on that everlasting remove to which we all are destined. I went home, dined at my old house, slept in my new lodgings, on a wet floor, and caught a rheumatism in my left shoulder.

Adieu, major. If you ever visit New York, beware of the first of May.

From this letter, which we assure our readers is of the first authority, it will sufficiently appear that the elegant tourist should so arrange his pleasures, (for business he ought to have none), as either to arrive at New York after, or quit it before, the first day of May. Previous to his departure, it will be proper for the traveller, if a gentleman, to furnish himself with the following indispensable conveniences:—

The New Mirror for Travellers, and Guide to the

Springs. **N. B.** Be careful to ask for the NEW MIRROR.

Two shirts. **N. B.** Dickies, or collars, with ruffles, will answer.

Plenty of cravats, which are the best apologies for shirts in the world, except ruffles.

Six coats, including a surtout and box-coat. **N. B.** If you can't afford to pay for these, the tailor must suffer — there is no help for him.

Forty pairs of pantaloons, of all sorts. Ditto, waistcoats.

Twelve pairs of white kid-gloves.

Twelve pairs of boots. N. B. If you wear boots altogether, stockings are unnecessary, except at balls — economy is a blessed thing.

Twelve tooth-brushes.

Twelve hair-brushes.

Six clothes-brushes — one for each coat.

A percussion-gun and a pointer-dog. **N. B.** No matter whether you are a sportsman or not — it looks well.

A pair of pistols, to shoot a friend with now and then.

An umbrella, which you can borrow of a friend and forget to return.

A portmanteau without any name or initials, so that if you should happen to take another man's, it may pass for a mistake. **N. B.** Never make such mistakes, unless there is some special reason for it.

A pocket-book, well filled with bank-notes. If you can't raise the wind with the genuine, you may buy a few counterfeits, cheap. Any money is good enough for travelling, and if one won't take it another will. Don't be discouraged at one refusal — try it again. If you are well-dressed, and have a gun and a pointer-dog, no one will suspect you. N. B. There are no police-officers in the steam-boats.

There is one class of travellers deserving a whole book by themselves, could we afford to write one for their especial benefit. We mean the gentlemen who, as the African negro said, " walk big way — write big book;" tourists by profession, who explore this country for the pleasure of their readers and their own profit, and travel at the expense of one people's reputation and of another's pockets; who pay for a dinner by libelling their entertainer, and for their passage in a steam-boat by retailing the information of the steward or coxswain; to whom the sight of a porpoise at sea affords matter for profitable speculation; who make more out of a flying-fish than a market-woman does out of a sheep's-head; and dispose of a tolerable storm at the price of a week's board. These are the travellers for our money, being the only ones on record, except the pedlers, who unite the profits of business with the pleasures of travelling — a consummation which authors have laboured at in vain until the present happy age of improvements, when sentimental young ladies wear spatterdashes and stout young gentlemen white kid-gloves, and when an opera-singer receives a higher salary than an archbishop and travels about with letters of introduction from kings!

Of all countries in the world, Old England, our kind, gentle, considerate old mamma, sends forth the largest portion of this species of literary "*riders*," who sweep up the materials for a book by the roadside. They are held of so much consequence as to be patronized by the government, which expends large sums in sending them to the North Pole, only to tell us, in a "big book," how cold it is there; or to Africa, to distribute glass beads, and repeat over and over the same things, through a score of huge quartos. With these we do not concern ourselves; but, inasmuch as it hath been alleged, however unjustly, that those who have from time to time honoured this country with their notice have been guilty of divers sins of ignorance, prejudice, and malignity, we here offer them a compendium of regulations, by the due observance of which they may in future avoid these offences, and construct a "big book" which shall give universal satisfaction.

Rules for gentlemen who "walk big way — make big book."

Never fail to seize every opportunity to lament, with tears in your eyes, the deplorable state of religion among "these republicans." People will take it for granted you are a very pious man.

Never lose an opportunity of canting about the sad state of morals among these republicans. People will give you credit for being very moral yourself.

Whenever you have occasion to mention the fourth of July, the birthday of Washington, or any other great national anniversary, don't forget to adduce it as proof of the bitter hostility felt by these republicans towards the English, and to lament these practices, as tending to keep up the memory of the Revolution, as well as to foster national antipathies.

Be very particular in noticing stage-drivers, waiters, tavern-keepers, and persons of the like importance, who, as it were, represent the character of the people. Whenever you want any profound information, always apply to them:— they are the best authority you can have.

If you happen to fall in company with a public man in the stage or steam-boat, take the first opportunity of pumping the driver or waiter. These fellows know every thing, and can tell you all the lies that have ever been uttered against him.

If you dine with a hospitable gentleman, don't fail to repay him by dishing up himself, his wife, daughters, and dinner, in your book. If the little boys don't behave respectfully towards you, and sneak into a corner with their fingers in their mouths, cut them up handsomely — father, mother, and all. Be sure you give their names at full length; be particular in noting every dish on the table; and don't forget pumping the waiter.

Tell all the old stories which the Yankees repeat of their Southern and Western neighbours, and which the latter have retorted upon them. Be sure not to forget the gouging of the judge, the roasting of the negro, the wooden nutmegs, the indigo coal; and, above all, the excellent story of the wooden bowls. Never inquire whether they are true or not; they will make John Bull twice as happy as he is at present.

Never write a line without having the fear of the reviewers before your eyes, and remember how poor Miss Wright got abused for praising these republicans and sinners.

Never be deterred from telling a story to the discredit of any people, especially republicans, on the score of its improbability. John Bull, for whom you write, will swallow any thing, from a pot of beer to a melo-drama. He is even a believer in his own freedom.

Never be deterred from telling a story on account of its having been told, over and over again, by every traveller since the discovery of America by the literati of Europe. If the reader has seen it before, it is only meeting an old friend; if he has not, it is making a new acquaintance. But be sure you don't forget to say that you saw every thing you describe. To quote from another is to give him all the credit, and is almost as bad as robbing your own house. There is nothing makes a lie look so much like truth as frequent repetition. If you know it to be false, don't let that deter you; for, as you did not invent it yourself, you cannot be blamed.

Abuse all the women in mass, out of compliment to your own countrywomen. The days of chivalry are past, and more honour comes of attacking than defending ladies in the present age of public improvements. Besides, all the world loves scandal, and a book filled with the praises of one nation is an insult to the rest of the world.

If the stage breaks down with you, give the roads no quarter.

If you get an indifferent breakfast at an inn, cut up the whole town where the enormity was encountered, pretty handsomely; if a bad dinner, deprive the whole nation of its morals; if a sorry supper, take away the reputation of the landlady, the cook, and the landlady's daughters without ceremony. Item, if they put you to sleep in a two-bedded room, although the other bed be empty, it is sufficient provocation to set them all down for infidels, thereby proving yourself a zealous Christian.

Never read any book written by natives of the country you mean to describe. They are always partial; and, besides, a knowledge of the truth fetters the imagination, and circumscribes invention. It is fatal to the composition of a romance.

Never suffer the hospitalities and kindness of these republicans to conciliate you, except just while you are enjoying them. You may eat their dinners and receive their attentions; but never forget, that if you praise the Yankees John Bull will condemn your book, and that charity begins at home. The first duty of a literary traveller is to make a book that will sell; the rest is between him and his conscience, and is nobody's business.

Never mind what these republicans say of you or your book. You never mean to come among them again; or, if you do, you can come under a different name. Let them abuse you as much as they please. "Who reads an American book?" No Englishman certainly, except with a view of borrowing its contents without giving the author credit for them. Besides, every true-born Englishman knows that the shortest way of elevating his own country is to depress all others as much as possible.

Never fail to find fault with everything, and grumble without ceasing. Else people won't know you for an Englishman.

Never mind your geography, as you are addressing yourself to people who don't know a wild turkey from Turkey in Europe. Your book will sell just as well, if you place New York on the Mississippi, and New Orleans on the Hudson. You will be kept in countenance by a certain British secretary of foreign affairs, who is said to have pronounced the right to navigate the St. Lawrence inadmissible to the United States, because it would give them a direct route to the Pacific.

You need not make any special inquiries into the state of morals, because every body knows that republicans have no morality; nor of religion, because every body knows they tolerate all religions, and of course can have none; nor of manners, because, as there is no distinction of ranks recognized in their constitution, it is clear they must all be blackguards. The person most completely qualified of any we ever met with for a traveller was a worthy Englishman, who, being very near-sighted, and hard of hearing, was not led astray by the villany of his five senses; and, curiously enough, his book contained quite as much truth as those of his more fortunate contemporaries who were embarrassed by eyes and ears.

If the tourist belongs to the order of the petticoat, the following articles are of the first necessity in a visit to the Springs.

Six fashionable hats, in bandboxes. N. B. The steam-boats are pretty capacious, and from Albany to the Springs you can hire an extra.

Two lace veils to hide blushes. If you never blush, there is no harm done.

An indispensable for miscellaneous matters. Beware of pockets and pick-pockets.

Two trunks of barèges, gros de Naples, and silks.
Two trunks of miscellaneous finery.
A dressing-case.
One large trunk containing several sets of curls well-baked, prepared by Monsieur Manuel.
The last Waverley.
Plenty of airs.
Ditto of graces.
Six beaux to amuse you on the journey. N. B. A poodle will do as well.
A dozen pairs of white satin shoes to ramble about in through the swamps at Saratoga and Ballston. Leather smells vilely, and prunello is quite vulgar.
Six dozen pairs of silk hose, the thinnest that can be had. There is nothing so beautiful as flesh-colour with open clocks.
A travelling-chain, the largest and heaviest that can be had, to wear round the neck. This will furnish the beaux with a hint for saying clever things about chains, darts, &c. The poodle can sometimes play with it.

☞ There is no occasion for a pocket-book, as all is paid by papa (or his creditors), and young ladies ought never to know any thing about the value of money. It sophisticates the purity of their unadulterated sentiments.

These principal requisites being procured, you take the steam-boat for Albany. If you are in a great hurry, or not afraid of being drowned in going ashore at West Point, or blown up by the way, take one of the fastest boats you can find. But, if you wish to travel pleasantly, eat your meals in comfort, associate with genteel company, sleep in quiet, and wake up alive, our advice is to take one of the SAFETY BARGES, where all these advantages are combined. It grieves us to the soul to see these sumptuous aquatic palaces, which constitute the very perfection of all earthly locomotion, almost deserted by the ill-advised traveller — and for what? That he may get to Albany a few hours sooner: as if it were not the distinguishing characteristic of a well-bred man of pleasure to have more time on his hands than he knows what to do with. Let merchants, and tradesmen, and brokers, and handicraft people, and all those condemned to daily labour, to whom time is as money, patronize the swift boats; and let those who are running away from justice affect them; but, for the man of leisure, whose sole business is to kill time pleasantly, enjoy himself at his ease, and dine free from the infamous proximity of hungry rogues who devour with their eyes what they can't reach with their hands, the safety barges are preferable even to the chariot of the sun. N. B. We dont mean to discourage people who may cherish a harmless propensity to being blown up. Every one to his taste.

The following hints will be found serviceable to all travellers in steam-boats.

In the miscellaneous company usually found in these machines, the first duty of a man is to take care of himself — to get the best seat at table, the best location on deck; and, when these are obtained, to keep resolute possession in spite of all the significant looks of the ladies.

If your heart yearns for a particularly comfortable

seat which is occupied by a lady, all you have to do is to keep your eye steadily upon it, and, the moment she gets up, don't wait to see if she is going to return, but take possession without a moment's delay. If she comes back again, be sure not to see her.

Keep a sharp lookout for meals. An experienced traveller can always tell when these are about being served up, by a mysterious movement on the part of the ladies, and a mysterious agitation among the gentlemen, who may be seen gradually pressing towards the cabin doors. Whenever you observe these symptoms, it is time to exert yourself by pushing through the crowd to the place of execution. Never mind the sour looks, but elbow your way with resolution and perseverance, remembering that a man can eat but so many meals in his life, and that the loss of one can never be retrieved.

The most prudent plan, however, is that generally pursued by your knowing English travellers, which is as follows: As soon as you have seen your baggage disposed of, and before the waiters have had time to shut the cabin-doors, preparatory to laying the tables, station yourself at one of them, in a proper situation for action. On the inside if you can, for there you are not in the way of the servants. Resolutely maintain your position in spite of the looks and hints of the servants, about "Gentlemen in the way," and "No chance to set the tables." You can be reading a book or a newspaper, and not hear them; or, a better way is to pretend to be asleep.

Keep a wary eye for a favourite dish, and, if it happens to be placed at a distance or on another table, you can take an opportunity to look hard at an open window as if there was too much air for you, shrug your shoulders, and move opposite the dish aforesaid.

The moment the bell rings, fall to: you need not wait for the rest of the company to be seated, or mind the ladies, for there is no time to be lost on these occasions. For the same reason, you should keep your eyes moving about, from one end of the table to the other, in order that if you see any thing you like you can send for it without losing time. Call as loudly and as often as possible for the waiter; the louder you call, the more consequence you will gain with the company. If he don't mind you, don't hesitate to snatch whatever he has got in his hands, if you happen to want it.

Be sure to have as many different things on your plate at one time as it will hold, and to use your own knife in cutting up all the dishes within your reach, and particularly in helping yourself to butter, though there may be knives on purpose. N. B. It is of no consequence whether your knife is fishy or not.

Don't wait for the dessert to be laid, but the moment a pudding or a pie is placed within your reach, fall to and spare not. Get as much pudding and pie, and as many nuts, apples, raisins, &c., on your plate as you can, and eat all together.

Pay no attention to the ladies, who have, or ought to have, friends to take care of them, or they have no business to be travelling in steam-boats.

The moment you have eaten everything within your reach, and are satisfied nothing more is forthcoming, get up and make for the cabin door with a segar in your hand. No matter if you are sitting at the middle of the inner side of the table, and disturb a dozen persons, or more. They have no business to be in your way. If it is supper-time and the candles are lighted, you had best light your segar at one of them, and puff a little before you proceed, for fear it should go out. N. B. If you were to take an opportunity to find fault with the meals, the attendants, and the boat, in an audible tone, as Englishmen do, it will serve to give people an idea you have been used to better at home.

Never think of pulling off your hat on coming into the cabin, though it happens to be full of ladies. It looks anti-republican; and, besides, has the appearance of not having been used to better company.

Never miss an opportunity of standing in the doorway, or on the stairs, or in narrow passages; and never get out of the way to let anybody pass, particularly a lady.

If there happens to be a scarcity of seats, be sure to stretch yourself at full length upon a sofa or a cushion, and, if any lady looks at you as if she thought you might give her a place, give her another look as much as to say, "I'll see you hanged, first."

If the weather is cold, get directly before the stove, turn your back, and open the skirts of your coat behind as wide as possible, that the fire may have fair play.

If you happen to be better dressed than your neighbour, look at him with an air of superiority; and don't hear him if he has the impudence to speak to you. If it is your ill-fortune to be dressed not so well, employ a tailor as soon as possible to remedy the inferiority.

Be sure to pay your passage, if you have any money.

If you have none, go to sleep in some out-of-the-way corner, and don't wake till the moon rises in the West.

Don't pay any attention to the notification that, "no smoking is allowed abaft the wheel;" but strut about among the ladies, on the quarter-deck and the upper gallery, with a segar in your mouth on all occasions. There are so many ignorant people that smoke on board steam-boats, that it will naturally be supposed you can't read, and of course don't know of the prohibition. If you can get to the windward of a lady or two, so much the better.

Whenever you are on deck by day, be sure to have this book in your hand, and, instead of boring yourself with the scenery, read the descriptions, which will be found infinitely superior to any of the clumsy productions of nature.

N. B. These rules apply exclusively to *gentlemen*, the ladies being allowed the liberty of doing as they please, in all respects except six.

They are not permitted to eat beefsteaks and mutton-chops at breakfast, unless they can prove themselves past fifty.

They must not sit at table more than an hour, unless they wish to be counted hungry, which no lady ought ever to be.

They must not talk so loud as to drown the noise of the engine, unless their voices are particularly sweet.

They must not enact the turtle-dove before all the company, unless they can't help it.

They must not jump overboard at every little noise of the machinery.

They must not be always laughing, except they have very white teeth.

With these exceptions, they may say and do just what they like, in spite of papa and mamma, for this is a free country.

PASSAGE UP THE HUDSON.

"This magnificent river,* which, taking it in all its combinations of magnitude and beauty, is scarcely equalled in the New, and not even approached in the Old, World, was discovered by Hendrik Hudson in the month of September, 1609, by accident, as almost every other discovery has been made. He was searching for a north-west passage to India when he first entered the bay of New York, and imagined the possibility that he had here found it, until, on exploring the river upwards, he came to fresh water, ran aground, and abandoned his hopes."

Of this man, whose name is thus identified with the discovery, the growth, and the future prospects of a mighty state, little is known; and of that little the end is indescribably melancholy. He made four voyages in search of this imaginary north-west passage, and the termination of the last (in 1610) is in the highest degree affecting, as related in the following extracts from the published collections of the New York Historical Society. The "Master" is Hudson.

"You shall vnderstand," says Master Abacuk Pricket, from whose account this is taken, "that our Master kept (in his house at *London*) a young man, named *Henrie Greene*, borne in *Kent*, of Worshipfull

---
* We quote from the unpublished *ana* of Alderman Janson.

Parents, but by his lend life and conuersation hee had lost the good will of all his friends, and had spent all that hee had. This man, our Master would haue to Sea with him, because hee could write well: our Master gaue him meate, and drinke, and lodging, and by meanes of one Master *Venson*, with much adoe got foure pounds of his mother to buy him clothes, wherewith Master *Venson* would not trust him: but saw it laid out himselfe. This *Henrie Greene* was not set downe in the owners' booke, nor any wages made for him. Hee came first aboard at *Grauesend*, and at *Harwich* should haue gone into the field, with one *Wilkinson*. At *Island* the Surgeon and hee fell out in *Dutch*, and hee beat him a shoare in *English*, which set all the company in a rage; so that wee had much adoe to get the Surgeon aboard. I told the Master of it, but hee bade mee let it alone, for (said hee) the Surgeon had a tongue that would wrong the best friend hee had. But *Robert Iuet* (the Master's Mate) would needs burne his finger in the embers, and told the Carpenter a long tale (when hee was drunke) that our Master had brought in *Greene* to cracke his credit that should displease him: which words came to the Master's eares, who when hee vnderstood it, would haue gone backe to *Island*, when he was fortie leagues from thence, to haue sent home his Mate *Robert Iuet* in a Fisher-man. But, being otherwise perswaded, all was well. So *Henry Greene* stood vpright, and very inward with the Master, and was a seruiceable man euery way for manhood: but for Religion, he would say he was cleane paper whereon he might write what he would. Now, when our Gunner was dead, and (as the order is in such cases) if the company stand in need of any thing that belonged to the man deceased, then is it brought to the Mayne Mast, and there sold to them that will giue most for the same: This Gunner had a gray cloth gowne, which *Greene* prayed the Master to friend him so much as to let him haue it, paying for it as another would giue: the Master saith hee should, and thereupon hee answered some, that sought to haue it, that *Greene* should haue it, and none else, and so it rested.

"Now, out of season and time, the Master calleth the Carpenter to goe in hand with an house on shoare, which at the beginning our Master would not heare, when it might haue been done. The Carpenter told him, that the Snow and Frost were such, as hee neither could, nor would goe in hand with such worke. Which when our Master heard, hee ferreted him out of his Cabbin, to strike him, calling him by many foule names, and threatening to hang him. The Carpenter told him that hee knew what belonged to his place better then himselfe, and that hee was no House Carpenter. So this passed, and the house was (after) made with much labour, but to no end. The next day after the Master and the Carpenter fell out, the Carpenter tooke his Peece and *Henry Greene* with him, for it was an order that none should goe out alone, but one with a Peece, and another with a Pike. This did moue the Master so much the more against *Henry Greene*, that *Robert Billet* his Mate must haue the gowne, and had it deliuered vnto him; which when *Henry Greene* saw, he challenged the Master's promise: but the Master did so raile on *Greene*, with so many words of disgrace, telling him, that all his friends would not trust him with twenty shillings, and therefore why should he? As for wages he had none, nor none should haue, if he did not please him well. Yet the Master had promised him to make his wages as good as any man's in the ship; and to haue him one of the Prince's guard when we came home. But you shall see how the deuil out of this so wrought with *Greene*, that he did the Master what mischiefe hee could in seeking to discredit him, and to thrust him and many other honest men out of the Ship in the end."

It appears that, (Greene having come to an understanding with others whom he had corrupted), a plot was laid, to seize Hudson and those of the crew that remained faithful to him, put them on board a small shallop which was used in making excursions for food or observations, and run away with the ship. Of the manner in which this was consummated the same writer gives the following relation:

"Being thus in the Ice on Saturday, the one and twentieth of Iune at night, *Wilson*, the Boatswayne, and *Henry Greene* came to mee lying (in my Cabbin) lame, and told mee that they and the rest of their Associates would shift the Company, and turne the Master, and all the sicke men into the shallop, and let them shift for themselues. For, there was not fourteen daies' victual left for all the Company, at that poore allowance they were at, and that there they lay, the Master not caring to goe one way or other: and that they had not eaten any thing these three dayes, and therefore were resolute, either to mend or end, and what they had begun they would goe through with it, or dye."

Pricket refuses, and expostulates with Wilson and Greene.

"*Henry Greene* told me then, that I must take my fortune in the Shallop. If there bee no remedie, (said I), the will of GOD bee done."

Pricket tries to persuade them to put off their design for two days, nay, for twelve hours, that he might persuade Hudson to return home with the ship; but, to this they would not consent, and proceeded to execute their plot as follows:—

"In the meane time *Henrie Greene* and another went to the Carpenter, and held him with a talke, till the Master came out of his Cabbin (which hee soone did): then came *Iohn Thomas* and *Bennet* before him, while *Wilson* bound his armes behind him. He asked them what they meant? They told him, he should know when he was in the Shallop. Now *Iuet*, while this was a doing, came to *Iohn King* into the Hold, who was prouided for him, for he had got a sword of his own, and kept him at a bay, and might haue killed him, but others came to helpe him: and so he came vp to the Master. The Master called to the Carpenter, and told him that he was bound; but, I heard no answere he made. Now *Arnold Lodlo*, and *Michael Bute* rayled at them, and told them their knauerie would shew itselfe. Then was the Shallop haled vp to the Ship side, and the poore, sicke, and lame men were called vpon to get them out of their Cabbins into the Shallop. The Master called to me, who came out of my Cabbin as well as I could, to the Hatchway to speake with him: where, on my knees I besought them, for the loue of God, to remember themselues, and to doe as they would be done vnto. They bad me keepe my selfe well, and get me into my Cabbin; not suffering the Master to speake with me. But when I came into my Cabbin againe, hee called to me at the Horne, which gaue light into my Cabbin, and told mee that *Iuet* would ouerthrow vs all; nay (said I) it is that villaine *Henrie Greene*, and I spake it not softly." . . . .

"Now were all the poore men in the Shallop, whose names are as followeth; *Henrie Hudson*, *Iohn Hudson*, *Arnold Lodlo*, *Sidrack Faner*, *Phillip Staffe*, *Thomas Woodhouse*, or *Wydhouse*, *Adam Moore*, *Henrie King*, *Michael Bute*. The Carpenter got of them a Peece, and Powder, and Shot, and some Pikes, an Iron Pot, with some meale, and other things. They stood out of the Ice, the Shallop being fast to the Sterne of the Shippe, and so, (when they were nigh out, for I cannot say they were cleane out), they cut her head fast from the Sterne of our Ship, then out with their Topsayles, and towards the East they stood in a cleere Sea."

The mutineers, being on shore some days after, were attacked by a party of Indians.

"*Iohn Thomas* and *William Wilson* had their bowels cut, and *Michael Perce* and *Henry Greene* being mortally wounded, came tumbling into the Boat together. When *Andrew Moter* saw this medley, hee came running downe the Rockes, and leaped into the Sea, and so swamme to the Boat, hanging on the sterne thereof, till *Michael Perce* tooke him in, who manfully made good the head of the Boat against the Sauages, that pressed sore vpon vs. Now *Michael Perce* had got an Hatchet, wherewith I saw him strike one of them, that he lay sprawling in the Sea. *Henry Greene* crieth *Coragia*, and layeth about him with his Truncheon: I cryed to them to cleere the Boat, and

Andrew Moter cryed to bee taken in: the Sauages betooke them to their Bowes and Arrowes, which they sent amongst vs, wherewith *Henry Greene* was slaine outright, and *Michael Perce* receiued many wounds, and so did the rest. *Michael Perce* cleereth the Boate, and puts it from the shoare, and helpeth *Andrew Moter* in: but, in turning of the Boat, I receiued a cruell wound in my backe with an Arrow. *Michael Perce* and *Andrew Moter* rowed the Boate away, which when the Sauages saw, they ranne to their Boats, and I feared they would haue launched them, to haue followed vs, but they did not, and our ship was in the middle of the channell, and could not see vs.

"Now, when they had rowed a good way from the shoare, *Michael Perce* fainted, and could row no more: then was *Andrew Moter* driuen to stand in the Boat head, and waft to the ship, which (at the first) saw vs not, and when they did, they could not tel what to make of vs, but in the end they stood for vs, and so tooke vs vp. *Henry Greene* was throwne out of the Boat into the Sea, and the rest were had aboard, the Sauage being yet aliue, yet without sense. But they died all there that day, *William Wilson* swearing and cursing in the most fearefull manner: *Michael Perce* liued two dayes after, and then died. Thus you haue heard the Tragicall end of *Henry Greene* and his Mates, whom they called Captaine, these foure being the only lustie men in all the ship."

After this, Robert Juet took the command, but "dyed, for meere want," before they arrived at Plymouth, which is the last we hear of them, except that Pricket was taken up to London to Sir Thomas Smith.

The unfortunate Hudson and his companions were never heard of more. Doubtless they perished miserably, by famine, cold, or savage cruelty. But the mighty river which he first explored, and the great bay to the north, by bearing his name, preserve his memory, and will continue to preserve it to the latest posterity. We thought we could do no less than call the attention of the traveller, for a few moments, to the hard fate of one to whom they are originally indebted for much of the pleasures of the tour to the Springs.

After the traveller has paid tribute to the memory of Henry Hudson by reading the preceding sketch of his melancholy end, he may indulge himself in contemplating the beautiful world expanding every moment before him, appearing and vanishing in the rapidity of his motion, like creations of the imagination. Every object is beautiful, and its beauties are heightened by the eye having no time to be palled with contemplating them too long. Nature seems in jocund motion hurrying by, and as she moves along displays a thousand varied charms in rapid succession, each one more enchanting than the last. If the traveller casts his eyes backwards, he beholds the long perspective of waters gradually converging to a point at the Narrows, fringed with the low soft scenery of Jersey and Long Island, and crowned with the little buoyant islands on its bosom. If he looks before him, on one side the picturesque shore of Jersey, with its rich strip of meadows and orchards, now backed by the wood-crowned hills, and again by perpendicular walls of solid rock, and on the other, York Island with its thousand little palaces, sporting its green fields and waving woods, by turns allure his attention, and make him wish, either that the river had but one side, or that he had more eyes to admire its beauties.

As the vessel wafts him merrily, merrily along, new beauties crowd upon him so rapidly as almost to confuse the impressions of the view. That noble ledge of rocks which is worthy to form the barrier of the noble river, and which extends for sixteen miles, shows itself in a succession of sublime bluffs, projecting out one after the other, looking like the fabled works of the giants. High on these cliffs, may be seen the woodman, pitching his billet from the very edge down a precipice of hundreds of feet, whence it slides or bounds to the water's edge, and is received on board its destined vessel. At other points, on some steep slope, you will see the quarriers, undermining huge masses of rocks that in the lapse of ages have separated from the cliff above, and setting them rolling down with thundering crashes to the level beach below. Here and there under the dark impending cliff, where nature has formed a little green nook or flat, some enterprising skipper who owns a little periauger, or some hardy quarryman, has erected his little cot. There, when the afternoon shadows envelop the rocks, the woods, and the shore, may be seen little groups of children sporting in all the glee of youthful idleness — some setting their shaggy dog to swimming after a chip, others worrying some patient pussy, others wading along the smooth sands, knee-deep in the waters, and others, perhaps, stopping to stare at the moving wonder champing by, then chasing the long ripple occasioned by its furious motion, as it breaks along the beach. Contrasting beautifully with this long mural precipice on the west, the eastern bank exhibits a charming variety of outline, in long, graceful, curving hills,—here sinking into little vales, each pouring forth a gurgling brook—there rising again into tree-clad eminences, presenting the image of a succession of mighty waves, suddenly arrested in their rolling career, and turned into mingled woods and meadows and fertile fields, rich in all the evidences of industry, and animated with cattle, sheep, and whistling ploughmen.

These precipices are said to be of the trap formation, a most important species of rock in geology, as whoever "understands trap" may set up for a master of the science. In many places, this trap formation is found apparently based on a horizontal stratum of primitive rock. This has somewhat shaken the trap theory, and puzzled geologists. But we leave them to settle the affair, and pass on to objects of more importance to the tourist, in a historical point of view at least.

At Sneden's Landing, opposite Dobb's Ferry, the range of perpendicular trap rocks, disappears. You again detect it, opposite Sing Sing, where it exhibits itself in a most picturesque and beautiful manner at intervals, in the range of mountains bordering the west side of the river, between Nyack and Haverstraw. At Sneden's commences a vast expanse of salt-meadows, generally so thickly studded with barracks and hay-stacks, as to present at a distance the appearance of a great city rising out of the famed Tappan Sea, like Venice from the Adriatic. Travellers, who have seen both, observe a great similarity — but, on the whole, prefer the hay-stacks. Here begins the Tappan Sea, where the river expands to a breadth of three miles, and where, in the days of log-canoes and pine skiffs, full many an adventurous navigator is said to have encountered dreadful perils in crossing over from the Slote* to Tarrytown. At present its dangers are all traditionary.

The western border of this beautiful expanse is mountainous; but the hills rise in such gradual ascent that the whole is cultivated to the very top, and exhibits a charming display of variegated fields. That the soil was once rich is established by the fact of this whole district being settled by the Dutch, than whom there never was a people better at smelling out rich vales and fat alluvial shores. Here the race subsists, unadulterated to the present time. The sons are cast in the same mould with the father and grandfather; the daughters depart not from the examples of their mothers and grandmothers. The former eschew the mysteries of modern tailoring, and the latter borrow not the fashion of their bonnets from the French milliners. They travel not in steamboats, or in any other newfangled inventions; abhor canals and railroads, and will go five miles out of the way to avoid a turnpike. They mind nobody's business but their own, and such is their inveterate attachment to home, that it is credibly reported there are men now living along the shores of the river, who not only have never visited the renowned Tarrytown, directly opposite, but who know not even its name.

They are deplorably deficient in the noble science

[* A creek just South of the present Piermont dock. It was called by the old Dutch folks, The Tappan Slote.]

of gastronomy, and such is their utter barbarity of taste, that they never eat but when they are hungry, nor after they are satisfied, and the consequence of this savage indifference to the chief good of life is that they one and all remain without those infallible patents of high-breeding, gout and dyspepsia. Since the period of the first settlement of this region, the only changes that have ever been known to take place are, first, those brought about by death, who, if report says true, has sometimes had his match with some of these tough old copperheads; secondly, in the aspect of the soil, which from an interminable forest has become a garden; and, thirdly, in the size of the loaves of bread, which from five feet long have dwindled down into the ordinary dimensions. For this unheard-of innovation, the people adduce in their justification the following undoubted tradition, which, like their hats and their petticoats, has descended from generation to generation without changing a syllable.

"Some time in the autumn of the year 1694, just when the woods were on the change, Yffrouw, or Vrouw, Katrinchee Van Noorden was sitting at breakfast with her husband and family, consisting of six stout boys and as many strapping girls, all dressed in their best, for it was of a Sunday morning. Vrouw Katrinchee had a loaf of fresh rye-bread between her knees, the top of which was about on a line with her throat, the other end resting upon a napkin on the floor; and was essaying with the edge of a sharp knife to cut off the upper crust for the youngest boy, who was the pet; when unfortunately it recoiled from the said crust, and, before the good vrouw had time to consider the matter, sliced off her head as clean as a whistle, to the great horror of Mynheer Van Noorden, who actually stopped eating his breakfast. This awful catastrophe brought the big loaves into disrepute among the people, but such was their attachment to good old customs, that it was not until Domine Koontzie denounced them as against the law and the prophets that they could be brought to give them up. As it is, the posterity of the Van Noordens to this day keep up the baking of big loaves, in conformity to the last will and testament of their ancestor, who decreed that the memory of this event should be thus preserved in his family."*

On the opposite side of the river, snugly nestling in a little bay, lies Tarrytown, famous for its vicinity to the spot where the British spy, André, was intercepted by the three honest lads of Westchester. If the curious traveller is inclined to stop and view this spot, to which a romantic interest will ever be attached, the following directions will suffice.

" Landing at Tarrytown,† it is about a quarter of a mile to the post-road, at Smith's tavern. Following the post-road due North, about half a mile, you come to a little bridge over a small stream, known by the name of Clark's Kill, and sometimes almost dry. Formerly the wood on the left hand, South of the bridge, approached close to the road, and there was a bank on the opposite side, which was steep enough to prevent escape on horseback that way. The road from the North, as it approaches the bridge, is nar-

---

* We quote from the manuscript *ana* of Alderman Janson, to which we shall frequently refer in the course of this work.

† Vide *ana* of Alderman Janson.

rowed between two banks of six or eight feet high, and makes an angle just before it reaches it. Here, close within the copse of wood on the left, as you approach from the village, the three militia lads, (for lads they were, being hardly one and twenty), concealed themselves, to wait for a suspicious stranger, of whom they had notice from a Mrs. Read, at whose house they had stopped on their way towards Kingsbridge. A Mr. Talmadge, a Revolutionary officer, and a member of the House of Representatives, some years since took occasion to stigmatize these young men, as *Cow Boys*, out on a plundering expedition. The imputation was false; they were in possession of passes from General Philip Van Courtlandt, to proceed beyond the lines, as they were called, and of course, by the laws of war, were authorized to be where they were.

"As Major André approached, according to the universal tradition among the old people of Westchester, John Paulding darted out upon him and seized his horse's bridle. André was exceedingly startled at the suddenness of this rencounter, and, in in a moment of unguarded surprise, exclaimed—'Where do you belong?'

"'Below,' was the reply, this being the expression commonly used to designate the lines of the British, who were then in possession of New York.

"'So do I,' was the rejoinder of André in the joyful surprise of the moment. It has been surmised that this hasty admission sealed his fate. But, when we reflect that he was suspected before, and that afterwards not even the production of his pass from General Arnold could prevail upon the young men to let him go, it will appear sufficiently probable that this imprudent avowal was not the original cause of his being detained and examined. After some discussion and the exhibiting of his pass, he was taken into the wood, and searched, not without a good deal of unwillingness on his part. It is said he particularly resisted the pulling-off of his right boot, which contained the treasonable documents. When these were discovered, it is also said that André unguardedly exclaimed, 'I'm lost!'; but, presently recollecting himself, added, 'No matter — they dare not hang me.'

"Finding himself discovered, André offered his gold watch and a purse of guineas for his release. These were rejected. He then proposed that they should secrete him, while one of the party carried a letter, which he would write in their presence, to Sir Henry Clinton, naming the ransom necessary to his discharge, and which they might themselves specify, pledging his honour that it should accompany their associate on his return. To this they likewise refused their assent. André then threatened them with a severe punishment for daring to disregard a pass from the commanding general at West Point; and bade them beware of carrying him to head-quarters, for they would only be tried by a court-martial and punished for mutiny. Still the firmness of these young men sustained them against all these threats and temptations, and they finally delivered him to Colonel Jameson. It is no insignificant evidence of the weight of the influences thus overcome, that Colonel Jameson, an officer of the regular army, commanding a point of great consequence, so far yielded to the production of this pass as to permit André to write to General

Arnold a letter, which enabled that traitor to escape the ignominious fate he deserved.

"While in custody of the three Westchester volunteers, André is said gradually to have recovered from his depression of spirits, so as to sit with them after supper, and chat about himself and his situation, still preserving his incognito of John Anderson. In the course of the evening which he passed in their company, he related the following singular little anecdote. It seems, the evening before he left London to embark for America, he was in company with some young ladies of his familiar acquaintance, when it was proposed, that, as he was going to a distant country on a perilous service, he should have his fortune told by a famous sibyl, at that time fashionable in town, in order that his friends might know what would become of him while away. They went accordingly, when the beldam, after the customary grimace and cant, on examining his palms, gravely announced, 'That he was going a great distance, and would either be hanged, or come very near it, before he returned.' All the company laughed at this awful annunciation, and joked with him on the way back. 'But,' added André, smiling, 'I seem in a fair way of fulfilling the prophecy.'

"It was not till André arrived at head-quarters, and concealment became no longer possible, that he wrote the famous letter to General Washington, avowing his name and rank. He was tried by a court-martial, found guilty on his own confession, and hanged at Tappan, where he met his fate with dignity, and excited in the bosoms of the Americans that sympathy as a criminal, which has since been challenged for him as a hero and a martyr. A few years since, the British consul at New York caused his remains to be disinterred and sent to England, where, to perpetuate if possible the delusion of his having suffered in an honourable enterprise, they were buried in Westminster Abbey, among heroes, statesmen, and poets. The thanks of Congress, with a medal, an annuity, and a farm, were bestowed on each of the three young volunteers, and, lately, a handsome monument has been erected by the corporation of New York, to John Paulding, at Peekskill, where his body was buried. The other two, Isaac Van Wart and David Williams, still survive.

" About half a quarter of a mile south of Clark's Kill bridge, on the high-road, formerly stood the great tulip, or white-wood, tree, which, being the most conspicuous object in the immediate vicinity, has been usually designated as the spot where André was taken and searched. It was one of the most magnificent of trees, one hundred and eleven feet and a half high, the limbs projecting on either side more than eighty feet from the trunk, which was ten paces round. More than twenty years ago it was struck by lightning, and its old weather-beaten stock so shivered that it fell to the ground, and it was remarked by the old people, that on the very same day they for the first time read in the newspapers the death of Arnold. Arnold lived in England on a pension, which we believe is still continued to his children. His name was always coupled, even there, with infamy; insomuch that when the Duke of Richmond, Lord Shelburne, and other violent opponents of the American Revolutionary war, were appointed to office, the late Duke of Lauderdale remarked that, 'If the king wished to employ traitors, he wondered that he should have overlooked Benedict Arnold.' For this he was called out by Arnold, and they exchanged shots, but without effect. Since then we know nothing of Arnold's history, till his death. He died as he lived during the latter years of his life, an object of detestation to his countrymen, of contempt to the rest of the world.

"There is a romantic interest attached to the incidents just recorded, which will always make the capture of André a popular story; and the time will come when it will be chosen as the subject of poetry and the drama, as it has been of history and tradition. There is already a play founded upon it, by Mr. William Dunlap, the writer and translator of many dramatic works. Mr. Dunlap has however, we think, committed a mistake, in which nevertheless he is countenanced by most other writers — that of making André his hero. There is also extant a history of the whole affair, written by Joshua Hett Smith, the person who accompanied André across the river from Haverstraw, and whose memory is still in some measure implicated in the treason of Arnold. It is written with much passion and prejudice, and abounds in toryisms. Neither Washington, Greene, nor any of the members of the court-martial, escape the most degrading imputations: and the three young men who captured André are stigmatized with cowardice, as well as treachery! The history is the production of a man who seems to have had but one object, that of degrading the characters of others, with a view of bolstering up his own. Washington and Greene require no guardians to defend their memory, at one time assailed by women and dotards, on the score of having, the one, presided at the just condemnation of a spy, the other, refused his pardon to the threats and bullyings of the enemy. The reputations of the three young captors of André have also been attacked, where one would least of all expect it — in the Congress of the United States, where, some years ago, an honourable member denounced them as *Cow Boys;* and declared to the house that Major André had assured him he would have been released, could he have made good his promises of great reward from Sir Henry Clinton. The characters of these men were triumphantly vindicated by the publication of the testimony of nearly all the aged inhabitants of Westchester, who bore ample testimony to the purity of their lives and the patriotism of their motives. The slander is forgotten, and if its author be hereafter remembered, no one will envy him his reputation."

Tarrytown is still farther distinguished by being within a mile or two of *Sleepy Hollow,* the scene of a pleasant legend of our friend Geoffrey Crayon, with whom in days long past we have often explored this pleasant valley, fishing along the brooks, though he was beyond all question the worst fisherman we ever knew. He had not the patience of Job's wife — and without patience no man can be a philosopher or a fisherman.

SING SING.

Sing Sing is a pleasant village, on the west side of the river, about six miles above Tarrytown. It is a very musical place, (as its name imports), for all the birds sing charmingly; and is blessed with a pure air, and delightful prospects. There is a silver mine a couple of hundred yards from the village, to which we recommend the adventurers in the South-American and North-Carolinian mines to turn their attention. They will certainly lose money by working it, but the money will be spent at home, and the village will benefit by their patriotism. If they get ruined, there is a state-prison close by where they will find an asylum. There is an old lady living in the neighbourhood, who recollects hearing her father say, that he had once, before the Revolutionary war, been concerned in this mine; and there is a sixpence still preserved in the family, coined from its produce, that only cost him two hundred pounds. A new state-prison is being built here, from marble procured on the spot, in which the doleful experiment of solitary confinement is to be tried. It will not do. It will only be substituting lingering torments for those of sudden death. Without society, without books, without employment, without anticipations, and without the recollection of any thing but crimes, insanity or death must be the consequence of a protracted seclusion of this sort. A few days will be an insufficient lesson, and a few months would be worse than death — madness or idiocy. It is a fashionable Sunday excursion with a certain class of idlers in New York, to visit this prison in the steam-boat. It is like going to look at their lodgings before they are finished. Some of them will get there if they don't mind. After all, we think those philanthropists are in the right, who are for abolishing the criminal code entirely, and relying on the improved spirit of the age and the progress of moral feeling.

Three or four miles east of Sing Sing, is the CHAPPAQUA SPRING, which at one time came very nigh getting the better of Ballston, Saratoga and Harrowgate, for it is a fact well authenticated, that one or two persons of good fashion came uncommonly near being cured of that incurable disease called " I dont know what," by drinking these waters. Upon the strength of this, some " public-spirited individuals " erected a great hotel for the public accommodation. We wish we knew their names, as we look upon every man who builds a tavern as a public benefactor, upon the authority of the famous prize-poet, heretofore quoted, who says : —

> " Thrice happy land! to glorious fates a prey,
> Where taverns multiply, and cots decay!
> And happy they, the happiest of their kind,
> Who ease and freedom in a tavern find!
> No household cares molest the chosen man
> Who, at the tavern, tosses off his can,
> Who, far from all the irksome cares of life,
> And, most of all, that care of cares, a wife,
> Lives free and easy, all the livelong year,
> And dies without the tribute of a tear,
> Save from some Boniface's bloodshot eye,
> Who grieves that such a liberal soul should die,
> And on that 'Canongate of Chronicles,' the door,
> Leave such a long unliquidated score."

POINT NO POINT.

Directly opposite to Sing Sing is Point no Point, a singular range of highlands of the trap formation, which is extremely apt to deceive the traveller who don't " understand trap", as the geologists say. In sailing along up the river, a point of land appears at all times, (except in a dense fog or a dark night, when we advise the reader not to look out for it), projecting far into the river. On arriving opposite, it seems to recede, and to appear again a little beyond. Some travellers compare this Point no Point to a great metaphysician, who reasons through a whole quarto, without coming to a conclusion. Others liken it to the great Dr. ——, who plays round his subject like children about a bonfire, but never ventures too near, lest he should catch it, and, belike, burn his fingers. Others again approximate it to the speech of a member of Congress, which always seems coming to the point, but never arrives at it. The happiest similitude however, in our opinion, was that of a young lady, who compared a dangling dandy admirer of hers to Point no Point, "Because," said she, "he is always pointing to his game, but never makes a dead-point."

If the traveller should happen to go ashore here, by following the road from Slaughter's Landing up the mountain, about half a mile, he will come suddenly upon a beautiful sheet of pure water nine miles in circumference, called Snedecker's Lake, a name abhorred of Poetry and the Nine. The southern extremity is bounded by a steep pine-clad mountain, which dashes headlong down almost perpendicularly into the bosom of the lake, while all the other portions of its graceful circle are rich in cultivated rural beauties. The Brothers of the Angle may here find pleasant sport, and peradventure catch a pike, the noblest of all fishes, because he has the noblest appetite. Alas!, how is the pride of human reason mortified at the thought that a pike, not one tenth the bulk of a common-sized man, can eat as much as half a score of the most illustrious gourmands!—and that too without dyspepsia, or apoplexy. Let not man boast any longer of his being the lord of the creation. Would we were a pike, and lord of Snedecker's Lake, for, as the great prize-poet sings in a fit of hungry inspiration:—

> "I sing the Pike! not him of lesser fame,
> Who gained at Little York a deathless name,
> And died a martyr to his country's weal,
> Instead of dying of a glorious meal—
> But thee, O Pike!, lord of the finny crew,
> King of the waters, and of eating, too.
> Imperial glutton, that for tribute seizest
> As many glittering small fry as thou pleasest,
> No surfeits on thy ample feeding wait,
> No apoplexy shortens thy long date;
> The patriarch of eating, thou dost shine;
> A century of gluttony is thine.
> Sure the old tale of transmigration's true:
> The soul of Heliogabalus dwells in you!"

STONY POINT.

This is a rough, picturesque point, pushing boldly out into the river, directly opposite to Verplanck's Point on the east side. The remains of a redoubt are still to be seen on its brow, and it was the scene of one of the boldest exploits of one of the boldest spirits of a revolution fruitful in both. The fort was carried at midnight at the point of the bayonet, by a party of Americans under General Anthony Wayne, the fire-eater of his day. In order to judge of this feat, it is necessary to examine the place and see the extreme difficulty of approach. The last achievement of "Mad Anthony"—(so he was christened by his admiring soldiers who would follow him any where)—was the decisive defeat of the Indians at the battle of Miami, in 1794, which gave rest to a long-harassed and extensive frontier, and led to the treaty of Greenville, by which the United States acquired an immense accession of territory. He died at Presque Isle on Lake Erie, in the fifty-second year of his age. It is believed that Pennsylvania yet owes him a monument.

There is a light-house erected here, on the summit of the point. We have heard people laugh at it as entirely useless, but doubtless they did not know what they were talking about. Light-houses are of two kinds, the useful and the ornamental. The first are to guide mariners, the others to accommodate the lovers of the picturesque. The light-house at Stony Point is of the latter description. It is a fine object either in approaching or leaving the Highlands, and foul befall the carping Smelfungus who does not thank the public-spirited gentleman, (whoever he was), to whom we of a picturesque turn are indebted for the contemplation of this beautiful superfluity. Half the human race, (we mean no disparagement to the lasses we adore), and indeed half the world, is only made to look at. Why not, then, a light-house? The objections are untenable, for if a light-house be of no other use, it at least affords a snug place for some lazy philosopher to loll out the rest of his life on the featherbed of a cosy sinecure.

We now approach the Highlands, and advise the reader to shut himself up in the cabin and peruse the following pages attentively, as it is our intention to give a sketch of this fine scenery, so infinitely superior to the reality, that Nature will not be able to recognise herself in our picture.

Genius of the picturesque sublime, or the sublime picturesque, inspire us! Thou that didst animate the soul of John Bull, insomuch that, if report says true, he did once get up from dinner, before it was half discussed, to admire the sublime projection of Anthony's Nose — thou that erewhile didst allure a first-rate belle and beauty from adjusting her curls at the looking-glass, to gaze for more than half a minute at beauties almost equal to her own — thou that dost sometimes actually inspirit that last best work of the ninth part of a man, the dandy, actually to yawn with delight at the Crow's Nest, and pull up his breeches at sight of Fort Putnam — thou genius of travellers, and tutelary goddess of book-making — grant us a pen of fire, ink of lightning, and words of thunder, to do justice to the mighty theme!

First comes the gigantic Donderbarrack — (all mountains are called gigantic, because the ancient race of giants was turned into mountains, which accounts for the race being extinct) — first comes the mighty Donderbarrack, president of hills — (we allow of no king-mountains in our book) — whose head is hid in the clouds, whenever the clouds come down low enough; at whose foot dwells in all the feudal majesty (only a great deal better) of a Rhoderick Dhu, the famous highland chieftain, Caldwell, lord of Donderbarrack, and of all the little hills that grow out of his ample sides like warts on a giant's nose. To this mighty chieftain all the steam-boats do homage, by ringing their bells, slowing their machinery, and sending their boats ashore to carry him the customary tribute, to wit, store of visitors, whom it is his delight to entertain at his hospitable castle. This stately pile is of great antiquity, its history being lost in the dark ages of the last century, when the Indian prowled about these hills, and shot his deer, ere the advance of the white man swept him away forever. Above — as the prize-poet sings —

> "High on the cliffs the towering eagles soar —
> But hush, my muse — for poetry's a bore."

Turning the base of Donderbarrack, the nose of all noses, Anthony's Nose, gradually displays itself to the enraptured eye, which must be kept steadily fixed on these our glowing pages. Such a nose is not seen every day. Not the famous hero of Slawkenbergius, whose proboscis emulated the steeple of Strasburg, ever had such a nose to his face. Taliacotius himself never made such a nose in his life. It is worth while to go ten miles to hear it blow — you would mistake it for a trumpet. The most curious thing about it is, that it looks no more like a nose than my foot. But, now we think of it, there is something still more curious connected with this nose. There is not a soul born within five miles of it, but has a nose of most jolly dimensions — not quite as large as the mountain, but pretty well. It is the custom for the passengers in steam-boats to salute it in passing with a universal blow of the nose: after which, they shake their kerchiefs at it, and put them carefully in their pockets. No young lady ever climbs to the top of this stately nose, without affixing her white cambric handkerchief to a stick, placing it upright in the ground, and leaving it waving there, in hopes that all her posterity may be blessed with goodly noses.

Immediately on passing the Nose the Sugar Loaf appears: keep your eye on the book for your life — you will be changed to a loaf of sugar if you don't. This has happened to several of the disciples of Lot's wife, who thereby became even sweeter than they were before. Remember poor Eurydice, whose fate was sung in burlesque by an infamous outcast bachelor, who, it is said, was afterwards punished, by marrying a shrew who made him mix the mustard every day for dinner.

WEST POINT.

" If the traveller," observes Alderman Janson, " intends stopping here, to visit the Military Academy and its admirable superintendent, I advise him to make his will before he ventures into the landing-boat. That more people have not been drowned in this adventurous experiment can only be accounted for on the supposition that miracles are growing to be but every-day matters. There is, I believe, a law regulating the mode of landing passengers from steam-boats, but it is a singular fact that laws will not execute themselves, notwithstanding all the wisdom of the legislature. Not that I mean to find fault with the precipitation with which people and luggage are tumbled together into the boat, and foisted ashore at the rate of fifteen miles an hour. At least five minutes in the passage to Albany is saved by this means, and so much added to the delights of the tourist, who is thereby enabled to spend five minutes more at the Springs. Who would not risk a little drowning, and a little scalding, for such an object? Certainly the most precious of all commodities, (especially to people who don't know what to do with it), is time; except, indeed, it may be, money to a miser who never spends any. It goes to my heart to find fault with any thing in this best of all possible worlds, where the march of mind is swifter than a race-horse or a steam-boat, and goes hand-in-hand with the progress of public improvement, like Darby and Joan, or Jack and Gill, blessing this fortunate generation, and preparing the way for a world of steam-engines, spinning-jennies, and machinery: insomuch that there would be no use at all for such an animal as man in this world any more, if steam-engines and spinning-jennies would only make themselves. But the reader will I trust excuse me this once, for venturing to hint with a modesty that belongs to my nature, that all this hurry — this racing — this tumbling of men, women, children, and baggage, into a boat, helter-skelter — this sending them ashore at the risk of their lives — might possibly be excusable if it were done for the public accommodation. But such is not the fact. It is nothing but the struggle of interested competition, the effort to run down a rival boat, and get all, instead of sharing with others. The public accommodation requires that boats should go at different times of the day, yet they prefer starting at the same hour, nay, at the same moment — eager to sweep off the passengers along the river, and risking the lives of people at West Point, that they may take up the passengers at Newburgh. The truth is, in point of ease and comfort, convenience and safety, the public is not now half so well off as during the existence of what the said public was persuaded to call a great grievance — the exclusive right of Mr. Fulton.

"There is a most comfortable hotel at West Point, kept by Mr. Cozzens, a most obliging and good-humoured man, to whom we commend all our readers, with an assurance that they need not fear being *cozened* by him. Nothing can be more interesting than the situation of West Point, the grand object to which it is devoted, and the magnificent views it affords in all directions. If there be any inspiration in the sublime works of nature, or if the mind, as some believe, receives an impulse or direction from local situation, there is not, perhaps, in the world, a spot more favourable to the production of heroes and men of science. Secluded from the effeminate, or vicious, allurements of cities, both mind and body preserve a vigorous freshness which is eminently favourable to the development of each without enfeebling either. Manly studies and manly exercise go hand-in-hand, and manly sentiments are the natural consequence. The bodies of the cadets are invigorated by military exercise and habits, while their intellects are strengthened, expanded, and purified, by the acquirement of those high branches of science, those graces of literature, and those elegant accomplishments, which when combined constitute the complete man. No one whose mind is susceptible of noble emotions can see these fine young fellows going through their exercises on the plain of West Point, to the sound of the bugle repeated by a dozen echoes of the mountains, while all the magnificence of nature concurs in adding beauty and dignity to the scene and the occasion, without feeling his bosom swell and glow with patriotic pride.

"If these young men require an example to warn or to stimulate, they will find it in the universal execration heaped upon the name and the memory of

Benedict Arnold, contrasted with the reverential affection, that will forever descend to the latest posterity as an heirloom, with which every American pronounces the name of Washington. It was at West Point that Arnold betrayed his country, and it was on the hills opposite West Point that Washington wintered with his army, during the most gloomy period of our Revolution, rendered still more gloomy by the treason of Arnold, so happily frustrated by the virtue of the American yeomanry. The remains of the huts are still to be seen on Redoubt Hill and its vicinity, and there is a fine spring on the banks of a brook near by, to this day called Washington's, from being the spring whence the water was procured for his drinking. It issues from the side of a bank closely embowered with trees, and is excessively cold. The old people in the vicinity, who generally live to about a hundred, still cherish the tradition of its uses, and direct the attention of inquirers to it, with a feeling than which nothing can more affectingly indicate the depth of the devotion to her good father implanted in the heart of America. Close to the spring are two of the prettiest little cascades to be found any where. Indeed, the whole neighbourhood abounds in beautiful views and romantic associations, and it is worth while to cross over in a boat from West Point to spend a morning here in rambling."

On the opposite side of the river from West Point, and about two miles distant, lies COLD SPRING, a pleasant, thriving little village. Perhaps the pleasantest ride in the whole country is from here to Fishkill Landing. A road has been made along the foot of the mountains. On one hand it is washed by the river

— on the other overhung by Bull and Breakneck Hills, the base of which latter has been blown up in places to afford room for it to pass. The prospects all along are charming, and, on turning the beak of Breakneck Hill, there opens to the north and northwest a view, which when seen will not soon be forgotten.

Nearly opposite Cold Spring, at the foot of two mountains and inaccessible except from the river, lies the CITY OF FAITH — a city by brevet; founded by an enterprising person, with the intention of cutting out Washington, and making it the capital of the United States — and indeed of the New World.* He has satisfied himself that the spot thus aptly selected is the point of navigation the nearest possible to the great Northern Pacific, and contemplates a railroad, from thence to the mouth of Columbia River. This must necessarily concentrate travel at this fortunate spot. After which his intention is to dig down the Crow's Nest and Butter Hill, or decompose the rocks with vinegar, in order that travellers may get at his emporium, by land, without breaking their necks. He has already six inhabitants to begin with, and wants nothing to the completion of this great project, but a bank — a subscription of half a dozen millions from the government — a loan of "the credit of the state," for about as much — and a little more faith in the people. We think the prospect quite cheering, and would rejoice in the prospective glories of the City of Faith, were it not for the apprehension that it will prove fatal to the Ohio and Chesapeake Canal,

[* There was such a scheme. The projector might have been a visionary; but he got up a fine map, and sold as many lots as he could.]

and swallow up the Mamakating and Lacawaxan. This business of founding cities is in America considered a mere trifle. They make a great noise about Romulus the founder of Rome, and Peter the founder of St. Petersburg! We knew a man who had founded twelve great cities, some of which, like Rome, are already in ruins; and yet he never valued himself on that account.

As you emerge from the Highlands, a noble vista is gradually disclosed to the view. The little towns of NEW CORNWALL, NEW WINDSOR, and NEWBURGH, are seen in succession along the west bank of the river, which here, as if rejoicing at its freedom from the mountain barrier, expands itself into a wide bay, with Fishkill and Matteawan on the east, and the three little towns on the opposite side, the picturesque shores of which rise gradually into highlands, bounded in the distance to the north-west by the blue summits of the Kaatskill Mountains. Into this bay, on the east, enters Fishkill Creek, a fine stream which waters some of the richest and most beautiful valleys of Dutchess County. Approaching the Hudson, it exhibits several picturesque little cascades, which have lately been spoiled by dams and manufactories, those atrocious enemies to all picturesque beauty, as the prize-poet exclaims in a fine burst of enthusiasm — poetical enthusiasm, consisting in swearing roundly.

> " Mill-dams be damned, and all his race accurs'd,
> Who damned a stream by damming it the first!"

On the west, and nearly opposite, enters Murderer's Creek, which, after winding its way through the delightful vale of Canterbury, as yet unvisited and undescribed by tourist or traveller, tumbles over a villanous mill-dam into the river. If the traveller has a mind for a beautiful ride in returning from the Springs, let him land at Newburgh, and follow the turnpike-road through the village of Canterbury, on to the *Clove,* a pass of the great range of mountains, through with the Ramapo plunges its way among the rocks. The ride through this pass is highly interesting, and the point where the Ramapo emerges from the southern side of the mountains is well worthy of attention. Here joining the Mauwy, it courses its way through a narrow vale of exquisite beauty, till it is lost on the Pompton Plains in the river of that name. The roads are as good as usual, but the accommodations are not the best in the world, and those who love good eating and good beds better than nature's beauties, (among whom we profess ourselves), may go some other way. Those who choose this route by way of variety, must by no means forget the house of Mynheer Roome, at Pompton village famed in song, where they will meet with mortal store of good things, including sweetmeats of divers sorts and cakes innumerable and unutterable, and hear the Dutch language spoken in all its original purity, with the true Florentine accent.

But let the traveller beware of talking to him about turnpikes, railways, or canals, all which he abhorreth. In particular, avoid the subject of the MORRIS CANAL, at the very name of which Mynheer's pipe will be seen to pour forth increasing volumes of angry smoke, and, like another Vesuvius, he will disgorge whole torrents of red-hot Dutch lava. In truth Mynheer Roome has an utter contempt for modern improvements, and we don't know but he is half-right. "Dey always cost more dan dey come to," he says; and those who contemplate the sober primitive independence of the good Mynheer, and see his fat cattle, his fat negroes, and his fat self, encompassed by rich meadows and smiling fields, all unaided by the magic of modern improvements, will be apt to think with him, "dat one half dese tings dey call improvements" add little, if anything, to human happiness, or domestic independence.

Within a couple of hundred yards of Mynheer Roome's door, the Pompton, Ramapo, and Ringwood, three little rivers in whose very bottoms you can see your face, unite their waters, gathered from the hills to the North and West, and, assuming the name of the first, wind through the extensive plain in many playful meanders almost out of character for Dutch rivers, till they finally disappear, through a break in the hills, towards the South. From Pompton there is a good road to Hoboken, by diverging a little from which the traveller may visit the falls of Passaic, which were once the pride of nature, who has lately resigned them to her rival, art, and almost disowns them now. But it is high time to return to Murderer's Creek, and Canterbury Vale, which hath been sung, (by the prize-poet so often quoted), in the following strains, which partake of the true mystical metaphysical sublime.

> "As I was going to Canterbury,
> I met twelve hay-cocks in a fury,
> And, as I gaz'd, a hieroglyphic bat
> Skimm'd o'er the zenith in a slip-shod hat."

From which the intelligent traveller will derive as clear an idea of the singular charms of this vale as from most descriptions in prose or verse.

The name of Murderer's Creek is said to be derived from the following incidents.

Little more than a century ago, the beautiful region watered by this stream was possessed by a small tribe of Indians, long since become extinct or incorporated with some other savage nation of the west. Three or four hundred yards from where the stream discharges itself into the Hudson, a white family, of the name of Stacey, had established itself in a log-house, by tacit permission of the tribe, to whom Stacey had made himself useful by his skill in a variety of little arts held in high estimation by the savages. In particular, a friendship subsisted between him and an old Indian called Naoman, who often came to his house and partook of his hospitality. The Indians never forgive injuries, nor forget benefits. The family consisted of Stacey, his wife, and two children, a boy and girl, the former five, the latter three years old.

One day, while Stacey was absent, Naoman came to his log-hut, lighted his pipe, and sat down. He looked very serious, sometimes sighed deeply, but said not a word. Stacey's wife asked him what was the matter, and if he was sick. He shook his head, sighed, but said nothing, and soon went away. The next day he came again, and behaved in the same manner. Stacey's wife began to think strange of this, and related it to her husband, who advised her to urge the old man to an explanation, the next time he came. Accordingly, when he repeated his visit the day after, she was more importunate than usual.

At last the old Indian said, "I am a red man, and the pale-faces are our enemies — why should I speak?"

"But my husband and I are your friends; you have eaten salt with us a thousand times, and my children have sat on your knee as often. If you have any thing on your mind, tell it me."

"It will cost me my life if it is known, and the white-faced women are not good at keeping secrets," replied Naoman.

"Try me, and see."

"Will you swear by your Great Spirit, you will tell none but your husband?"

"I have none else to tell."

"But will you swear?"

"I do swear by our Great Spirit, I will tell none but my husband."

"Not if my tribe should kill you for not telling?"

"Not if your tribe should kill me for not telling."

Naoman then proceeded to inform her that, owing to some encroachments of the white people below the mountains, his tribe had become irritated, and were resolved that night to massacre all the white settlers within their reach; and bade her find her husband at once, notify him of the danger, and, as secretly and speedily as possible, take their canoe, and paddle over the river to Fishkill for safety. "Be quick, and do nothing that may excite suspicion," said Naoman as he departed. The good wife sought her husband, who was on the river, fishing, and told him the story. As no time was to be lost, they proceeded to their boat, which was, unluckily, filled with water. It took some time to clear it out, and meanwhile Stacey recollected his gun, which had been left behind. He hurried back to the house, and returned with it. All this took up considerable time, and costly time it proved to this poor family.

The daily visits of old Naoman, and his more than ordinary gravity, had excited suspicion in some of the tribe, who had accordingly paid particular attention to the movements of Stacey. One of the young Indians who had been kept on the watch, seeing the whole family about taking to their boat, ran to the little Indian village, about a mile off, and gave the alarm. Five Indians ran down to the riverside where their canoes were moored, jumped in, and paddled after Stacey, who by this time had got some distance out into the bay. They gained on him so fast, that twice he dropped his paddle and took up his gun. But his wife prevented his shooting, by telling him that, if he fired and they were afterwards overtaken, they would meet no mercy from the Indians. He accordingly refrained, and plied his paddle, till the sweat rolled in big drops down his forehead. All would not do; they were overtaken within a hundred yards of the shore, and carried back with yells of triumph.

When they got ashore, the Indians set fire to Stacey's house, and dragged himself, his wife, and his children, to their village. Here the principal old men, (Naoman being one of them), assembled to deliberate on the affair. The chief among them stated that some one of the tribe had undoubtedly been guilty of treason, in apprising Stacey, the white man, of the designs of the tribe, whereby he took the alarm, and had wellnigh escaped. He proposed to examine the prisoners, as to who gave the information. The old men assented to this; and Naoman among the rest. Stacey was first interrogated by one of the old men, who spoke English, and interpreted to the others.

Stacey refused to betray his informant. His wife was then questioned, while two Indians stood threatening the two children with tomahawks. She attempted to evade the truth, by declaring that she had a dream the night before, which had alarmed her, and that she had persuaded her husband to fly. "The Great Spirit never deigns to talk in dreams to a white-face," said the old Indian: "Woman, thou hast two tongues and two faces. Speak the truth, or thy children shall surely die." The little boy and girl were then brought close to her, and the two savages stood over them, ready to execute their bloody orders.

"Wilt thou name," said the old Indian, "the red man who betrayed his tribe? I will ask thee, three times." The mother answered not. "Wilt thou name the traitor? This is the second time." The poor mother looked at her husband, and then at her children, and stole a glance at Naoman, who sat smoking his pipe with invincible gravity. She wrung her hands and wept; but remained silent. "Wilt thou name the traitor? 'Tis the third, and last, time." The agony of the mother waxed more bitter; again she sought the eye of Naoman, but it was cold and motionless: a pause of a moment awaited her reply, and the next moment the tomahawks were raised over the heads of the children, who besought their mother not to let them be murdered.

"Stop," cried Naoman. All eyes were turned upon him. "Stop," repeated he, in a tone of authority. "White woman, thou hast kept thy word with me to the last moment. I am the traitor. I have eaten of the salt, warmed myself at the fire, shared the kindness, of these Christian white people, and it was I that told them of their danger. I am a withered, leafless, branchless trunk: cut me down if you will. I am ready." A yell of indignation sounded on all sides. Naoman descended from the little bank where he sat, shrouded his face with his mantle of skins, and submitted to his fate. He fell dead at the feet of the white woman, by a blow of the tomahawk.

But the sacrifice of Naoman, and the firmness of the brave Christian mother, did not suffice to save the lives of the other victims. They perished — how, it is needless to say; and the memory of their fate has been preserved in the name of the pleasant stream on whose banks they lived and died, which to this day is called Murderer's Creek.

NEW CORNWALL, AND NEW WINDSOR.

It is bad policy to call places, new. The title will do very well for a start, but, when they begin to assume an air of antiquity, it becomes quite unsuitable. It is too much the case with those who stand godfathers to towns in our country. They seem to think, because we live in a new world, every thing must be christened accordingly. The most flagrant instance of this enormity is New York, which, although ten times as large, and ten times as handsome as York in England, is destined by this infamous cognomen of, "new," to play second to that old worn-out town, which has nothing in it worth seeing except its great minster. The least people can do, after condemning a town to be called *new*, is to paint their houses every now and then, that the place may do honour to its title. But, between ourselves, Monsieur Traveller, the whole thing is absurd. Some score of centuries hence, we shall have a dozen clutter-headed antiquaries disputing whether New York and old York were not one and the same city; and it is just as likely as not, that the latter will run away with all the glories of the queen of the new world. Why not call our cities by a name absolutely fresh to human ears, — Conecocheague, Amoonoosuck, Chabaquidick, or Kathtippakamuck? There would then be no danger of their being confounded with those of the old world, and they would stand by themselves in sesquipedalian dignity, till the end of time, or till people had not breath to utter their names.

"New Cornwall," as Alderman Janson truly observes, "is assuredly not one of the largest towns on the river; but it might be so, and it is not its fault that it is not six times as large as Pekin, London, Paris, or Constantinople, as it can be clearly proved that it might have extended half a dozen leagues towards any of the four quarters of the earth, without stumbling over any thing of consequence except a river and a mountain. If its illustrious founders, (whose names are unknown), instead of confining their energies to building a few wooden houses which they forgot to paint even with Spanish-brown, had cut a canal to the Pacific Ocean, made a railroad to Passamaquoddy and a tunnel under the Atlantic, and erected three hundred thousand handsome brick houses with folding doors and marble mantel-pieces, without doubt it might have been at this moment the greatest city in the known world. I am aware that a certain ignoramus of a critic denies all this, inasmuch as the river is in the way towards the East and therefore it cannot extend in that direction. But I suppose this blockhead never heard of turning the course of the Hudson into the channel of Fishkill Creek, and so at the same time improving the navigation of both, and affording ample space for the growth of the city by digging down Fishkill Mountains. Nay, we dare affirm he is totally ignorant of the mode of sucking a river, or even a sea, dry, by means of sponges, whereby it may be easily passed over dry-shod, a method still pursued by the people of Terra Incognita, and those that carry their heads below their necks, mentioned by Herodotus. We therefore affirm that the only reason why this is not the greatest city in the universe is because the founders did not do as I have just said. If the aforesaid blockhead of a critic denies this, may he never be the founder of a great city, or even a great book. He ought to know, blockhead as he is, that, in this age of improvement, every thing is possible; and that the foundations of a great city may be laid any where, in despite of that old superannuated baggage, 'Nature,' whom nobody minds nowadays. Only give me a bank, and the liberty of issuing as much paper as I please, without the disagreeable necessity of redeeming it; or, only let the state of New York '*loan me its credit*' for a million or so, and I will engage to turn Nature topsy-turvy, or commit any other enormity in the way of conferring benefits on the community. If Archimedes had known any thing about banks, he would have required no other basis for the lever with which he was to raise the world. But, unfortunately for the march of mind and the progress of public improvements, the banking capital of this portion of the republic was diverted to one of the most singular objects, by one of the most singular conspiracies, on record.

"It seems" continues the alderman, "that the people of New York, with rather more discretion than they have since displayed in similar cases, became at one time rather shy of the paper-money of certain country banks, and among others of the bank in question. Whereupon the directors, as Fame loudly reported at that time, did incontinently get together and determine to starve the good citizens of New York into swallowing their notes, by cutting off their supplies of Goshen butter. Accordingly, as the aforesaid goddess did loudly trumpet forth to the world, divers agents, directors, clerks, and cashiers, were sent into the rich bottoms of Orange County, to contract for all the butter made, or to be made, during that remarkable year. The consequence was that a horrible scarcity took place in New York, the burghers whereof had for a long time nothing to butter their parsnips with but fair words. But the sturdy people of the metropolis held out manfully, refusing for a long time to swallow the aforesaid bank-notes, until being at length actually reduced to the necessity of substituting Philadelphia butter, they gave in at last, and agreed to swallow any thing rather than that. Hereupon the butter and the notes of the district came to market in great quantities, and such was the sympathy which grew up between them, that the latter actually turned yellow, and assumed the exact colour of the former. In memory of this renowned victory over the New-Yorkers, the county was called Orange, from the hue of the butter, and all the milkmaids to this day wear orange-coloured ribbons, as they sit milking their cows and singing Dutch songs."

This is not the place for dilating on the manifold advantages of banks and paper-money, which last we look upon as the greatest discovery of modern times, and, indeed, of all times whatever. But we hope the enlightened traveller will, for a few moments, withdraw his eyes from the beauties of the scenery, to attend to some of the most prominent blessings of paper-money and banks.

In the first place, the institution of paper-money has called forth the talents of divers persons in the fine arts, as is exemplified in the numerous attempts at imitation, which is the basis of the fine arts. Before the sublime invention of paper-money, it was not worth while for a man to risk his neck or his liberty, for the paltry purpose of counterfeiting a silver dollar; but now since the forgery of a single note, and the successful passing it away, may put a thousand dollars in the pocket, there is some stimulus to the exercise of genius. Besides, a man can carry in his pocket-book forged notes, to the amount of hundreds of thousands of dollars, without exciting attention; whereas the same amount in counterfeit specie, would require a dozen wagons or a steam-boat, and inevitably excite suspicion.

Thus it will be found that this branch of the fine arts has improved and extended prodigiously under the institution of paper-money; insomuch that the works of our best artists have been frequently imitated so successfully as to impose upon the most experienced eye. In addition to this singular advantage, it cannot be denied, that every dollar thus created by this spirit of emulation in the fine arts adds so much to the public wealth, and forms an accession to the circulating medium. When at last its circulation is stopped, by a discovery, it will generally be found in the hands of some ignorant labourer, so poor that the loss of a few dollars is a matter of little consequence, as he would at all events be poor, either with or without them. Besides, he deserves to suffer for his ignorance, like every-body else in the world.

Another great blessing of paper-money is, that it makes all hands believe themselves richer than they really are, as is exemplified in the following authentic story of a Connecticut farmer, which we extract from the annals of that state.

The farmer had a sow and pigs, just at the time a little bank was set up in a village hard by. The bank, by making money plenty, raised the price of his sow and pigs, some fifty per cent. This tempted him to sell them, which he did, for a high price,—as much as fifty dollars. The next spring, he wanted another sow and pigs, for his winter pork. In the mean while, the paper of the little bank, having been issued with too great liberality, had depreciated very considerably, and he was obliged to give seventy-five dollars for a sow and pigs. Very well—the sow and pigs were now worth seventy-five dollars. About this time, the legislative wisdom chartered another bank, in another neighbouring town, having a church and a blacksmith's shop—but no whipping-posts, they being abolished for the benefit of honest people. This made money still more plenty than before, and our honest farmer was again tempted to sell his sow and pigs, for a hundred dollars. He was now worth fifty dollars more than when he commenced speculating, but then the mischief was that he wanted a sow and pigs. Very well. The multiplication of paper had its usual effect in diminishing its value, and it so happened that he was obliged to buy a sow and pigs for a hundred and fifty dollars. He calculated he had now made a hundred dollars by his speculation, but still he had nothing to show for it but his sow and pigs. To make an end of our story, our honest farmer was once more tempted to speculate, by an offer of two hundred dollars for his sow and pigs, and began to talk of buying an addition to his farm, when unluckily the bank failed, and the good man's speculation ended in having exchanged his sow and pigs for nothing. But he had enjoyed the delight of imaginary wealth all this time, which every body knows is far better than the reality, as it brings all the pleasures without any of the cares of riches. How often do we see men, rolling in actual wealth, suffering more than the pangs of poverty, by the anticipation of it;—but who ever saw one who *fancied* himself rich haunted by a similar bugbear?

Banking capital is in truth a capital thing. All other capital is real; this is ideal, and every body knows the pleasures of imagination far transcend those of reality. It is better than the music of Amphion or Orpheus, for the former only whistled up the walls of a city, and the latter set the trees and bears dancing; while your banking capital can build houses, and furnish them too; and not only put the *bulls* and *bears* on tiptoe, but make an ass as wise as Solomon. In short, not to delay the traveller too long from the beauties of nature, had the old philosophers known any thing of paper-money, they would no longer have disputed about the *magnum bonum*, which is neither a vile Brummagem razor, nor a clear conscience, but an abundance of paper currency.

NEWBURGH is the capital of Orange County. It is a thriving village, and a great place for holding conventions. The steam-boats stop here just long enough to give people a fair chance of breaking their shins, in coming aboard, and getting ashore. The two tides of people, meeting, occasion a pleasant bustle, very amusing to the spectator, but not to the actor. There is a bank here, the notes of which are yellow, in compliment to the butter. The houses are mostly painted yellow for a similar reason, and the men wear yellow breeches when they go to church on Sundays. The complexions of the young women are a little tinged with this peculiarity; but they are very handsome notwithstanding, though they can't hold a candle to the jolly Dutch girls at Fishkill on the opposite side of the river. Newburgh is not illustrious for any particular delicacy of the table, which might give it distinction, and therefore we advise the intelligent traveller not to trouble himself to stop there. In order to eat his way through a country with proper advantage, the enlightened tourist should be apprised beforehand of these matters, else he will travel to little purpose.

From Newburgh to Poughkeepsie, the river presents nothing particularly striking; but the shores are every where varied with picturesque points of view. Neither is there any thing remarkable in the eating way. The traveller may therefore pass on to Poughkeepsie, Pokepsie, or Ploughkeepsie, as the Honourable Frederick Augustus De Roos is pleased to call it in his Travels of Twenty-One Days.

Poughkeepsie is the capital of Dutchess County, so called in honour of the Duchess of York, daughter of the famous Chancellor Clarendon. If the Count de Grammont tells the truth, she had very little honour to bestow upon the county in return. The origin of the word, Poughkeepsie, is buried in the remote ages of antiquity; but it is supposed to be either Creek or Greek. It is not, however, mentioned by either Ptolemy or Strabo. This omission may be supposed to indicate that it was not in being at that time. But, the fact is, the ancients were, like their successors the moderns, deplorably ignorant of this country, as well as of the noble science of gastronomy, and expended as much money upon a goose's liver as would furnish a dozen tables with all the delicacies of a Parisian Restaurant. They stuffed the goose with figs — a fig for such stuffing! Yet must we not undervalue the skill of the Romans, who were worthy to conquer the world, if it were only for discovering the inimitable art of not only roasting a goose alive, but eating it alive afterwards. The fattening of worms with meal was also a matchless excellence of these people. But it is the noble and princely price of their meals which most excites our envy and applause; and in this respect it is that the immortal Apicius, who spent two millions of dollars in suppers, deserved to give his name to all modern gourmands. Neither the death of Curtius, nor of Cato of Utica, nor of any other Roman worthy, can touch the heel of the shoe of that of the thrice-renowned Apicius, who starved himself to death, for fear of being starved, he having but about four hundred thousand dollars left to spend in fattening worms, enlarging livers, and roasting geese alive. It was a glorious era, when a supper cost half a million of dollars; and it was worth while for a man to visit Rome from the uttermost ends of the earth, only to see these people eat. Truly, we say again, they deserved the empire of the world.

The highest price we ever paid for a supper in Poughkeepsie, was — we are ashamed to mention it — was seventy-five cents. But then we had no live geese, stuffed worms, or diseased livers. Alas! we shall never conquer the world if we go on in this way!

Somewhere between Poughkeepsie and Hudson, inclusive, is said to be a great hot-bed of politics, and some of the greatest politicians of the state infest this quarter. In proof of this, it is always found that they are on the right, that is to say, the strongest, side. We are told, but do not vouch for the fact, that they consult the weathercock on the court-house steeple, and change their coats accordingly. If the wind blows from the North-East, they put on their domestic woollens; if from the South, or West, these being warm winds, they change their domestic woollens for light regent's-cloth; and if the wind veers about as it sometimes does, without settling in any quarter, they throw by their coats entirely, until it blows steadily. He who has but one coat to his back is obliged to turn it to suit the wind and weather. This is the case with but few, as they are all too good politicians to be reduced to such extremity. This may be true or not; we speak but by hearsay, and people ought not to believe every thing. Certain it is, however, that every saddler in the town publicly advertises himself as "saddler and *trimmer*," whether in allusion to his politics or not, we cannot say. If the former be the case, it shows a most profligate state of public sentiment. What would the unchangeable, inflexible patriots of New York and Albany, who don't turn their coats above once or twice a year, say to such open profession of versatility!

Nevertheless, Poughkeepsie abounds in the most delectable of all the works of nature, always excepting canvas-back ducks, or geese roasted alive; to wit, damsels ineffably beautiful: that is, if nature may dispute with a French milliner the honour of producing a fashionable woman, or a woman fashionably accoutred. We ourselves sojourned here, erewhile, that is to say, some five and thirty years ago, and have not yet got rid of the scars of certain deep wounds, received from the sharp glances of beauty's eyes. A walk on the romantic bluffs which overhang the river, of a summer evening, when the boats are gliding noiselessly by at your feet, the beautiful landscape softening in the touching obscurity of twilight, and the skyward line of the Kaatsbergs melting into nothing, with one of these fair damsels hanging on your arm, is a thing to be remembered for many a year, a mighty pretty morsel to put into "time's wallet," only it is apt to give a man the heart-ache for at least ten years afterwards. Many an invincible dandy from the west side of Broadway, who never felt the pangs of love, except for his own dear self, has suffered more than his tailor from one of these evening walks, and lived to lament, in broadcloth and spatterdashes, the loss of such sweet communion, such innocent, yet dangerous delights. As the prize-poet says:—

> "Past times are half remember'd dreams;
> The future, ev'n at best, but seems;
> The present is — and then — is not;
> Such is man — and such his lot.
> Behind, he cannot see for tears;
> Before, is nought but hopes and fears;
> One cheats him with an empty bubble,
> The other always pays him double.
> 'Tis a vile farce of scenes ideal,
> Where nought but misery is real."

From Poughkeepsie to Hudson, the eastern bank of the river exhibits a uniform character of picturesque beauty. Villages, and landing-places at the mouths of large brooks, are scattered at distances of a few miles, and all is cultivated and pastoral repose. The western shore is more bold in its features, bounded at intervals by the blue peaks of the Kaatsbergs in the distance. Here lies Kingston, already risen from its ruins, and exhibiting few traces of that wanton and foolish barbarity which stimulated the British commander to set fire to it, during the Revolutionary war. Here, too, lies ATHENS, about which our learned Thebans have had such hot disputes; some maintaining that Boston, others that Philadelphia, and others that New York, was the real Athens of America. In vain have they wasted their ink, their time, and their readers' patience, on the theme. Here lies the true Athens of America, unknown and unnoticed by the learned, who are always looking for Babylon at Nineveh, and Nineveh at Babylon; and wasting centuries of speculation in searching for something right under their nose, like the great bookworm Magliabecchi, who spent three days in looking for a pen, which he carried in his mouth all the time.

What is it constitutes the identity of a man? His

name. And what, we would ask, constitutes the identity of a city? The same. Would New York be New York, or Albany, Albany — by any other name? and would any thing be necessary to change New York into Albany, and Albany into New York, except to exchange their names? What nonsense is it then for people to be denying that Athens is Athens, and not Boston, Philadelphia, or New York, which had better be content with their own true baptismal names, than to be usurping those of other cities. We trust we have settled this question forever, and that, hereafter, these great overgrown, upstart cities will leave our little Athens in the undisturbed possession of its name and honours. If any city of the United States could dispute this matter without blushing, it would assuredly be New York, which has a "Pantheon," for vending oysters; an "Acropolis," for ready-made linen; an "Athenian Company," for manufacturing coarse woollens; and a duck-pond, called the Piræus. Nor are Boston and Philadelphia without very specious claims; the former having an Athenæum, and a market-house with a front in imitation of the Temple of Minerva, because Minerva is the goddess of wisdom, and all market-women are thrifty, or in common acceptation, wise; while the latter has its two magnificent fanes of Plutus, god of paper-money, he being the only Pagan divinity to whom the Christians erect temples.

KAATSKILL.

Those who are fond of climbing mountains in a hot day, and looking down till their heads turn, must land at the village of Kaatskill, whence they can procure a conveyance to the hotel at Pine Orchard, three thousand feet above the level of the river, and have the pleasure of sleeping under blankets in the dog-days. Here the tourist may enjoy a prospect of unbounded extent and magnificence, and receive a lesson of the insignificance of all created things. Standing near the verge of the cliff, he looks down, and no object strikes his view, except at a distance of fifteen hundred feet below. Crawling there, man is but an atom, hardly visible; the ox is but a mouse; and the sheep are little white specks in the fields, which themselves are no bigger than the glasses of a pair of green spectacles. The traveller may judge of the insignificance even of the most stately objects, when told that a fashionable lady's hat and feathers dwindles in the distance to the size of a moderate mushroom! It is, we trust, needless to caution the tourist against falling down this dizzy steep, as in all probability he would come to some harm.

There are two cascades not far from the Pine Orchard, which want nothing but a little more water to be wonderfully sublime. Generally there is no water at all, but the proper application of half a dollar will set it running presently.

> " *Music** has charms to soothe the savage breast,
> To raise floodgates, and make the waters flow."

Messrs. Wall and Cole, two fine artists, admirable in different, we might almost say, opposite, styles, have illustrated the scenery of the Kaatskill by more than one picture of singular excellence. We should like to see such pictures gracing the drawing-rooms of the

---

* Music — figurative for the jingling of silver — the only modern music that works such miracles.

wealthy, instead of the imported trumpery of British naval-fights, or coloured engravings, and, above all, in the place of that vulgar, tasteless, and inelegant accumulation of gilded finery, which costs more than a dozen fine landscapes. These lovers of cut-glass lamps, rose-wood sofas, and convex mirrors, have yet to learn that a single bust or picture of a master adorns and enriches the parlour of a gentleman, in the eyes of a well-bred person, a thousand times more than the spoils of half a dozen fashionable warehouses.

But, after all, there is nothing in this world like a good appetite and plenty of good things to satisfy, or rather satiate, it; for merely to *satisfy* the appetite is to treat it as one would that of a horse. In this respect, and this only in our estimation, are the tops of high mountains entitled to consideration. It is amazing what a glorious propensity to eating is generated by the keen air of these respectable protuberances. People have been known to eat up every thing in the house at a meal, and report says that a fat waiter once disappeared in a very mysterious manner. The stomach expands with the majesty and expansion of the prospect, to a capacity equally majestic, and the worthy landlord at the Pine Orchard (between ourselves) has assured us that he has known a sickly young lady, who was travelling for an appetite, discuss venison for breakfast like an alderman. Certain half-starved critics, will, without doubt, sharpen their wits as sharp as their appetites, and, putting gray goose-lance in rest, tilt at us terribly, for thus exalting the accomplishment of eating above all others, and inciting people to inordinate feats of the trencher.

But we will shut their mouths at once and forever, by asking a simple question,— whether the *sine qua non* of rich and idle people's comfort and happiness is not *exercise*, without which they cannot enjoy either their wealth or their leisure? Having answered this question, we will ask them another, to wit: whether there be any exercise, not to say hard work, equal to that which the inward and outward man undergoes in the final disposal of a sumptuous dinner or supper? How he puffs, and blows, and sighs, and snoozes, and, heaven forgive us! belches,— and twists and turns, enjoying neither stillness nor motion, until he has quieted this mighty mass of ingredients. In short, it is the hardest exercise in the world, and of course must be highly beneficial to health. This is what constitutes the unrivalled excellence of eating, and its superiority over all other carnal delights; since we have the pleasures of taste in the first place, and, in the second, the benefit of real training to prepare us for a new meal. Hence it was, that a famous eating philosopher, hearing a peasant grumbling that he could not, like him, live without work, replied in the following impromptu —

"I labour to digest **one** dinner, more
Than you, you blockhead, do, to earn a score."

"The town of Kaatskill, and the neighbouring country," observes Alderman Janson in his manuscript *ana*, "is the seat of many Dutch families, whose ancestors settled there in the olden time. Honest, industrious, and sober — what a noble trio of virtues! — they pursue the even tenor of their way, and would continue to do so for generations to come, were it not for the late attempts to corrupt them with canals and great state-roads; and, above all, by locating a fashionable hotel in the very centre of their stronghold, the Kaatskill Mountain. Since the introduction of these pestilent novelties, divers rebellious movements against the good old customs have been noticed. It is not long since, that several old ladies, whose descent ought to have forever saved them from the temptation of such enormities, have introduced the fashion of drinking tea by candle-light; and that a young fellow — a genuine descendant of Rip Van Winkle — being out shooting, met a Dutch damsel in a fashionable bonnet, whereat he was so frightened that he fired his gun at random, and ran home to tell his mother that he had seen a strange wild beast, that looked, for all the world, " like I don't know what." It is a sore thing to see the venerable customs of antiquity thus gradually beaten from their last intrenchments in the mountains. All this comes of steam-boats, manufactories, and other horrible enormities of this improving age."

HUDSON.

" A very respectable town, or rather, city," says Alderman Janson: " so called after the renowned Hendrik Hudson of blessed memory. It is opposite to Athens, and ought to have been noticed immediately after it. But if the traveller wishes particularly to view the city, he has only to mention his desire, and the steam-boat will turn back with him, for they are very obliging. Hudson furnishes one of those examples of rapid growth, so common, and so peculiar, to our country. It goes back no farther than 1786, and is said now to contain nearly two thousand inhabitants. But towns, like children, are very apt to grow more in the first few years, than in all their lives after. Hudson, however, has a bank, which is a sort of wet-nurse to these little towns, giving them too often a precocious growth, which is followed by a permanent debility. The town is beautifully situated, and the environs are of the most picturesque and romantic description. There are several pretty country-seats in the neighbourhood. Here ends, according to the law of Nature, the ship-navigation of the river; but, by a law of the Legislature, a company has been incorporated with a capital of one million of dollars — how easy it is to coin money in this way! — to make a canal to New Baltimore; for what purpose, only legislative wisdom can explain. There was likewise an incorporated company, to build a mud-machine for deepening the river. But the river is no deeper than it was, and the canal to New Baltimore is not made, probably because the million of dollars is not forthcoming. One may pay too dear for a canal, as well as for a whistle. That canals are far better than rivers is not to be doubted; but, as we get our rivers for nothing, and pay pretty dearly for our canals, I would beg leave to represent in behalf of the poor rivers, that they are entitled to some little consideration, if it is only on the score of coming as free gifts. Hudson is said to be very much infested with politicians, a race of men, who, though they have never been classed among those who live by their own wits and the little wit of their neighbours, certainly belong to the genus."

From hence to Albany the Hudson gradually decreases in magnitude, changing its character of a mighty river for that of a pleasant pastoral stream. The high banks gradually subside into rich flats, portentous of Dutchmen, who light on them as certainly as do the snipes and plovers. " Wisely despising," observes Alderman Janson, " the barren mountains which are only made to look at, they passed on up the river from Fort Amsterdam, till they arrived hereabouts, and here they pitched their tents. Their descendants still retain possession of the seats of their ancestors, though sorely beset, by the march of the human mind and the progress of public improvement on one hand, and on the other by interlopers from the modern Scythia, the cradle of the human race in the new world, Connecticut. These last, by their pestilent scholarship, and mischievous contrivances of patent ploughs, patent threshing-machines, patent corn-shellers, and patent churns, for the encouragement of domestic industry, have gone near to overset all the statutes of St. Nicholas. The honest burghers of Coeymans, Coxsackie, and New Paltz, still hold out manfully; but, alas! the women — the women are prone to apostasy, and hanker after novelties. A Dutch damsel can't, for her heart, resist a Connecticut school-master with his rosy cheeks and store of book-learning; and even honest yffrouw herself chuckles a little amatory Dutch at his approach, simpering mightily thereat, and stroking down her apron. A goose betrayed — no, I am wrong — a goose once saved the capitol of Rome; and it is to be feared a woman will finally betray the citadels of Coeymans, Coxsackie, and New Paltz, to the schoolmasters of Connecticut, who circumvent them with outlandish scholarship. These speculations," quoth the worthy alderman,* "remind me of the mishap of my unfortunate great uncle, Douw Van Wezel, who sunk under the star of one of these errant grammarians.

"Douw and little Alida Vander Spiegle had been play-mates since their infancy — I was going to say school-mates, but at that time there was no such thing as a school, so far as I can learn, in the neighbourhood, to teach the young varlets to chalk naughty words on walls and fences, which is all that learning

---

* We ought, long before this, to have apprised the reader, that Alderman Nicholas Nicodemus Janson was the flower of the magistracy of Coxsackie, and died full of years and honours, on his patron St. Nicholas' day, in the year of our Lord one thousand eight hundred and twenty-seven. He was our great-uncle by the mother's side, and many are the happy days we remember to have passed in his honest old Dutch house, which, according to custom, has lately been turned into a tavern. He was indisputably the greatest scholar of the age, in the opinion of his neighbours, who ought to know him best, and as compared with divers great authors of the present time, of whom he was wont to say, that he furnished one with all the botany, and another with all the geology, he ever had in his life. He left behind him twenty-six large volumes of manuscripts, which he devised to the writer of this book, as he expressed it, "In special token of my affectionate remembrance, considering them as by far the most valuable of my possessions." The rest of the heirs never disputed the legacy; and, what is quite unaccountable, the executors turned it over to us with the utmost promptitude, while some other legatees remain unpaid to this day. These gentlemen will be astonished, if not mortified, to hear, that we have lately been offered more for these invaluable manuscripts than all the rest of the worthy alderman's property is worth. But we disdain to sell what was bestowed upon us freely; and it is our intention, when we are grown too old to travel, to publish the whole twenty-six volumes, under the title of "Reminiscences," at our own expense, charging the public nothing for the insides, and only two dollars a volume for the binding: — to the which course we are vehemently incited by the example of a certain worthy of Coxsackie, who, being desirous the public should enjoy the full benefit of a famous nostrum of his for the cure of all things, did actually give away the said nostrum for nothing, only charging four shillings for the bottles: — whereby all the country was cured, without any expense, and the worthy philanthropist got rich, with a clear conscience.

is good for, for aught I see. Douw was no scholar, so there was no danger of his getting into the state-prison for forgery; but it requires little learning to fall in love. Alida had however staid a whole winter in York, where she learned to talk crooked English, and cock her pretty little pug-nose at our good old customs. They were the only offspring of their respective parents, whose farms lay side by side, squinting plainly at matrimony between the young people. Douw and Alida went to church together every Sunday; wandered into the church-yard, where Alida read the epitaphs for him; and it was the talk of every-body that it would certainly be a match. Douw was a handsome fellow for a Dutchman, though he lacked that effeminate ruddiness which seduces poor ignorant women. He had a stout frame, a bluish complexion, straight black hair, eyes of the colour of indigo, and as honest a pair of old-fashioned mahogany-baluster legs, as you would wish to see under a man. It was worth while to make good legs then, when every man wore breeches, and some of the women too, if report is to be credited. Alida was the prettiest little Dutch damsel that ever had her stocking filled with cakes on new-year's eve, by the blessed St. Nicholas. I will not describe her, lest the whole army of my readers should fall in love with her, or at all events weep themselves into Saratoga fountains, when they come to hear of the disastrous fate of poor Douw, whose destiny it was — but let us have no anticipations; sufficient for the day is the evil thereof.

" It was new-year's eve, and Douw was invited to see out the old year at Judge Vander Spiegle's, in the honest old Dutch way, under the special patronage of St. Nicholas, to whom whoever fails in due honour and allegiance, this be his fate: never to sip the dew from the lips of the lass he loveth best, on new-year's eve, or new-year's morn; never to taste of hot spiced Santa Cruz; and never to know the delights of mince-pies and sausages, swimming in the sauce of honest mirth and home-felt jollity. St. Nicholas!, thrice-jolly St. Nicholas! Bacchus of Christian Dutchmen, king of good fellows, patron of holiday fare, inspirer of simple frolic and unsophisticated happiness, saint of all saints that deck the glorious calendar! — thou that first awakenest the hopes of the prattling infant; dawnest anticipated happiness on the school-boy; and brightenest the wintry hours of manhood — if I forget thee whatever betide, or whatever fantastic, heartless follies may usurp the place of thy simple celebration, may I lose with the recollection of past pleasures the anticipation of pleasures to come, yawn at a tea-party, petrify at a soirée, and perish finally, overwhelmed, in a deluge of whip-syllabub and floating-island! Thrice, and three times thrice, jolly St. Nicholas! On this, the first day of the new year, 1826, with an honest reverence and a full bumper of cherry-bounce, I salute thee! Io, St. Nicholas! May thy sleigh-bells tinkle for ever!

"There were glorious doings at the judge's among the young folks, and the old ones too, for that matter, till one or two or perhaps three in the morning, when the visitors got into their sleighs and skirred away home, leaving Douw and the fair Alida alone, or as good as alone, for the judge and the yffrouw, were as sound as a church in the two chimney-corners. If wine, and French liqueurs, and such trumpery, make a man gallant and adventurous, what will not hot spiced Santa Cruz achieve! Douw was certainly somewhat flustered — perhaps it might be predicated of him that he was as it were a little tipsy. Certain it is, he waxed brave as a Dutch lion. I'll not swear but that he put his arm round her waist, and kissed the little Dutch girl — but I *will* swear positively that before the parties knew whether they were standing on their heads or feet, they had exchanged vows and become irrevocably engaged. Whereupon Douw waked the old judge, and asked his consent, on the spot. "Yaw, yaw" — yawned the judge, and fell fast asleep again in a twinkling. Nothing but the last trumpet would have roused the yffrouw till dawn.

"In the morning, the good yffrouw was let into the affair, and began to bestir herself accordingly. I cannot count the sheets, and table-cloths, and towels, the good woman mustered out, nor describe the preparations made for the expected wedding. There was a cake baked, as big as Kaatskill Mountain, and mince-pies enough to cover it. There were cates of a hundred ignoble names, and sweetmeats enough to kill a whole village. All was preparation, expectation, and prognostication. A Dutch tailor had constructed Douw a suit of snuff-colour, that made him look like a great roll of leaf-tobacco; and a York milliner had exercised her skill in the composition of a wedding-dress for Alida, that made the hair of the girls of Coeymans and Coxsackie stand on end. All was ready, and the day appointed. But, alas! I wonder no one has yet had the sagacity to observe, and proclaim to the world, that all things in this life are uncertain, and that the anticipations of youth are often disappointed.

"Just three weeks before the wedding, there appeared in the village of Coxsackie a young fellow, dressed in a three-cornered cocked-hat, (with a queue at least a yard long hanging from under it, tied up in an eel skin), a spruce blue coat, (not much the worse for wear), a red waistcoat, corduroy breeches, handsome cotton stockings with a pair of good legs in them, and pumps with silver buckles. His arrival was like the shock of an earthquake, he being the first stranger that had appeared within the memory of man. He was of a goodly height, well-shaped, and had a pair of rosy cheeks, which no Dutch damsel ever could resist, for, to say the truth, our Dutch lads are apt to be a little dusky in the epidermis.

" He gave out that he was come to set up a school, and teach the little chubby Dutch boys and girls English. The men set their faces against this monstrous innovation; but the women! the women! they always will run after novelty, and they ran after the school-master, his red cheeks, and his red waistcoat. Yffrouw Vander Spiegle contested the empire of the world within doors with his honour the judge, and bore a divided reign. She was smitten with a desire to become a blue-stocking herself, or, at least, that her daughter should. The yffrouw was the bellwether of fashion in the village; of course many other yffrouws followed her example, and in a little time the lucky school-master was surrounded by half the grown-up damsels of Coxsackie.

" Alida soon became distinguished as his favourite scholar; she was the prettiest, the richest girl in the school; and she could talk English, which the others were only just learning. He taught her to read poetry — he taught her to talk with her eyes — to write love-letters — and, at last, to love. Douw was a lost man, the moment the school-master came into the village. He first got the blind side of the daughter, and then of the yffrouw: but he found it rather a hard matter to get the blind side of the judge, who had heard from his brother in Albany, what pranks these Connecticut boys were playing there. He discouraged the school-master; and he encouraged Douw to press his suit, which Alida had put off, and put off, from time to time. She was sick — and not ready — and indifferent — and sometimes as cross as a little Fury. Douw smoked his pipe harder than ever at her; but she resisted like a heroine.

"In those times of cheap simplicity, it was the custom of the country for the school-master to board in turn with the parents of his scholars, a week or a fortnight at a time, and it is recorded of these learned Thebans, that they always staid longest where there was a pretty daughter, and plenty of pies and sweetmeats. The time at last came round, when it was the school-master's turn to spend the allotted fortnight with Judge Vander Spiegle, sorely to the gloomy forebodements of Douw, who began to have a strong suspicion of the cause of Alida's coldness. The schoolmaster knew which side his bread was buttered, and laid close siege to the yffrouw, by praising her good things, exalting her consequence, and depreciating that of her neighbours. Nor did he neglect the daughter whom he plied with poetry, melting looks, significant squeezes, and all that — although all that was quite unnecessary, for she was ready to run away with him at any time. But this did not suit our schemer: he might be divorced from the acres, if he married without the consent of the judge. He however continued to administer fuel to the flame, and never missed abusing poor Douw to his face, without the latter being the wiser for it, he not understanding a word of English.

"By degrees he opened the matter to the yffrouw, who liked it exceedingly, for she was, as we said before, inclined to the mysteries of blue-stockingism, and was half in love with his red waistcoat and red cheeks. Finally, she told him, in an ingenuous way, that as there were two to one in his favour, and the old judge would, she knew, never consent to the marriage while he could help it, the best thing he could do was to go and get married as soon as possible, and she would bear him out. That very night Douw became a disconsolate widower, although, poor fellow, he did not know of it till the next morning. The judge stormed and swore, and the yffrouw talked, till at length he allowed them to come and live in the house, but with the proviso that they were never to speak to him, nor he to them. A little grandson in process of time healed all these internal divisions. They christened him Adrian Vander Spiegle, after his grandfather, and, when it came to pass that the old patriarch died, the estate passed from the Vander Spiegles to the Longfellows, after the manner of men.

"Poor Douw grew melancholy, and pondered ofttimes whether he should bring his action for breach of promise, fly the country forever, turn Methodist, or marry under the nose of the faithless Alida, 'on purpose to spite her.' He finally decided on the latter, married a little Dutch brunette from Kinderhook, and prospered mightily in posterity, as did also his neighbour, Philo Longfellow. But it was observed that the little Van Wezels and the little Longfellows never met without fighting; and that, as they grew up, this hostility gathered additional bitterness. In process of time the village became divided into two factions, which gradually spread wherever the Yankees and the Dutch mixed together; and finally, like the feuds of the Guelphs and Ghibellines, divided the land for almost a hundred miles round."

ALBANY.

Leaving Coxsackie, the traveller gradually approaches those rich little islands and *flats*, beloved by the honest Dutchmen of all parts of the world, in the midst of which are seen the long comfortable brick mansions of the Cuylers, the Schuylers, the Van Rensselaers, and others of the patroons of ancient times. "I never see one of these," quoth Alderman Janson, "without picturing to myself the plentiful breakfasts, solid dinners, and manifold evening repasts, which have been, and still are, discussed in these comfortable old halls, guiltless of folding doors and marble mantel-pieces, and all that modern trumpery which starves the kitchen to decorate the parlour, and robs the stranger of his hospitable welcome for the sake of glitter and trash. I never think of the picture so delightfully drawn by Mrs. Grant, in the

'Memoirs of an American Lady,' of the noble patriarchal state of 'Uncle Schuyler' and his amiable wife, without contrasting it with the empty, vapid, mean, and selfish pageantry of the present time, which satiates itself with the paltry vanity of display, and stoops to all the dirty drudgery of brokerage and speculation, to gather wealth, only to excite the gaping wonder, or secret envy, of vulgar rivals. By St. Nicholas, the patron of good fellows, but the march of the human intellect is sometimes like that of a crab, backwards!"

"The city of Albany," continues the worthy alderman, "was founded, not by Mars, Neptune, Minerva, nor Vulcan, nor by any of the wandering vagabond gods of ancient times. Neither does it owe its origin to a runaway hero like Æneas, nor to a runaway debtor, like a place that shall be nameless. Its first settlers were a race of portly burghers from old Holland, who, sailing up the river in search of a resting-place, and observing how the rich flats invited them as it were to their fat and fruitful bowers, landed thereabouts, lighted their pipes, and began to build their dwellings without saying one word. Tradition also imports, that they were somewhat incited to this by seeing divers large and stately sturgeons jumping up out of the river, as they are wont to do most incontinently in these parts. These sturgeons are, (when properly disguised by cookery so that you cannot tell what they may be), most savoury and excellent food, although there is no truth in the story hatched by the pestilent descendants of Philo Longfellow, that the flesh of the sturgeon is called Albany beef, and that it is sometimes served up at Rockwell's,

Cruttenden's, and other favourite resorts of tourists, as veal-cutlets. Out upon such slanders! By St. Nicholas, the Longfellows lie most immoderately. The worthy burghers of Albany never deceived a Christian in their lives. As their old proverb says:

> ' 'Twould make an honest Dutchman laugh,
> To say a sturgeon is a calf.'

"The Indians, according to the learned Knickerbocker, perceiving that the new-comers were, like themselves, great smokers, took a vast liking to them, and brought out the pipe of peace, without saying a word, and presently a cloud of smoke overspread the land, like the haze of the Indian summer. An old chief at length looked at Mynheer Van Wezel, the leader of the party, and gave a significant grunt. Mynheer Van Wezel looked at the old Indian and gave another grunt equally significant. Thus they came to a mutual good-understanding, and a treaty was concluded, without exchanging a single word, or any other ceremony than a good sociable smoking-party. Some of the descendants of Philo Longfellow insinuate that Mynheer Van Wezel took an opportunity of presenting his pistol, well charged with Schiedam, to the old chief and his followers, and that it operated marvellously in bringing about the treaty. But there is not a word of truth in the story. This good-understanding was produced by the magic virtues of silence and tobacco. This example shows how easy it is to be good friends, if people will only hold their tongues; and it moreover forever rescues the excellent practice of smoking from the dull jests of effeminate puppies, who affect to call it vulgar. If modern negotiators would only sit down and smoke a familiar pipe together every day for five or six months, my life upon it there would be less ink shed, and blood shed, too, in this world. By St. Nicholas, the saint of smokers!, there is nothing comparable to the pipe, for soothing anger, softening down irritation, solacing disappointment, and disposing the mind to balmy contemplation, poetical flights, and lofty soarings of the fancy; insomuch that any young bard, who will tie his shirt with a black ribbon and take to smoking and drinking gin and water like my Lord Byron, will in a short time write equal to his lordship, allowing for accidents."

"Thus," continues the alderman, "was the city of Albany founded, and originally called *All-bonny*, as the Dutch people still pronounce it, from the bonny river, the bonny woods, bonny pastures, and bonny landscapes by which it was environed. But, blessed St. Nicholas!, how is it sophisticated, since, by the posterity of Philo Longfellow; by politicians, tourists, and lobby-members; by widening streets, building basins, and digging canals! The old Dutch church, where the followers of Mynheer Van Wezel first offered up their simple orisons, is pulled down, and in its room a nondescript with two tin steeples erected, wherein they preach nothing but English. The young men who descend from the founders are not Dutchmen at all, and the damsels are nought. Not one in a hundred can read a Dutch Bible! In a little while the children of that roving Ishmaelite, Philo Longfellow, will sweep them from their inheritance, and the land shall know them no more. The very houses have changed their position, and it is written, that an old mansion of Dutch brick which whilom projected its end in front, on Pearl Street, did one night incontinently turn its broadside to the street, as if resolved like its master to be in the fashion, and follow the march of public improvement."

As the prize-poet sings — corroborating the sentiments of the worthy alderman —

> "All things do change in this queer world;
> Which world is topsy-turvy hurl'd!
> Tadpoles to skipping bull-frogs turn,
> And whales in lighted candles burn;
> The worm of yesterday, today,
> Flies, a rich butterfly, away;
> The city belles all turn religious,
> And say their prayers in hats prodigious;
> St. Tammany becomes Clintonian,
> And Adams-men downright Jacksonian.
> Thus all our tastes are wild and fleeting,
> And most of all our taste in eating:
> I knew a man — or rather, savage,
> Who went from ducks* to beef and cabbage!"

As Albany is a sort of depot, where the commodities of the fashionable world are warehoused (as it were) a night or two, for exportation to Saratoga, Niagara, Montreal, Quebec, and Boston, we shall here present to our readers a short system of rules and regulations, for detecting good inns, and, generally, for travelling with dignity and refinement.

And first, as to smelling out a comfortable inn.

Never go where the stage-drivers or steam-boat men advise you.

Never go to a newly-painted house — trap for the greenhorns. A butcher's-cart, with a good fat butcher, handing out turkeys, venison, ducks, marbled beef,

---

* *Quære.* — Canvas-backs? — if so, there is no hope for him.

celery, and cauliflowers, is the best sign for a public-house.

Never go to a hotel that has a fine gilt-framed picture of itself hung up in the steam-boat. Good wine needs no bush — a good hotel speaks for itself, and will be found out without a picture.

Always yield implicit obedience to a puff in the newspapers in praise of any hotel. It is a proof that the landlord has been over-civil to one guest at the expense of all the others. No man is ever particularly pleased anywhere, or with any body, unless he has received more attention than he deserves. Perhaps you may be equally favoured, particularly if you hint that you mean to publish your travels. Even publicans sigh for immortality.

Never seem anxious to get lodgings at any particular place. The landlord will put you in the garret if you do, unless you come in your own carriage.

If you have no servant, always hire one of the smartest-dressed fellows of the steam-boat to carry your baggage, and pass him off, if possible, till you are snugly housed at the hotel, as your own. Your accommodations will be the better for it; and when the mistake is discovered, they can't turn you out of your room, you know.

Grumble at your accommodations every morning. It will make you appear of consequence, and, if there are better in the house, in time you will get them.

Take the first opportunity to insinuate to the waiters, one at a time, that, if they remember you, you will remember them when you go away. You will have every soul of them at your command. N. B. You need not keep your promise.

Respecting the best public-houses in Albany, there are conflicting opinions. Some think Rockwell's, some Cruttenden's, the best. We dont know much of Rockwell, but Cruttenden, thrice-jolly Cruttenden, we pronounce worthy to be landlord to the whole universe. Fate intended him to keep open house, and if she had only furnished him with money enough, he would have done it at his own expense, instead of that of other people. He is the Falstaff of hosts, for he not only drinks himself, but causes others to drink, by virtue of his excellent wines, excellent jokes, and excellent example. However, as we profess the most rigorous impartiality, we give no opinion whatever on the relative merits of the two houses, having — for which we hope to be forgiven — more than once got royally fuddled at each. If, however, the traveller is particular, as he ought to be in these matters, he has only to inquire where a certain worthy member from New York puts up during the session. He will be morally certain of finding good fare and good lodgings there.

Lastly, never go away from a place without paying your bill, unless you have nothing to pay it with. *Necessitas non habet,* &c. — A man must travel nowadays, or he is absolutely nobody; and if he has no money, it must be at the expense of other people. In case you set out on a *foray* of this kind, it is advisable to have two trunks, one a small one for your own clothes and those of other people, the other a strong, well-braced, well-riveted, large-sized one, filled with brick-bats. Be sure to talk "big" about having married a rich wife as ugly as sin, for the sake of her money; about your great relations; and, if your modesty won't permit you to pass for a lord, don't abate a hair's-breadth of being second cousin to one. When the landlord becomes troublesome, or inattentive, and begins to throw out hints about the colour of a man's money, hire a gig, take your little trunk, give out that you are going to visit some well-known gentleman in the neighbourhood, for a day or two, and leave the great trunk behind for the benefit of mine host. It is not expected you will send back the gig.

"Albany,"—we again quote from the *ana* of Alderman Janson, the prince of city magistrates—"Albany is the capital of the state of New York, having been the seat of government for almost half a century. Formerly the legislature met in New York; but in process of time it was found that the members, being seduced into huge feeding by the attractions of oysters, and turtle and calf's-head soup, did, half the time, doze all through their afternoon session, and enact divers mischievous laws, to the great detriment of the community. Thereupon they resolved to remove to Albany; but, alas!, luxury and dissipation followed in their train, so that after a while they fell asleep oftener than ever, and passed other laws, which nothing but their being fast asleep could excuse. In my opinion, it would tend greatly to the happiness of the community, and go far to prevent this practice of legislating with the eyes shut, if these bodies were to meet in council like the Indians, under the trees in the open air, and be obliged to legislate, standing. This would prevent one man from talking all the rest to sleep, (unless they slept, like geese, poised on one leg), and thereby arrest the passage of many pernicious enactments for mending rivers, mending manners, mending charters, mending codes, making roads, and making beasts of burden of the people and fools of themselves. Truly saith the wise man, ' Too much of a good thing is good for nothing;' and too much legislation is a species of sly, insidious oppression, the more mischievous as coming in the disguise of powers exercised by the servants, instead of the masters, of the people. Commend me to King Log, rather than King Stork. Every legislative body, in my opinion, should have a majority of good honest, sleepy, patriotic members, whose pleasure it should be to do nothing for most part of the time during the session. Your active men are highly noxious in a government; they must always be doing something, meddling with every one's concerns, and so busy in keeping the wheels of government going, that they don't care how many people they run over. They are millstones in motion, and when they have no grist to grind will set one another on fire. To my notion, the most useful member that ever sat in Congress was one who never in his life made any motion except for an adjournment, which he repeated every day just before dinner-time. Truly, the energy and activity of a blockhead are awful."

" Once upon a time," (so says the fable, according to Alderman Janson), " the empire of the geese was under the government of an old king Gander, who, though he exercised an absolute sway, was so idle, pampered, and phlegmatic, that he slept three fourths of his time, during which the subject geese did pretty much as they pleased. But for all this he was a prodigious tyrant, who consumed more corn than half of his subjects, and moreover obliged them to duck their heads to him whenever they passed. But the chief complaint against him was, that though he could do just as he pleased, it was his pleasure to sit still and do nothing.

"Whereupon it came to pass one day, that his subjects held a town-meeting, or it might be a convention, and dethroned him, placing the government in the hands of the wise geese. Feeling themselves called upon to justify the choice of the nation, by bettering its condition, the wise geese set to work, and passed so many excellent laws, that in a little time the wisest goose of the community could hardly tell whether it was lawful to say boo to a goose, or hiss at a puppy-dog, or kick up a dust in a mill-pond of a warm summer morning. When the time of these wise geese expired, other geese still wiser were chosen to govern in their stead, for such was the prodigious march of mind among them, that there was not a goose in the whole empire but believed himself ten times wiser than his father before him. Each succeeding council of wise geese of course considered itself under obligation to give a push to the march of mind, until at length the mind marched so fast that it was in great danger of falling on its nose, and continually ran against posts, or fell into ditches.

"Thus each generation of wise geese went on making excellent laws to assist the march of mind and the progress of public improvement, until, in process of time, there were no more good laws to pass, and it became necessary to pass bad ones to keep their hands in, and themselves in their places. 'Gentlemen,' said a little, busy, bustling, active, managing, talkative young goose, who was resolved nobody should insinuate that *he* could not say boo to a goose — 'gentlemen, it does not signify, we must do something for the march of mind and the progress of public improvement, or the citizen-geese will reduce us all to nought, and choose other wise geese in our stead. They are already the happiest geese in the world; we must make them a little too happy, or they will never be satisfied.' Hereupon each of the wise geese burned to do something to assist the march of the mind and the progress of public improvement. One proposed a law to forbid geese to stand upon one leg at night and nuzzle their bills in their own feathers, this being a dangerous practice inasmuch as it exposed them to be surprised the more easily by foxes. Another offered a resolution, to oblige all the geese to lay their eggs the other end foremost and hatch them in half the usual period, whereby much time would be saved, and there would be a mighty increase of population. (This last motion was made by an old-bachelor goose, who had made the subject of population his chief study). A third proposed a law forbidding the young goslings to paddle in the water, till they were old enough to get out of the way of the great bull-frogs and snapping-turtles. A fourth moved to pick one half the geese of one half their feathers, and give them to the other half of the geese, for the encouragement of domestic industry and the national independence. After these laws had been debated about six months, they were passed without opposition, it being discovered, to the great surprise of the house, that there was no difference of opinion on the subject.

"Had these edicts been propounded by old king Gander, there would have been the devil to pay among the geese, and such a hissing as was never heard before. But there is a vast difference between being governed by a master and a slave. We see the proudest monarchs and the most headstrong tyrants submitting to the whim of a valet, or a gentleman-usher, or any other mere menial, when they would resist the will of their subjects on all occasions. So with the people, and so it was with the republic of the geese: they allowed themselves to be perpetually cajoled, and laughed at the idea of the possibility of having their chains riveted by their own servants. So the married geese set to work to lay their eggs according to law. But nature is an obstinate lady, and there is no legislating her into reason. The eggs and the goslings came into the world just as they did before. The goslings, contrary to law, would be dabbling in the water, and getting now and then caught by the snapping-turtles, and there was no such thing as punishing the little rogues after they were dead. In short, of all these laws, there was but one which actually went into operation, namely, that for picking one half of the geese for the benefit of the other half.

"But it was never yet known that either men or geese were content with a broken loaf when they could get the whole. The half of the republic of the geese, for whose benefit the other half had been picked, in process of time waxed fat, and strong, and wealthy, whereas the moiety that had been stripped of a good share of their feathers for the encouragement of domestic industry waxed proportionably poor and meagre, and their breast-bones projected awfully, like unto cut-waters. The fat geese now began to grumble that there was a great want of patriotism in the rules of the goosian republic, in not properly encouraging domestic industry, since nothing was clearer than that, if half a loaf was good, the whole loaf was better. So they petitioned — and the petition of the strong is a demand — they petitioned that the geese who had lost half their feathers for the public good should be called upon to yield the other half, like honest, patriotic fellows. The law was passed accordingly. But public discontent is like a great bell; it takes a long time in raising, but makes a mighty noise when once up. The geese which had been picked for the good of the republic had chewed the cud of their poverty in silence, but they spit venom in private among themselves; and this new law to pluck them quite naked brought affairs to a crisis. In matters of legislation, wealth and influence are every thing. But where it comes to *club-law*, or a resort to the right of the strongest, poverty always carries the day. The poor plucked geese accordingly took back by force what they had been deprived of by legislation, with interest; and, finding after a little while that it was necessary to have a head of some kind or other, unanimously recalled old king Gander to come and sleep over them again. He reigned long and happily — poised himself so nicely, by doing nothing, and keeping perfectly still, that he sat upright while the wheel of fortune turned round under him, and the occasional rocking of his kingdom only made him sleep the sounder."

MORAL.

"Leave the people to manage their private affairs in their own way as much as possible, without the interference of their rulers. The worst species of tyranny is that of laws, making sudden and perpetual changes in the value of property and the wages of labour, thus placing every man's prosperity at the mercy of others."

According to Alderman Janson, "Albany has the merit, or the reputation, of having first called into activity, if not into existence, a race of men perhaps the most useful of any invented since the days of Prometheus, who make it their sole business to enlighten the legislature: and especially on subjects of finance, banking, and the like. They are called by way of honourable distinction LOBBY-MEMBERS, because they form a sort of third estate, or legislative chamber in the lobby. They are wonderful adepts at *log-rolling*, and of such extraordinary powers of persuasion, that one of them has been known to lay a wager that he would induce a member of the inner house to reconsider his vote, in a private conference of half an hour. Such is the wonderful disinterestedness of these patriots that they never call upon the people to pay them three dollars a day, as the other members do: on the contrary, they not only bear their own expenses, but give great entertainments, and sometimes, it is affirmed, help a brother-member of the inner house along with a loan, a subscription, and even a free gift — out of pure good-nature and charity.

" Their ingenuity is exercised for the benefit of the good people of the state, in devising all sorts of projects, for making roads, digging canals, and sawing wood; all which they will execute for nothing, provided the legislature will let them make their own money out of rags, and, what is still better, 'Loan them the credit of the state,' for half a million or so. It is astonishing what benefits these *lobby-members* have conferred on this great state, filling it with companies for furnishing the people with every convenience, from bad money that won't pass, to coal that won't burn — whereby people, instead of wasting their resources in necessaries, may spend them in superfluities. Moreover, they have reflected great honour upon the state abroad, it being a common saying, that whoever wants his scheme '*log-rolled*,' or his project for the benefit of the community adopted by a legislature, must send to Albany for a gang of lobby-members. I thought I could do no less than say what I have said in behalf of these calumniated people, whom I intend to employ next winter, in getting an incorporation to clear Broadway of free gentlemen of colour, ladies' fashionable bonnets, and those 'infernal machines,' that whiz about, spirting water, and engendering mud from one end of the street to the other, thereby making it unnavigable for sober, decent people.

" In former times," continues the alderman, " Albany was a cheap place, where an honest man could live on a small income, and bring up a large family reputably, without running in debt, or getting a note discounted. But domestic industry and the march of public improvement have changed the face of things, and altered the nature of man as well as of woman. The father must live in style, whether he can afford it or not — the daughters must dress in the extremity of bad fashions, learn to dance, to paint, and to torture the piano — and the sons must disdain the ignominious idea of being useful. The race of fine ladies and fine gentlemen — (fine feathers make fine birds) — has multiplied an hundred-fold, and we are credibly informed that the former have entered into a solemn league and covenant, not to marry any man who cannot afford to live in a three-story house with folding doors and marble mantel-pieces. The ancient Dutch economy and the simple habits of Dutchmen have given place to speculation and folly; and the possession of a moderate independence is sacrificed to the idle anticipation of unbounded wealth. The race of three-cornered cocked-hats is almost extinct — the reverend old-fashioned garments so becoming to age are replaced by dandy coats — the good housewives no longer toil or spin, (and yet I say unto thee, gentle reader, that the gardens of the Euphrates were not so party-coloured as one of these) — tavern-keepers charge double, hack drivers treble, milliners quadruple — tailors have put off the modesty of their natures — and the old market-women have grown extortionate in cabbages and turnips. Nay, I have it from the best authority, that an old burgher of the ancient regime, was not long since ousted, by the force of conjugal eloquence, out of a patriarchal coat, which he had worn with honour and reputation upwards of forty years, and instigated by the devil to put on a fashionable frock in its place."

We also learn from the manuscripts of Alderman

Janson of blessed memory, that, "In the year 1783, on the 26th of August, one Baltus Blydenburgh, on being called upon by Teunis Van Valer for money which he owed him, declined paying it, on the ground that it was not in his power. At first Teunis thought he was joking, but, on being solemnly assured to the contrary, he threw up his hands and eyes to heaven, and cried out in Dutch, "Well, den, the world is certainly coming to an end!", and departed into the streets, where he told every body he met, that Baltus Blydenburgh could not pay his debts, and that the city was going to be swallowed up like Sodom and Gomorrah. The story spread, and the panic with it, insomuch that the good careful old wives packed up all their petticoats and looking-glasses, and were preparing to depart to the other side of the river. Such a thing as a man's not paying his debts had never before been known in Albany, and beyond doubt the city would have been entirely deserted, had it not been for the arrival of a grandson of Philo Longfellow, from New York, who assured them there was no danger of an earthquake; for, to his certain knowledge, if running in debt for more than people were able to pay would produce earthquakes, there would not be a city in the United States left standing. Whereupon," continues Alderman Janson, "the citizens were mightily comforted, and went to work getting in debt as fast as possible." He adds, that, up to the year 1783, there was not a school-master in Albany that could tell the meaning of the word "bankrupt," and concludes with the following affecting apostrophe: "Alas! for honest old Albany! All this comes of 'domestic industry,' 'the march of public improvement,' and the innovations of the posterity of Philo Longfellow!"

The grand canal ends at Albany, where there is a capacious basin for canal-boats. "The canal and locks," quoth the worthy alderman, "cost upwards of eight millions of dollars, the locks, especially, having been very expensive; whence the favourite song of the people of New York state is:

> ' I LOCK'D up all my treasure.' "

At Albany, wise travellers going to the Springs or to Niagara generally quit the water, and take to land-carriage; since no man, who is either in a hurry, (as all people who have nothing to do are), or who thinks it of any importance to wear a head on his shoulders, would venture on the canal. *Festina lente* is the maxim of the canal-boats; they appear always in a hurry, and yet go at a snail's pace. Four or five miles an hour would do very well when people were not so busy about nothing as they are now, but, body o' me!, fifteen miles an hour is indispensable to the new regime. By this saving of time, a traveller may be safely said to live twice as long as he could do before the march of mind and the progress of public improvement. The following are among the principal rules adopted by very experienced travellers on leaving Albany by land.

Whenever you come to two turnpike-roads, branching off in different directions, you may be pretty certain they both head to the same place, it being a maxim with the friends of public improvement, that, as two heads are better than one, (though one of them be a calf's-head), so are two roads, even though both are as bad as possible. In this country there are always at least two nearest ways to a place of any consequence.

Never inquire your way of persons along the road, but steer by the map, and then if you go wrong it will be with a clear conscience.

Never ask the distance to any place of "one of the posterity of Philo Longfellow," as Alderman Janson calls them, for he will be sure to ask you if you are going there, before he answers your question; nor of the descendants of the Van Wezels, for, ten to one, the first will tell you it is ten miles, and when you have gone half a dozen of them, the next will apprise you, after scratching his head in the manner of Scipio, that it is nigh about twenty. You will never get to the end of your journey, if you believe these fellows.

Never stop at the tavern recommended by the tavern-keeper at whose house you stopped last. They make a point of honour of not speaking ill of each other, a practice which we would particularly recommend to the liberal professions.

When you enter a tavern, begin by acting the great man — ask for a private room — call the landlord, his wife, and all his household, as loud as you can — set them all going, if possible, and find fault, not only with every thing you see, but with every thing they do. Examine the beds, and be particular in looking under them, to see if there is no robber concealed there. If there is any distinguished person living in the neighbourhood, inquire about him particularly, and regret you have not time to stay a day or two with him. If you happen to be travelling in a hack-carriage, make the driver take off his number and put up a coat of arms. Be sure to let the driver know that you will send him about his business if he whispers a word of the matter, and be so particular in looking to the horses, and inquiring if they have been taken care of, that every body will take it for granted they belong to you. As a good portion of the pleasure of travelling consists in passing for a person of consequence, these directions will be found of value in bringing about this desirable result.

When people stop by the side of the road to stare at your equipage, be sure to loll carelessly back, and take not the least notice of them. They will think you a great man, certainly; whereas, if you look at them complacently, they will only set you down as a gentleman.

Be careful, when you go away, not to express the least satisfaction to landlord or landlady at your entertainment, but let them see that you consider yourself ill-treated. They will take it for granted you have been used to better at home.

If you travel in a stage-coach, look as dignified as possible, and, if any body asks you a civil question, give him an uncivil look in return, (as is the fashion with the English quality-cockneys), unless the person looks as if he might tweak your nose for assuming airs.

Always, if possible, set out in a stage with a drunken driver, because there is some reason to calculate he will be sober in time. Whereas, if he sets out sober, it is pretty certain he will be drunk all the rest of the journey.

If you meet with a stranger who seems inclined to be civil extempore, take it for granted he means to pick your pocket or diddle you in some way or other. Civility is too valuable an article to be given away for nothing.

If you travel in a handsome equipage, no matter whether your own or not, be careful not to enter a town after dark, or leave it before the people are up; else one half of them won't have an opportunity of seeing you.

Always plump into the back seat of a stage-coach without ceremony, whether there are females to be accommodated or not. If any *man* happens to claim the place you have taken, you can only get out again you know, and look dignified.

Always be in a bad-humour when you are travelling. Nothing is so vulgar as perpetual cheerfulness. It proves a person devoid of well-bred sensibility.

Touching the payment of bills, our friend Stephen Griffin, Esq., assures us that, on the continent of Europe, none but an English cockney-traveller, with more money than wit, ever thinks of paying a bill without deducting one half. Here, in this honest country, it would be unreasonable in the traveller to deduct more than one third, that being the usual excess along the roads, and at public places much frequented by people having a vocation to travelling for pleasure. If, however, you wish to pass for a great man, pay the bill without looking at it. We were acquainted with a great broker, who always pursued this plan, and the consequence was, that hostlers, chambermaids, and landlords, one and all, looked upon him as the greatest man in America, and nobody could be waited on, or accommodated at the inns, until he was properly disposed of. There is, on the contrary, a meritorious class of travellers, whose business is to get away from hotels and public-houses without paying at all; who drink their bottle of Bingham, Marston, or Billy Ludlow, every day, scot-free. This requires considerable original genius, much knowledge of the world, and great power of face, with a capacity of changing names. Your *alias* is a staunch friend to worthies of this class. The best school for this species of knowledge is the Quarter-Sessions, or the police-court, where a regular attendance of about a twelvemonth will hardly fail of initiating the scholar into all the mysteries of the noble art of running in debt, an art than which there is not one more vitally important to the rising generation.

Before we leave Albany, we would caution the traveller against anticipating any thing extraordinary in the way of eating at this place. In vain may he sigh for canvas-backs, or terrapins. A turtle sometimes finds its way there, and now and then a cargo of oysters; but in general there is little or nothing to detain the enlightened, travelled gourmand. The fare will do well enough for legislators and lobby-members, but, for a refined and cultivated palate, what can be expected from a people who are said to follow the antiquated maxim of the old song:

"I eat when I'm hungry, and drink when I'm dry,"—

a maxim in itself so utterly vulgar and detestable, that it could only have originated in the fancy of some half-starved ballad-monger, who considered the mere filling of his stomach as the perfection of human happiness. Any fool can eat when he is hungry and drink when he is dry, provided he can get any thing to eat or drink; this is the bliss of a quadruped, devoid of the reasoning faculty. But to enjoy the delight of eating without appetite, to be able to bring back the sated palate to a relish of some new dainty, to reanimate the exhausted energies of the fainting stomach, and waken it to new exstacies of fruition; to get dyspepsias, and provoke apoplexies, is the privilege of that man alone, whose reason has been refined, expanded, and perfected by travel and experience. The happiest man, in our opinion, we ever knew, was a favoured being who possessed the *furor* of eating in greater perfection than all the rest of humankind. He would eat a whole turkey, a pair of canvas-backs, and a quarter of mutton, at a sitting, and finish with a half-bushel of peaches. He was indeed an example to his species; but he was too good for this world, and was maliciously taken off by an unlucky bone, at a turtle feast at Hoboken, where he excelled even himself, and died a blessed martyr. The only consolation remaining to his friends is, that he was afterwards immortalized in the following lines of the famous prize-poet, who happened to be at the feast which proved so disastrous.

>"Here lies a man whom flesh could ne'er withstand;
>But bone, alas!, did get the upper hand.
>Death in the shape of turtle, venison, fowl,
>Oft came and shook his scythe with ghastly scowl,
>But hero-like he damned him for a bore,
>And cried, undaunted, 'waiter bring us more!'
>At last death came in likeness of a bone,
>And the pot-valiant champion was o'erthrown.
>If death one single ounce of flesh had had,
>'Twould have been all over with him there, egad;
>A broil of him our hungry friend had made,
>And turtle-clubs been never more dismay'd
>By the gaunt imp of chaos and old night,
>Who spoils full many a glorious appetite."

"At Albany," as Alderman Janson observes, "ends the proper sloop-navigation of the Hudson. It is true they do manage to get them up as far as Troy, and Lansingburgh, and even Waterford. But nature never intended they should go farther than Albany. It was in full confidence of this that the first colony pitched upon Albany as the site of a great city, which was destined in a happy hour to become the capital of the state. Unfortunate adventurers!, they never dreamed of the march of the human mind, and the progress of public improvements; or of companies incorporated for the performance of miracles. They never surmised the possibility of a river like the Hudson, the master-piece of the Creator of the universe, being improved by an act of the legislature; nor did it ever enter into their matter-of-fact brains that the posterity of Philo Longfellow would found a city as it were right over their heads at Troy, and thus intercept the rafts coming down the river to Albany. What a pity it is that people cannot see a little farther into millstones! What glorious speculations we should all make!—except that, every body being equally enlightened as to the future, there would be no speculation at all, which would be a terrible thing for those useful people who, having no money themselves, disinterestedly go about manufacturing excellent projects, to drain the pockets of those who have. Money is, in truth, like an eel; it is easy to catch it, but to hold it fast afterwards is rather a difficult matter. And here I am reminded of the fate of an honest codger of my acquaintance, who had become rich by a long course of industry and economy, and who at the age of forty-five set himself down in a smart, growing town, not a hundred miles from I forget where, to enjoy the life of a gentleman.

"Martin Forbush, that was his name, lived a whole year in his dignified retirement, at the end of which he became rather dyspeptic, and began to get out of humour with the life of a gentleman. Of all the castles ever built in the air, the castle of indolence is the worst. Ease 'is not to be bought with wampum, or paper-money,' as Horace says; a man must have some employment, or pursuit — or at least a hobby-horse — or he can never be contented on earth. To one who has been all his life making money, the mere enjoyment of his wealth is not worth a fig. Even the great good, eating, has its limits. To be sure, nothing is wanting to the happiness of a rich man but that his appetite should increase with his means of indulging it. But, alas!, it would seem that every pleasure in life is saddled with its penalty, and that the gratification of the senses carries with it the elements of its own punishment. The very food we devour rises up in judgment against us. The turtle is revenged by apoplexy, dyspepsia, epilepsy, and catalepsy. Enough. The subject is too heart-rending.

"While honest Martin was thus dying by inches, of a gentleman's life, and pining away both corporeally and mentally under the incubus of idleness, as good luck would have it, a stirring, long-headed, ingenious, speculative, poor devil, came to settle in the town, which, as nature had done little or nothing for it, was the finest place that could be for public improvements of all kinds. He was inexhaustible in plans for laying out capital to the greatest advantage; he never saw a river that he could not make navigable, a field that he could not make produce four-fold, or a fall of three feet perpendicular that was not the fairest site in the world for mills and manufactories. All he wanted was money, and that he contrived to make others supply, which was but reasonable. It would have been too much for him to furnish both the dollars and the wit.

"The first thing such a public-spirited person does, on locating himself among the people whom he has come to devour, is to find me out all those snug fellows, who have ready money in their purses and dirt to their boots — men that have a few thousands lying by them, or stock that they can turn at once into cash, or land that they can mortgage for a good round sum. Having smelled out his game, our advocate for public improvement takes every opportunity of pointing out capital speculations, and hinting that if he only had a few thousands to spare, he could double them in the course of two or three years. Martin pricked up his ears. He longed, past all longing, to be turning a penny to advantage. It would give a zest to his life; it would employ his time, which he did not know what to do with. In short, he listened and was overcome. He determined to immortalize his name as a great public benefactor, and double his money at the same time.

"There was a river about a hundred yards wide, running close to the skirts of the town, which the apostle of public improvements assured Martin was the finest place for a bridge that was ever seen. It seemed to be made on purpose. There was not the least doubt but it would yield in tolls from thirty to fifty per cent on the first cost. Nothing was wanting but legislative authority for this great work. He would go to Albany, next session, and get an act passed for that purpose, if he only had the means; but just now he was a little short, one of his principal debtors having disappointed him.

"Honest Martin, rather than miss such a capital speculation, agreed to advance the needful, and, at a proper time, the redoubtable Timothy Starveling, or Starling, as he called himself, set out upon his mission to the paradise of lobby-members. Timothy took lodgings at the first hotel, kept open house, treated most nobly with honest Martin Forbush's cash, and wound himself into the confidence of two senators and five members. But before the matter was decided the money was run out, and therefore Timothy Starveling wrote a most mysterious letter to Martin, hinting at extraordinary expenses; accommodating members with loans — small matters, that told in the end; conciliating influential people; oiling the wheels; and heaven knows what else. Martin understood not one word of all this, but, rather than lose his money and his project, he sent his agent a fresh supply of cash. The bridge, notwithstanding, stuck not a little by the way, owing to the opposition of some who had not been properly enlightened on the subject; but, by dint of *log-rolling,* it floundered through at last. Timothy got it tacked to a Lombard and a steam-saw-mill, and the business was accomplished. He then, upon the strength of his charter, bought a carriage and horses, and rode home in style.

"Well, they set to work, and the bridge was built with Martin's money. But it brought him in no tolls, owing to the circumstance of there being no road at the end of it. Martin scratched his head; but Timothy was nowise dismayed. All they had to do was to make a turnpike-road, from the end of the bridge to the next town, which was actually laid out, though not actually built, and there would be plenty of tolls. 'Roads make travellers,' quoth Timothy, and Martin believed it. Another act of the legislature became necessary, and another mission for Timothy. The opposition was, however, much more difficult to overcome than on the former occasion, owing to an ill-natured definition given by a country member, to wit: 'A turnpike-bill is a law to enable the few to tax the many, for a bad road kept in bad repair.' It cost Martin a pretty penny to get permission for a road, and it cost him a prettier penny still to make it. However, made it was, at last. Timothy superintended, and Martin paid. The tolls were not sufficient to hire an old woman for opening the gates. Few people were tempted by their occasions to pass that way, and those few forded the river, it being shallow, and saved their coppers.

"But those who think Master Timothy Starveling was at his wit's end here, reckon without their host. You might as well catch a cat asleep, as Timothy at a nonplus. 'We'll petition for an act to deepen the river, and thus kill two birds with one stone. By improving the navigation we shall bring vast quantities of produce down, which will make the town the grand emporium of this part of the country, and at the same time so deepen the channel that it will not be fordable.' Martin thought the idea prodigious, and the same game was played a third time by Timothy at Albany. They improved the navigation of the river at no small cost, by deepening the channel. But rivers are unmanageable commodities. As fast as they deepened it filled up again, and one heavy rain deposited more mud and sand than could be removed in a year. In short, before the river became navigable, or the road and bridge brought in their thirty to fifty per cent., the purse of Martin Forbush ceased to jingle at the touch. It was as empty as my pocket.

"One day, when Master Timothy Starveling came to Martin for a small trifle to complete the project, the latter worthy gentleman crawled forth with his eyebrows elevated, his forehead wrinkled, and his shoulders almost as high as his head; and, turning his breeches-pockets insides out, looked with most rueful significance at the great advocate of public improvements. 'Pooh,' said the former, 'there is a remedy for all things, even for an empty pocket; look here,' (pulling out the charter for the bridge), 'I've got an iron in the fire yet, I thank you.' Whereupon he showed Martin a clause in the act, which, with a very little stretching and twisting, might be fairly interpreted into a privilege for banking. Martin was now pretty desperate, and caught at the idea. They got together all the paupers of the town, who subscribed their thousands and tens of thousands; gave their notes as security for the payment of their subscriptions; and chose Martin, president, and Timothy, cashier. Then, announcing to an astonished world, which wondered where the money came from, that the stock was all 'paid in, or secured to be paid,' they proceeded to the business of issuing notes, without taking their redemption into account. For a while they went on prosperously. There will always be found a sufficient number of honest fools in every community for rogues to work upon, and the good people were rejoiced in their hearts, to find money so plenty. But, in an evil hour, there appeared at the bank of Diddledum, a spruce young fellow in boots and spurs, with a bundle of bank-notes, who announced himself as the cashier of the neighbouring bank, of Fiddledum, and demanded the payment of his bundle in specie. There never was, nor was there now, nor ever would have been, a dollar of specie in the bank of Diddledum. This ungentlemanly and malicious *run*, being what no one, not even Timothy Starveling, Esquire, cashier, had ever dreamed of, the spruce young gentleman in boots and spurs was civilly requested to wait till they could have a meeting of the directors. But the young gentleman forthwith went to a notary and got all the notes protested; after which he placed them in the hands of a lawyer, who commenced a suit on each of them, in order to save expense. The spruce young gentleman in boots and spurs then departed for the happy village, which had grown so fast under the refreshing auspices of the bank of Fiddledum, that every body said it would soon outgrow itself. There were sixty new houses, three great hotels, and six distilleries, all built by men who were not worth a groat. How blessed is paper-money, how blessed its legitimate offspring, public improvements!

"But, blessed as it is, it proved the downfall of Timothy Starveling, Esquire, cashier of the bank of Diddledum. That night, the bank closed its doors, to open no more, and the ingenious Timothy, as was supposed, in attempting to cross the river on horseback, to avoid the 'public sentiment,' was swept away by the stream, which had been swelled to a torrent by heavy rains, and never appeared again. At least, his hat was found, several miles down the river; but himself and his horse could never be discovered, although the 'Morgan Committee' took up the affair.

"Martin Forbush was stripped of all his hard earnings. He surrendered his bridge, his road, and his navigation-improvements to his creditors — and much good did it do them. He went back to his old shop, to begin the world anew. In process of time he became once more an independent man. But he never again turned gentleman, and consequently never got the dyspepsia. He never burnt his fingers afterwards with public improvements, and nobody could ever persuade him to make a speculation. He even forgave Timothy Starveling, and was wont to say, 'Plague take him! — he robbed me of all my money, but then he cured me of the blue devils.'"

We would advise the fashionable tourist, (and to none other is this work addressed), who of course is hurrying directly to the Springs, to go by the way of the Cohoes and Waterford, and as far as possible to hug the bank of the Hudson. "Leaving Albany," says Alderman Janson, "you come upon those rich flats, that present a soft Arcadian scene, beautified with all the products of nature and industrious man. The meadows are peopled with luxurious Dutch cattle, resting in the shade of spreading elms that dot the landscape here and there. The fields of yellow wheat just ripening in the sunny month of July, the acres of stately corn with its dark green leaves, flaunting like ribbons about the brow of youth — bounded on one side by the swelling, rolling hills, on the other by the glassy river,—all together make a scene worthy of the golden age, and of the simple virtuous patriarchs who yet inhabit there, smoking their pipes, and talking Dutch, in spite of the changes of fashion, and the vagaries of inflated vanity, which instil into the hearts of the foolish the belief, that alteration is improvement, and that one generation of men is wiser than another. It is thus that youth laughs at age, and that the forward urchin, who knows nothing of the world but the vices and follies of a boy, thinks himself wiser than his grandfather of fourscore."

Infandum, regina—we despise Latin scraps, ever since the publication of the Dictionary of Quotations. But who has not heard of Troy?—not that famous city which Jacob Bryant maintained never had an existence, although it has made more noise in the world than the greatest matter-of-fact cities extant—not the city which thousands of travellers have gone to see, and come away, without seeing—not the city which sustained a ten years' siege, and was at last taken by a wooden horse;—no, verily, but the indubitable city of Troy, on the banks of the Hudson, which is worth three thousand beggarly Scamanders, and six thousand Hellesponts? We are aware that this excellent town, which contains at this moment Helens enough to set the whole world on fire, is pronounced by that great geographer and traveller, Lieutenant De Roos, to be in New England. Perish the thought! New England never had such a town to its back; one so full of enterprising people, continually plotting against the repose of Dame Nature. Alexander once seriously contemplated cutting Mount

Athos into a statue; King Stephanus Bombastes lost his wits with the idea of making Bohemia a maritime power — whence it was, that Corporal Trim very properly called him, 'This unfortunate king of Bohemia'; and a great advocate of public improvements is now so unluckily mad on the subject, that he fancies himself a great chip, floating in all weathers on the great northern canal. But all these are nothing to the Trojans, who, it is said, seriously contemplate a canal, parallel with the Hudson, from Troy to New York, if they can only get the legislature to pass an act against its freezing. Alas! poor river gods! what will become of them? As sings the famous prize-poet, who, we hereby solemnly affirm, in our opinion deserves to have his whiskers curled on the very pinnacle of Parnassus, —

> "Noah be hang'd, and all his race accursed,
> Who in sea-brine did pickle timber first!"

He means to say, that your salt-water rivers are no longer to be tolerated, and ought to be forthwith legislated out of existence, and doomed to oblivion. It is a great thing to discover what your modern poets would be at. They are the true "children of mist." But, to continue our quotation: —

> "O Trojan Greeks!, who dwell at Ida's foot,
> Pull up this crying evil by the root;
> Rouse in the mighty majesty of mind,
> Pull up your mighty breeches tight behind,
> Then stretch the red right arm from shore to shore,
> And swear that rivers shall endure no more!"

"It is almost worth while," says Alderman Janson, "to sacrifice a few hours of the delights of the Springs, for the purpose of ascending Mount Ida, and seeing the romantic little cascade, a capital place for manufactories. In the opinion of some people, this is all that water-falls are good for nowadays. I would describe it, but for fear of drawing the attention of some prowling villain, who would perhaps come and build a cotton-mill, and set all the pretty little rosy-cheeked Helens of Troy tending spinning-jennies, from sunrise to sunset, and long after, at a shilling a day, instead of leaving them to the enjoyment of the few hours of rest and careless hilarity which God in his wisdom hath appropriated to the miserable pack-horses of this age of improvements. The domestic industry of females is at home, by the fireside, in the society of their families, surrounded and protected by their household gods; not in woollen and cotton mills, herded together by hundreds, and toiling without intermission at the everlasting spinning-jenny, without leisure to cultivate the domestic virtues, or opportunity for mental improvement. Of all the blockheads this side of the moon, in my opinion the farmers of these United States are the greatest, considering the pains taken by the members of Congress and others to enlighten them. What in the name of all the thick-sculled wiseacres, past, present and to come, do they want of a 'woollen bill,' and what do the blockheads expect from getting perhaps a penny or two more a pound for their wool, except to pay twice as much a yard for the cloth which is made out of it? Why don't they learn wisdom from their own sheep?

"A cunning old fox one day put his head through the bars of a sheepfold, and addressed the flock as follows: 'Gentlemen, I have a proposition to make, greatly to your advantage; I'll give you a penny a pound more for your wool (if you'll only let me shear you) one of these days, provided meantime you'll pay me a dollar more a yard for the cloth I make out of it.' Whereupon an old ram of some experience cried 'Baah!', and all the rest of the sheep followed his example."

In speaking of Troy, Alderman Janson, who was a great hunter of manuscripts, states that he saw there a curious poem, written by a schoolmaster of Troy about forty years ago, in imitation of Homer's Batrachomyomachia.

As a specimen, the worthy alderman has copied the invocation, which we insert, with a view of indicating the corruption of the public press at that period. We congratulate our readers at the same time on the improvement which the march of mind hath brought about in this as well as every thing else.

"Thee we invoke, O sacred nine!—
No, not the sacred nine, but thee,
The youngest sister of the nine, unknown in ancient song!—
Thee, the TENTH MUSE!, begot, as legends tell,
By printer's devil on a famous shrew
(Who had kill'd nine husbands with eternal clacking,)
Up in a garret high, between two newspapers,
One Jackson t'other Adams.
There thou didst learn thy alphabet,
'Mid billingsgate most dire;
Loud blustering lies, and whispered calumnies,
Were thy first lessons in the art of speech;
Next, impudence became thy dry-nurse,
And did teach thy genius apt, to mouth with high pretence
Of art and literature, science profound,
And taste preëminent, stol'n from the man in the moon,
Or God knows where. There thou didst learn
To judge by virtue of thine ignorance;
To criticise a classic in false grammar,
And in bad English all the world defy.
There too, as stories go, thou didst become
A connoisseur in Flemish and Italian schools,

Albeit thou never sawest a picture in thy life,
Save on a sign-post at a tavern door;
Able to scan, with taste infallible,
A bust or statue, by approvéd rules,
Gathered from frequent contemplation deep
Of barbers' blocks, and naked blackamoors,
Stuck up by wicked wights to lure our youth
To shave their beards, and chew tobacco — pah!
There too, thou learn'dst to quaff oblivion's bowl,
Filled to the brim with foaming printers' ink;
To forget to-morrow what the day before
Thou sworest was gospel; to say, unsay,
And praise a man one hour, whom in the next
Thou didst consign to ignominious shame,
In phrase most trim and delicate, though stolen
From an old fish-wife, drunk, and in a passion.
There too, amid the din of politics and lies,
Thou learn'dst to be a judge inflexible
Of public virtue and of private worth;
To moot nice points of morals; and decide
On things obscure, that for long ages past
Have puzzled all mankind, and dried the brains
Of luckless sages to the very bottom,
Bare as mud-puddles in a six months' drought.

"Hail MUSE THE TENTH, worth all the other nine!
Presiding genius of our liberties,
We hail THEE on our knees, and humbly beg,
Thou'lt not forget who 'twas, in modern days,
First call'd thee from oblivion, and install'd thee
Goddess of men, whom gods and men do fear."

The alderman boasts that the poem is soon to be published simultaneously in five different languages, in five different countries, by five different booksellers, with five puffs of five first-rate journals in each language. We think the friends of the author had better advise him to leave out the invocation.

"There is a rock," continues the worthy alderman, in great wrath, "on Mount Ida, all covered with diamonds, better than you can make of charcoal, where I would recommend the ladies to stop, and supply themselves for the Springs, instead of flaunting about in chemical jewels, as is the fashion now. And here I must beg leave to digress a little, to offer my testimony against the progress of knowledge, which, when accompanied by a corresponding progress in vice and dishonesty, is a curse rather than a blessing. If there is a thorough-going rascal and cheat in this world, it is chemistry, who is perpetually practising deceptions upon mankind. The scoundrel can imitate, or disguise, every thing. He can make a piece of glass into diamonds, rubies, sapphires, and topazes, so that none but a jeweller, who is commonly as great a rogue as himself, can detect them. He can make excellent beer, without either malt or hops; and, what is worthy of remark, it will not poison a man half as soon as arsenic or copperas. He can make tea out of turnip-tops, so as to deceive a China merchant; he can make gas out of coal-cinders, and money out of gas; he can extract the red ink out of a check, and leave the black ink untouched; he can change a banknote of one dollar into one of a hundred; he can adulterate confectionery, and poison half mankind without their being a whit the wiser, except they learn something after death. In short, it is my humble opinion that, if the worthy revisers of our laws had decreed to hang every professor of chemistry, except such as could demonstrate their entire ignorance of the science and would put their scholars to learning trades, it would prevent the ladies from wearing false jewels, and add greatly to the honesty of the rising generation. It is bad enough for women to wear false curls, false faces, and false hearts, without deceiving us with false jewels. One can bear the disappointment in the temper and the complexion, but to be taken in by the diamonds is heart-breaking."

"Troy," according to Alderman Janson, "is already accommodated with a bank or two, without which our poor little helpless villages would be like children without nurses. But people are never content in this world, notwithstanding the march of mind and the progress of public improvement, and the Trojans are at this moment petitioning the legislature for another bank, utterly forgetful of the old proverb that too much of a good thing is good-for-nothing. Were I to define a legislature of the present approved fashion, I would say, it was a public body exclusively occupied with private business; for, in truth, were we to look closely at their proceedings, we should find almost all of them spending the whole of their time in passing bills for banks, incorporating companies for the most frivolous purposes, mending old charters, and making new ones. In the mean while, the general interests of the people are neglected, and laws affecting the whole community either not passed at all, or passed so full of imperfections that it is more trouble to mend them afterwards than to make new ones. A plague on this busy spirit which is called the spirit of improvement, but which is nothing more than an impertinent disposition to meddle with the concerns of other people, and so substitute our own theoretical notions in place of the practical experience of others. Why not, 'let very well alone'?

"I once had two near neighbours, who lived in a couple of old-fashioned Dutch houses, which, though they made no great figure without, were very snug and comfortable within, and accorded very well with the circumstances of the owners, which were but moderate. One of the houses had sunk a few inches at one of the corners, in consequence of some defect in the foundation; but this had happened twenty years before, and the building had ever since remained perfectly stable, being reckoned not the least injured, or the worse for this little eccentricity of shape. The other house had some trifling defect in the chimney, which, although it might as well not have been there, was of no serious importance. Both occupants lived perfectly content, and, if a wish would have removed these imperfections, they would hardly have taken the trouble to utter it.

"In process of time, however, the spirit of improvement got into our part of the town, and some great little busybody suggested, to the owners of the two houses, the perfect ease with which the sunken corner and the crooked chimney might be remedied at a trifling expense. At first, they wisely shook their heads; but the advice was repeated every day, and every-body knows that the perpetual repetition of the same thing is like the dropping of water—it will wear away a stone at last. My two neighbours at length began to talk over the matter seriously together, and one day came to consult me. 'Let very well alone,' said I; and they went away, according to custom, to do exactly contrary to the advice they came to solicit. The owner of the house with the sunken corner, and he of the crooked chimney, the next day went to work under the direction of the disciple of public improvements, to remedy these mortal annoyances which they had borne for more than twenty years with the most perfect unconcern. One got a great jackscrew under the delinquent corner; the other raised a mighty beam against his chimney; and to work they went, screwing and pushing with a vengeance. In less than fifteen minutes, the crooked chimney, being stubborn with age, and withal somewhat infirm, instead of quietly returning to the perpendicular, broke short off, and falling through the roof, upon the garret floor, carried that with it, and the whole mass stopped not to rest, till it found solid bottom in the cellar. It was well that the dame and all the children were out of doors, witnessing the progress of the experiment. Here was an honest, comfortable little Dutch house, sacrificed to the improvement of a crooked chimney.

" The man of the sunken corner succeeded, to his utter satisfaction, in placing the four angles on a level, and was delighted with his improvement; until, going into his house, he beheld with dismay, that the shock given to the old edifice, and the disturbance of its various parts which had been cemented by time into one solid mass, had cracked his walls so that they looked like a fish-net, broken the window-sills, moved the ends of the beams in their ancient resting-places, and, in short, wrecked the whole establishment. It was become like a sieve, and, the next time it rained, the whole family came out like drowned rats. There was not a dry square foot in the house, nor a dry thread on its occupants.

" The poor man set himself to work to remedy these inconveniences, and from time to time laid out a great deal of money, in stopping crannies, and setting the dislocated limbs. But all would not do — the whole frame of the edifice had been shaken to its centre by the disturbance of its parts. There was no mending it; and nothing was left but to pull it down, and build a new one, with all the modern improvements. The lord of the crooked chimney also resolved to do the same. But the man who begins to dig a new cellar very often commences undermining his own prosperity. The houses were at last finished, and very fine houses they were — but they did not belong to the owners. They were mortgaged for more than half they were worth, and, in process of time money growing very scarce, they were sold for just enough to satisfy the creditors. The end of all was, that my good neighbours had exchanged the little houses, with the sunken corner and crooked chimney, for an immense mansion, without walls or chimney. They were literally turned out of doors. 'I wish we had let very well alone,' said they to me, as they departed to the wilderness, to begin the world anew." Truly, mine uncle, the worthy alderman, was at least three thousand years behind the spirit of the age. Is it not better to live in fine houses belonging to other people, than in little old-fashioned ones of our own? We wish the alderman were alive to answer this question.

If the traveller, in his impatience to arrive at the Springs, thinks we get on too slowly, let him leave us and our book behind him, and take the consequences. Does he think we are a high-pressure steam-boat, to travel fifteen miles an hour without stopping a moment to look round and consider? Or, is he so desperately unlettered and behindhand with the spirit of the age, as to entertain, in the barren waste of his mind, the notion that the business of book-making is like that of brick-making, a plain, straightforward handicraft affair, wherein a man has nothing to do but mind his own business? Belike he does not know that, to make a book, it is necessary to tell all that other people have told before — to expand the little grains of gold-dust, which other painstaking authors have picked up with infinite labour, till, like the gold-beater, he makes them cover the leaves of a whole folio. Perhaps he has never heard of Johannes Secundus, who spun a whole volume of poetry out of a kiss — nor of the ever-to-be-renowned and never-to-be-forgotten writer, who divided the half of an idea into six parts, and manufactured a volume out of each portion — nor of the still-greater genius, whom we place on the tip of the highest hair in the head of Milton, Shakspeare, Cervantes, and Voltaire, who composed sixteen works without any idea at all. Preserve us! — any fool may write with his head full of ideas; but no one knows the troubles of an author who is obliged to pick up his crumbs by the way-side — to diverge to the right and to the left — to levy contributions upon every thing and every-body he meets — to skim the froth of wit, and dip up the sediment of wisdom — to repeat the same thing in a hundred different ways, and disguise it each time in such a manner that the most inquisitive blue-stocking cannot detect it, even with the aid of her spectacles and the reviewers. This — this is travail, this is mighty toil; and it is the industrious writers of such books that should be rewarded with money and immortality, since the labourer is always worthy of his hire. He works premeditatingly, and, as it were, with malice aforethought; he makes, by dint of hard and long exertion, the most meagre soil productive, while your boasted genius merely scratches the surface of the rich alluvium, and, behold!, the product is a hundred-fold. Therefore it is, we say again, and repeat it three hundred times, that if the travelling reader is not willing to wait with us till we have finished descanting on the Trojans, let him go on and welcome. We wash our hands of him, and there is an end of the matter.

Nobody knows the difficulty under which we unfortunate authors labour in writing a book, to avoid running our heads against the rascally ancients, or the still more rascally moderns, who got the start of us, and stole all our ideas before they came down to posterity. They have not left us a single original idea to our backs, but have swallowed up every thing with a most insatiable appetite; insomuch that the writers of the present day are, for the most part, obliged to become absurd or unintelligible, in order to strike out a miserable, half-starved novelty, which perishes peradventure at the end of a year, in spite of the dry-nursing and stall-feeding of diurnal puffers. The art of printing has ruined literature, and destroyed the value of learning. Before this mischievous invention, which is justly ascribed to the devil, a manuscript was a treasure, and the writer of it a phenomenon. It was read at the Olympic games, and the author was crowned with bays and considered on a footing with the victors in the chariot races and boxing matches. Then, a manuscript was a bonne-bouche for epicures on high days and holidays; now, a book is no more of a rarity than bacon and greens in Virginia, and the clodhopper of this country returns from his daily labours to a newspaper, as to his usual supper-fare. Then, too, the fortunate man who got possession of the precious papyrus or the invaluable parchment roll, had it all to himself, and could borrow what he pleased, without being called upon to pay the penalty of being cut up in a review. There was no such thing as plagiarism, at least there was no finding it out, which is quite synonymous. Even in later days, after the pernicious and diabolical art of multiplying books to infinity prevailed, we find, that a criminal who could read might plead the benefit of clergy, and, if it was decided, "*legit ut clericus,*" he was only burnt in the hand, instead of being hanged. But now, in good faith, if (I say not every man who can read, but) every man who has written a book, were to escape hanging, Jack Ketch would hold a sinecure, and there would be great robbing of the gallows. It is, without doubt, greatly to be lamented, that the practice of burning books by the hands of the common hangman and cutting off the ears of their authors is no longer in fashion. In this way the world got rid of some of these crying nuisances, and many were thereby discouraged from inflicting any more of them upon their unfortunate fellow-creatures. But now, forsooth, such is the license allowed or claimed, that the least morsel of a man will set him down pen in hand, intermeddle with the deepest matters, run away with a subject he knows not what to do with when he has got it, and thereby prevent some great scholar from thereafter doing it justice. Verily, little men should never meddle with great matters, as the fable aptly advises.

A cunning, dexterous angler once threw his line into a deep clear stream, where he waited patiently and watchfully, till he saw a fine trout slowly come forth from his profound recess under the cool shady bank, and float cautiously towards the bait. But, just as he was about swallowing it, a little rascally minnow, not as long as my finger, darted before him, took hold of the hook, and skirred away with it to the shallowest part of the brook. The trout swam slowly back to his retreat, and the angler, pulling up the minnow and taking it in his hand, exclaimed: " Thou art so small and contemptible, that I would let thee go again, were it not that thy impertinent meddling lost me a fine trout." So saying, he cast it indignantly on the sand, where it perished miserably in the noontide sun.

It is refreshing to see the advances made in dress, and other evidences of the " march of mind, and the progress of public improvement," in Troy, and in all our little villages and thriving towns. Every church is as fine as a fiddle on Sundays, and what it wants in heads it makes up in hats. The fashions of New York are adopted with as much facility in a country village as the dress of a Parisian opera-dancer is imitated in New York, and the same rules are followed in adapting them to the figure and person. If, for instance, a belle is about six feet high, she is content with a hat six feet in circumference, with the contents of one milliner's shop on it, by way of ornament. But if she is but four feet one, it is agreeable to the fashionable rules of proportion to make up in hat for the deficiency in height. She must have a hat twice as large as the lady of six feet, and two milliners' shops at least to ornament its vast expanse. This is according to the law of nature, which bestows the largest tops on the lowest trees, and gives to the cabbage a head bigger than that of a sunflower. Some egregious cynics will have it, that a lady ought to wear a hat somewhat in reference to the size of the town she inhabits, and never one larger than the town itself, as we are informed has been the case in two or three instances. It is observed that the toadstool — the only thing in nature whose proportions resemble a fashionable woman of the present dynasty — never spreads its umbrella beyond the stump which it proceeds from, and it is argued that this rule should govern a lady's bonnet. But it is difficult to persuade the sex to adopt the old-fashioned notions about taste and proportion, which have been entirely superseded by the march of mind and the progress of public improvement. And so much the better. A woman who never changes, even from bad to worse, is no better than a rusty weathercock, which never shows which way the wind blows. Nevertheless people, and particularly women and bantams, ought never to carry their heads too high, as the following pregnant example showeth.

One day, a little bantam-cock, with a high topknot, who was exceedingly vain because he had so many feathers to his legs that he could hardly walk, seeing a goose duck her head in passing under a bar at least six feet high, thus accosted her: "Why, thou miserable, bare-legged caitiff! thou shovel-nosed, web-footed, pigeon-toed scavenger of the highways! thou fool of three elements! not content with ignominiously crawling under a fence, thou must even nod thy empty pate, by way of confessing thy inferiority. Behold how we bantams do these things!" So saying, with a great deal of puffing and fluttering, with the help of his bill, he managed to gain the top of the fence, where he clapped his wings, and was just on the point of crowing in triumph, when a great hawk, that was sailing over his head, pounced down on him, and, seizing him by the topknot, carried him off without ceremony. The goose, cocking her eye, and taking a side view of the affair, significantly shook her feathers, and, the next time she passed under a bar, bowed her head lower than ever.

The march of mind and progress of public improvement in the country towns and villages appears, moreover, in the great progress made in good eating, and other elegant luxuries. The great republican patent of nobility, dyspepsy, is almost as common in these, as in New York, where our valet, a gentleman of colour, is grievously afflicted with it, and has taken to white mustard-seed. We have eaten such dinners among the burghers of Troy as would have made old Homer's mouth water, could he have seen them. They actually emulated those of a first-rate broker, who does not owe above twice as much as he ever expects to pay, and can therefore afford to be liberal. This giving of good dinners at the expense of other people is a capital expedient in economy, particularly deserving of imitation. What can be more delightful than to see our companions enjoying themselves in the most glorious of all sublunary delights, at the expense of any body that will lend us money?—thus making friends, and gaining immortal glory as a generous fellow, without a penny of one's own in pocket! People are always so grateful too for good dinners, insomuch that we have known a "damned liberal, open-hearted fellow," as he was called, who had ruined three or four of his acquaintances, by giving fine banquets at their cost, that was actually invited afterwards, three times, to take potluck with some of his stall-fed friends, who had grown fat upon him. We remember being at one of this bountiful gentleman's treats, when the following toast was drunk with great applause, while he was called out by an impertinent creditor: " Long live our hospitable entertainer! — if he don't outlive his money." On the subject of these village feasts and sylvan luxuries, see Spafford's Gazetteer,* for many honest and excellent remarks. As a fellow-labourer in enlightening travellers, we heartily and seriously recommend his work to the public patronage. Let it not be understood that we singled out Troy as particularly distinguished in these elegant extravagances. Even if it were, the inhabitants deserve no credit above their neighbours, seeing there are two or three banks in the town; — and what would be the use of banks, if people did not spend their money faster than they earn it?

It will hardly be worth the traveller's while to visit Troy, except to partake of these good dinners; for, after reading our book, he will know more about it than he could learn in ten visits, and, being now so near the focus of all worldly delights, the Springs, every moment becomes precious. Let him therefore keep on the west side of the river, crossing the Mohawk just below the Cohoes Falls, of which he will have a fine view from the bridge. Here he may stop fifteen minutes to look at the locks which connect the

[* Horatio Gates Spafford, LL.D., published " A Gazetteer of the State of New York ", in 1824.]

great canal with the Hudson, as a flight of steps connects the upper and lower stories of a house. "Without doubt," observes our old-fashioned friend, Alderman Janson, whom we quote as the great apostle of antediluvian notions, "without doubt, canals and locks are good things in moderation; but, somehow or other, I think I have a prejudice in favour of rivers, where they are to be had; and where they are not, people may as well make up their minds to do without them. In sober truth, it is my firm opinion, (and I don't care whether any body agrees with me or not), that the great operation of a canal is, merely to concentrate on its line, and within its immediate influence, that wealth, population, and business, which, if let alone, would diffuse themselves naturally, equally, and beneficially through every vein and artery of the country. The benefits of a canal are confined to a certain distance, while all beyond is actually injured, although nobody can escape paying his proportion of the expenses of its construction."

"I was once," continues the alderman, "a little mad myself in the canal way, like most people, and actually made a pilgrimage in a canal-boat all the way to Buffalo. I found every-body along the sides of the canal delighted with the vast public benefits of these contrivances; they could sell the product of their lands, and the lands themselves, for twice or thrice as much as formerly. I rubbed my hands with great satisfaction, and was more in love with canals than ever. Returning, I diverged from the line of the canal, into some of the more remote counties, and found all the people scratching their heads. 'What is the matter, good people all, of every sort? What can you want, now that the great canal is finished?' 'The devil take the great canal,' cried all with one voice: 'every body is mad to go and settle on the canal.' 'To be sure they are, my good friends and fellow-citizens, and that is the beauty of a canal; it raises the price of land, within a certain distance, to double what it was before.' 'Yes, and it lowers the price of land not within a certain distance in an equal, if not greater, proportion. Nobody thinks of coming here to settle now — they are all for the canal.' Oho, thought I; then a canal has two sides, as well as two ends."

The alderman then goes on to moralize on the difficulty of increasing the actual quantity of good in this world — maintaining that what is gained in one place is lost in another; that public improvements are, for the most part, private speculations; and that the accumulation of wealth in a particular tract of country, or in the hands of a small portion of a community, is always at the expense of the larger portions of each, and renders the one bloated, the others impotent. This position he illustrates by the following fable.

"A long time ago, when men were not much wiser than pigs are nowadays, the head became exceedingly dissatisfied at seeing the blood circulating freely through all parts of the body, even to the tips of the fingers and ends of the toes, without discrimination, and prayed to Jupiter to remedy this democratic, levelling economy of nature. The gods always grant foolish prayers, and accordingly Jupiter decreed that the blood should no longer circulate to the extremities, but confine itself to certain favoured parts, such as the head, the heart, the liver, and the lungs, which in a little time became so overcharged and unwieldy that they could hardly perform their ordinary functions. The head grew giddy, the heart palpitated with oppressive struggles, the liver expanded into turgid inactivity, and the lungs puffed like a pair of bellows. Meanwhile the extremities, shut off from the stream of life thus withdrawn to pamper the other parts, gradually shrivelled up, and lost their elasticity, insomuch that the hands could no longer perform their functions, or the legs support the overgrown head above them. 'O Jupiter!' cried the head, 'restore the circulation of the blood to its former channels, and let nature again have her way.' 'Fool!', replied Jupiter, laughing—'dost thou think it as easy to restore, as to disturb, the order of nature? Hadst thou let her alone, each limb and organ of the frame to which thou belongest would have equally partaken of the support of life, and all would have grown with a happy, harmonious proportion, into healthful, mature, and vigorous manhood. Now it is too late. Even the gods cannot remedy the consequences of folly, however they may remove its causes. Thou hast grown prematurely, and it is ordained that such never live long. The mushroom of a night is the ruin of a day.' A rush of blood to the brain brought on apoplexy, and the decree of the gods was fulfilled."

The ride along the glorious Hudson, from the Mohawk to where the road turns Westward to the Springs, presents a perpetual succession of enchanting scenes. But by this time the inquisitive traveller is, doubtless, full of anticipations of the delights of these ethereal fountains, where a thousand nymphs, more beautiful, or at least better dressed, than ever haunted legendary stream or crystal spring of yore, quaff the inspiring beverage, till — till one is astonished what becomes of it! We will therefore delay him no longer. Perish the beauties of nature! What are they all when compared with those exquisite combinations of art and nature, which puzzle the understanding to decide which had the most to do in their production, the milliner or the goddess!

BALLSTON.

The first view of Ballston generally has the same effect upon visitors that matrimony is said to have upon young lovers. It is very extraordinary, but the first impression — we mean of Ballston — is that it is the ugliest, most uninviting spot in the universe. But this impression soon wears away, as the tourist daily associates with beautiful damsels, the lustre of whose unfading and ineffable charms diffuses itself as it were over the whole face of nature, converting the ugly swamp into a green meadow, the muddy brook into a pellucid rivulet meandering musically along, the mounds of sand into full-bosomed hills, and Sans Souci into the palace of the fairy Feliciana, where, as every-body knows, people were so happy they did not know what to do with themselves. We defy any man to be surrounded by beautiful women, even though it were in utter darkness, without having his imagination exclusively saturated with ideas of grace and loveliness, let the surrounding objects be what they may. For, as the poet has it: —

> 'The eye of beauty, like the glorious sun,
> Casts a reflected lustre all around,
> Making deformity itself partake
> In its wide-glowing splendours.'

The localities of Ballston and Saratoga are ennobled and illustrated by this singular influence of beauty. It must be confessed, if they depended only on their own intrinsic capabilities they would be no way extraordinary. Yet, to do them justice, they are not altogether desperate as to pretensions. If the marshes were only meadows, dotted with majestic elms; the sand-hills richly cultivated with fields of wheat and corn; the sluggish brook a pastoral, purling river; the pine trees stately forests of oak and hickory, and their stumps a little more picturesque;—neither Ballston nor Saratoga need be ashamed to show itself any day in the week, not excepting Sunday. As it is, candour itself must admit that their attractions are altogether reflected from the ladies' eyes.

Being now arrived at the head-quarters, the very focus and hot-bed of elegance, fashion, and refinement, it becomes us to be more particular in our directions to the inexperienced traveller, who peradventure hath never sojourned at a watering-place. For this purpose we have with great pains, and at the expense of a vast deal of actual observation and thought, collected, digested, and codified, a system of rules and regulations, derived from the best sources, and sanctioned by the example of people of the very first tournure as well as the most finished education: to wit, brokers of eminence, retired bankrupts living upon their means, aspiring apprentices, and dandies of the first pretensions. For the purpose of being more succinct, clear, and explicit, we have divided our code into chapters, comprising a complete set of precepts for the government of every class of persons, beginning, however, with a few general rules and standing directions of universal application.

CHAPTER I.

OF LODGINGS.

The first requisite on arriving at either Ballston or Saratoga is to procure lodgings. In the choice of a house, the traveller will do well to consult the newspapers, to see if the landlord has a proper conception of the art of puffing himself, without which, we affirm without fear of contradiction, no man has any legitimate claim to fashionable notoriety. A fellow who has not interest to raise a puff must be something worse than a swindler or a murderer. We are aware that certain wiseacres, with even less money than wit, and less knowledge of the world than a bookworm, have been pleased on divers occasions to ridicule this system of puffs and recommendations, as exclusively appertaining to quackery in medicine. But let us tell them to their teeth, that a system applicable to quack doctors has been found, by actual experience, to answer just as well for quack lawyers, quack parsons, quack politicians, quack philosophers, quack poets, quack novelists, quack publicans, and quacks of all sorts, sizes, dimensions, qualities, appurtenances, and pretensions. "Let them laugh that win," said the renowned Pedagogus, who once compiled a book in which he made the unparalleled and gigantic improvement of spelling words as they are pronounced, instead of pronouncing them as they are spelled. By selling his book at a great discount, he got all the school-masters — we beg pardon — principals of gymnasia, and of polytechnic, philotechnic, chirographic, and adelphic academies, to recommend it. Honest Thomas Dilworth forthwith hid his powdered head, especially when, in addition to this, upwards of three hundred great politicians, who were, *ex officio*, scholars and philosophers, recommended the book as a most valuable work, distinctly marking the progress of mind and the astonishing strides of the gigantic spirit of the age. All the rational people then living, of whom however there were not above a hundred millions, laughed most consumedly at the sage Pedagogus and his certificates; but he only replied, "Let them laugh that win." The sage Pedagogus, in the course of twenty years, sold upwards of six million copies of his book, and made his fortune. Where was the greater wisdom? in the sage Pedagogus, or in the people that laughed at him?

Therefore it is we say again, and again, repeating it three thousand times to all who will listen, go to the house that has the greatest number of puffs to its back, although it may, and doubtless does, sometimes happen, that they are indited by some honest man of the quill, who has settled his bill by bartering his praise for the landlord's pudding.

CHAPTER II.

OF DRINKING THE WATERS.

There is no doubt, in the opinion of those who have observed the vast progress of the human mind since the discovery of the new planet Herschel and the invention of self-sharpening pencils, that the ancients laboured under the disease of a constipated understanding. Else they could never have differed as they did about the *summum bonum*, or great good, holding at least three hundred different opinions, some of which were inexpressibly absurd; as, for instance, that which pointed out the practice of virtue as the only foundation of happiness. But, ever since the discovery of the new planet and the self-sharpening pencil, and, above all, the invention of the chess-playing automaton, all rational animals, from the philosopher to the learned pig, unite in pronouncing a good appetite, with the wherewithal to satisfy it, to be the real, and only, *summum bonum*, the fountain of all our knowledge, as well as the source of all substantial happiness. How is it that the said pig is taught the noble science of A, B, C, except through the medium of his appetite? and what impels the animal, man, to the exertion of his faculties, bodily and mental, but his appetite? Necessity, says the old proverb, is the mother of invention. Now, what is necessity, but hunger? The vital importance of a good appetite cannot be better illustrated than by the following passage from the works of M. Huet, bishop of Avranches, the most learned man of his age, if not the most learned man of any age. "Whenever," says he, " I receive letters late in the evening, or very near the time of dining, I lay them by for another opportunity. Letters generally convey more bad news than good; so that, on reading them either at night or at noon, I am sure to spoil my *appetite,* or my repose."

It is doubtless in the pursuit of this chief good, a good appetite, and the means of satisfying it, that thousands of people flock to the Springs, from all quarters. It is in this quest they exchange the delight of making money, for the honour of spending it; it is for this the matron quits the comforts of her domestic circle, to mingle in the crowd by day, and sleep at night in a room six feet by nine, opening on a passage where the tread of human feet is never intermitted, from sunset to sunrise — from sunrise to sunset. It is for this the delicate and sensitive girl musters her smiles, nurtures her roses, and fills her bandboxes. It is for this the snug citizen, who, as he waxes rich, becomes poor in appetite and weak of digestion, opens his accumulated hoards, and exchanges the cherished maxims of saving, for those of spending his money. It is for this the beau reserves the last few hundreds that ought to go to the paying of his tailor, determined to enjoy the delights of eating, though the artist starve, in spite of goose and cabbage. In short, it is for this, and this alone, that his grace of York, of blessed memory, allowed to his cook, the thrice-renowned and immortal Monsieur Ude, twelve hundred pounds sterling a year of the money that ought to have gone to the paying of his creditors, to whom his grace bequeathed only the worst half of the *summum bonum,* a good appetite, with nothing to eat.

Next to a good appetite for dinner, a keen relish for

breakfast constitutes the happiness of our existence. In order to attain to this, the first requisite is to rise early in the morning, and wait a couple of hours with as much impatience as possible, drinking a glass of Congress water about every ten minutes, and walking briskly between each, till the walk is inevitably increased to a trot, and the trot to a gallop when the preliminaries of a good appetite for breakfast are completed. Philosophers and chemists have never yet fairly accounted for this singular propensity to running, produced by the waters, nor shall we attempt to solve the difficulty. It is sufficient for us that the great good is attained, in the acquisition of a sharp appetite for breakfast. And here we will stop a moment, to notice a ridiculous calumny of certain people, who, we suspect, prefer brandy and water to all the pure waters of the Springs: to wit, that it is the morning air and exercise that produces this propensity to running, and the keen appetite consequent upon it. The refutation of this absurd notion is found in the fact that the waters of Ballston do not occasion people to run half as fast, and that consequently they don't eat half as much as they do at Saratoga. In truth, it is worth a man's while to go there only to see people eat: the amatory philosophers, in particular, who maintain that some young ladies live upon air, others upon the odour of roses, and others upon the Waverley novels, should not fail.

CHAPTER III.

OF EATING.

It is not necessary to be very particular on this head, as the rules we have given in respect to the deportment of the elegant tourist, in steam-boats, will sufficiently apply to the Springs. We will merely observe that great vigilance and celerity is necessary, in both places, inasmuch as the viands have a habit of vanishing before one can say Jack Robinson. One special rule, which we cannot by any means omit mentioning, is, never to stop to lose time in considering what you shall eat, or to help your neighbours; if you do, you are a gone man.

We remember to have seen a spruce John Bull, (who, from his carrying a memorandum-book and making frequent notes, was no doubt a forger of books of travels), who, the first morning he attended breakfast at Congress Hall, afforded us infinite diversion. He had placed his affections most evidently on a jolly smoking steak, that, to say the honest truth, was the object of our own secret devoirs, and stood leaning on the back of a chair, directly opposite, waiting for that bell which excels the music of the spheres or of the veritable Signorina, in the ears of a true amateur. At the first tinkling of this delightful instrument, a nimble young fellow, from the purlieus of the Arcade,* with a body no bigger than a wasp, slipped in be-

[* This building was put up in the year 1826. Commencing about 120 feet from Broadway on the Northerly side of Maiden Lane, it was from 50 to 60 feet wide, and ran through to John Street. It had two stories and an attic, with a partially-glazed roof. Divided into a number of small fancy stores, it failed as a speculation.]

tween, took the chair, and transferred a large half of the steak to his own uses. The Signior John Bull looked awfully dignified, but said nothing, and departed in search of another steak, in a paroxysm of hunger. He had swallowed eight tumblers of Congress that morning. In the mean while, he had lost the chance of getting any seat at all, until he was accommodated at a side-table, where we detected him making several notes in his memorandum-book, which, without doubt, bore hard upon the Yankees. It is astonishing how much the tone of a traveller's book depends upon the tone of his stomach. We once travelled in Italy with an English book-maker by trade, who occasionally read portions of his lucubrations to us, and we always had occasion to notice this singular connexion of the brain and the stomach. If he got a good breakfast, he let the Italians off quite easy; if his dinner was satisfactory, he grumbled out a little praise; but if he achieved a good supper and bed, he would actually overflow in a downright eulogium. But woe to Italy if his breakfast was scanty — his dinner indifferent — his supper wanting — and his bed peopled with fleas. Ye powers! how he cut and slashed away! The country was naught — the men all thieves and beggars — the women no better than they should be — the morals good-for-nothing — the religion still worse — the monks a set of lazy dogs — and the pope was sure to be classed with his old playmate, the devil. Of so much consequence is a good dinner to the reputation of nations. It behooves, therefore, all tavern-keepers to bear in mind, that they have in trust the honour of their country, and that they should be careful to stuff all travellers by profession, and all professors of the noble art of puffing, with the good things of their larders — to station a servant behind the back of each of their chairs, with special orders to be particularly attentive — and to give them the best beds in the house. So shall their country flourish in diurnals and immortal books of travel, and taverns multiply and prosper evermore. There is no place in the world where this rule of feeding people into good-humour is more momentous than at the Springs, where the appetite becomes so gloriously teasing and imperative, that it is credibly reported, in the annals of the bon-ton, that a delicate young lady did once eat up her beau, in a rural walk before breakfast. Certain it is, the unfortunate young gentleman was never heard of, and his bills at Congress Hall, and at the tailors, remain unpaid even unto this day.

The reader will please to have a little patience here, while we stop to take a pinch of snuff before we commence another chapter.

CHAPTER IV.

OF FASHIONABLE TOURNURE, AND THE BEHAVIOUR BECOMING IN YOUNG LADIES AT THE SPRINGS.

1. YOUNG ladies should never flirt very violently, except with married men, or those engaged to be married, because nobody will suspect they mean any harm in these cases, and, besides, the pleasure will be enhanced by making their wives and mistresses tolerably unhappy. Pleasure, without giving pain to somebody, is not worth enjoying.

2. Young ladies should take special care of their bishops. The loss of a bishop is dangerous in other games besides chess.

3. Young ladies should take every occasion to indulge to excess in drinking — we mean the waters — because it is good for their complexions.

4. Young ladies should always sit down, whenever they are tired of dancing, whether other ladies in the set have had their turn or not; and they should never sit down till they are tired, under the vulgar idea of giving those a chance of dancing who have had none before. It is the very height of tournure to pay not the least attention to the feelings of other people — except indeed they are of the first fashion.

5. If a young lady don't like the people standing opposite to her in the dance, she ought to quit her place and seek another, taking care to give the said people such a look as will explain her motive.

6. Young ladies should be careful to remember on all occasions, that, according to the most fashionable decisions, it is the height of good breeding to be ill-bred, and that what used to be called politeness is considered by the best society as great a bore as the tunnel under the Thames.

7. Young ladies should never forget that blushing is a sign of guilt.

8. Young ladies, and indeed old ladies too, must always bear in mind that fine feathers make fine birds; and that the more feathers they wear, the more they approximate to high ton. It is of no sort of consequence, according to the present mode, whether the dress is proper for the occasion or not. A walking dress ought to be as fine as one for an assembly, for

the peacock spreads his tail equally on the top of a hen-roost and on the gate of a palace. The infallible rule for dressing is, to get as much finery, and as many colours, as possible, and put them all on at once. It looks like economy to wear only a few ornaments at a time, and, of all things on the face of the earth, nothing is so low, vulgar, and *bourgeois*, as economy. No lady who utters the word, even in her sleep, can ever aspire to tournure. We knew an unfortunate damsel, who ruined herself for ever in good society, by being overheard to say that she could not afford to buy a Cashmere. She was unanimously left out of the circle thenceforth and forevermore.

9. In going into a ball or supper room where there is a great crowd, young ladies should not wait the motions of the married ones, but push forward as vigorously as may be, in order to get a good place; and not mind a little squeezing — it makes them look rosy. Nothing that can possibly happen is so mortifying as to be obliged to take up with an out-of-the-way seat at a supper-table, or the lower end of the room in a cotillon. We have known ladies go into a decline in consequence.

10. Young ladies should always say they are engaged, when asked to dance by a person they don't choose to dance with. It is a pious fraud, justified by the emergency of the case.

11. In walking up and down the public drawing-room, it is always fashionable to keep up a bold front. For this purpose, it is advisable for five or six young ladies to link arm-in-arm, and sweep the whole room. If any body comes in the way, elbow them out without ceremony, and laugh as loud as possible to show it is all a joke.

12. Young ladies should be sure to laugh loud, and talk loud in public, especially when they say an ill-natured thing about somebody within hearing whom nobody knows. Such people have no business at the Springs. Epsom salts is good enough for them. If they must have Congress-water, let them go to Lynch & Clark's, and not bore good society.

13. Young ladies should dress as often, and in as great a variety, as possible. Besides passing away the time, it sometimes achieves wonders. We have known an obstinately undecided, undetermined, hesitating, vacillating, prevaricating beau, who had resisted all the colours of the rainbow, at last brought to the ground by a philosophical, analytical, and antithetical disposition of pink, yellow, green, white, black, blue, fawn, Marie-Louise, bronze, and brass-coloured silks and ribbons, that proved irresistible. As some fish are only to be caught by particular baits at certain seasons, so some men are caught by particular colours. We ourselves could never resist a flesh-coloured gauze, and silken hose of the same. Young ladies had much better study the nature of these affinities, instead of going to hear lectures on political economy, chemistry, and anatomical dissections. The only part of a man they have any concern with is the heart. Women are like bees — because ——. We will give a ball and supper to the fortunate person who shall solve this conundrum: Why are women like bees?*

[* The quidnuncs of the day appear to have taken this up as a genuine conundrum. The New-York Mirror for October 4, 1828, quoting "The Statesman", gives the following answers: — 1. Because they deal most in *sweets* during the *honey-moon.* — 2. Because they *swarm* most briskly in pleasant weather. — 3. Because they are generally upon the *wing.* — 4. Because they are fond of *combs.*]

14. Next to dress, (which is, or ought to be, the first object of a lady's care), is the management of the person; for which the following directions will be found highly useful. The first essential to gracefulness is a total departure from nature. What is the use of being taught, if ladies do not exhibit the effects of teaching, the whole object of which is to counteract the natural vulgarity of nature? If nature gave them a grave or pensive disposition, they must try and thwart it by perpetual laughing. If she bestowed on them a playful, animated mind, the effort should be to appear sad, sorrowful, sentimental, and sleepy. If she gave them a light, airy, elastic step, all they have to do is to creep softly along, with downcast look, and silent, solemn inactivity. If, on the contrary, she vouchsafed them an outline like a dumpling, it is proper and indispensable to dance, bounce, skip, and curvet, like an India-rubber ball. In short, nature must be frustrated in some way or other, and there is an end of it. Without a little caprice, a little affectation, and a great deal of fashionable nonsense, a young lady is intolerable. Talk of nature, and sincerity, and singleness of heart! A natural woman is no more fit for use than a raw calf's-head. She must be worked up with the spices of fashion, or a refined man who has travelled will pronounce her entirely destitute of tournure.

15. The first requisite for a young lady, in walking, riding, sitting, lolling, or dancing, is, that she should do it according to the fashion, whether it is set by an opera-dancer, or by a person of high ton, who does as she does because she can't do any better. If the said opera-dancer, from the mere force of habit, strides

along, and lifts up her feet half a yard high, the young ladies must do the same. If the aforesaid person of rank walks with a wriggle, a jerk, a stoop, or a lean on one side, or fiddles along with the elbows and hips; if she does all this, because from some physical incapacity she cannot do otherwise, still the young ladies, by the laws of fashion, must do the same, and creep, or wriggle, or jerk, or stoop, or walk cramp-sided, or fiddle along with elbows and hips, as the law directs. Whatever is fashionable is graceful, beautiful, proper, and genteel, let the grumbling and vulgar mob, who affect to follow nature, say what they will. In short, it is now a well-established doctrine, that the whole tenour of a fashionable education ought to be to defeat the vulgar propensities implanted by nature. To direct, control, or, what is still more ridiculous, to facilitate, the expansion of natural beauties, qualities, or propensities, is, to use a fashionable phrase just come out at Almack's, " All bosh." It is only the poets who make such a rout about following nature, and the sincerity of their declarations may be tested by the contrast between their precepts and their example. Some one of these ranting, rhyming cavillers, who is ashamed of his name, some time ago bored the English world with the following philippic against this imitative quality which is the distinguishing characteristic of people of fashion, who, on reading it, will no doubt smile at the vulgar indignation of this parvenu. It is extracted, with an alteration or two to suit present purposes, from an obscure poem, not long since published in London, the name of which, if we remember rightly, was " May Fair."

"The thinking mind this miracle must strike,
  Scanning the moderns, that they're all alike:
  True character is merged, for every soul,
  Runs the same gauntlet, gains the self-same goal.
  In the world's jostle is the stamp worn out,
  As from the coins we carry long about.
  They're all the same without, the same within,
  Alike in dullness, and alike in sin;
  All in one way they sit, ride, walk, or stand,
  Speak with one voice, nay, learn to write one hand.
  Drest to the mode, our very nurseries show,
  The baby lady, and the infant beau:
  In rival lustre maid and mistress meet,
  And elbow one another in the street.
  As much like nature are the things we see,
  As yon clipped, dusty pole, is like a tree,
  Green, waving, glorious, beautiful, and free."

Did ever mortal read such low stuff! It is almost as vulgar and old-fashioned as Juvenal. But this is not the worst. Hear the villain!

" Our women, too, no varied medium keep;
  Like storms they riot, or like ditches sleep.
  Pale, cold, and languid, wrapped in sullen state,
  Or flush'd, warm, eager, full of learnéd prate,
  Blue-bottle-flies, they buzz about and shine,
  Cramming ten senseless words in one long line.
  These haunt the galleries of the cheap antique,
  (Who cares for naked figures — they're but Greek!)
  And knowing man's no longer to be found,
  Except in monkey shape, above the ground,
  'Tend anatomic lectures, there to see,
  Not what he is, but what he ought to be;
  Display their forms in the gymnastic class,
  And get ethereally drunk with gas."

We have given these extracts to show our fashionable readers (and we despise all others) what human nature in the form of a poet is capable of: as well as to laugh at his presumption in finding fault with what constitutes the charm of fashion — its uniformity. By its magic influence on dress and demeanour, it reduces grace and deformity, beauty and ugliness, youth and age, activity and decrepitude, talent and stupidity, to a perfect level. All look alike, act alike, talk alike, feel alike, think alike, and constitute as it were one universal identity. "Can any mortal mixture of earth's mould" compare with a fashionable lady of the winter of 1828, except her fashionable cook or chambermaid? Were not the latter, like Achilles, a little vulnerable about the heel and ankle, this beautiful symmetry of the whole sex would be complete. But perfection is not to be looked for in this world — not even in the world of fashion.

Next to the arts of dress and behaviour, the most important thing to be studied is the system of graduating the thermometer of attention to the claims of the beaux. This is a matter of no small difficulty, and requires great *tact*, as the reviewers say. The following general rules will be found useful; but only long experience, or frequent parental admonition, can perfect this indispensable accomplishment.

First. Always proportion your attentions to the claims of the gentlemen who aspire to them. These claims are of great variety. One man may claim consideration from the tying of his neckcloth — another from the cut of his coat — another from his accomplishments, such as fiddling, dancing, talking English-French, or French-English, or writing sleepy verses. Others come forward with the appendage of a gig and tandem, or a curricle — others with that of a full purse, or great expectations — and others preposterously expect consideration from the qualities of their heads and hearts. These last deserve no mercy. The following list is carefully graduated according to the latest discoveries in the great science of bon-ton.

Number one of the classes of beaux, entitled to the first consideration, consists of the thrice-blessed who are accommodated with full purses. These constitute the first-born of Egypt; they are the favourite offspring of fortune, and carry with them a substitute for wit, valour, and virtue, in their pockets. They are entitled to the first-fruits of every prudent, well-educated young lady. Yet it is not actually incumbent on a young lady to fall in love with them at first sight. If the fortunate gentleman is worth fifty thousand dollars, he is only entitled to a gentle preference, a look and a smile occasionally. If he is the meritorious possessor of a hundred thousand, the preference must be demonstrated by double the number of looks and smiles. Two hundred thousand merit a downright penchant; three hundred thousand justify the lady in being very unhappy; and half a million secures her pardon if she dies for love. N. B. If it comes to this extremity, the mother is justified in charging the half a million with practising upon the young lady's affections, and insisting on his marrying her.

Secondly. The next class of pretenders are the gentlemen who carry off belles, as the champions at the Olympic games gained their triumphs, by virtue of their horses. A single horse goes for little or nothing; a gig and mounted servant is something, and the owner somebody; a tandem and livery makes a *distingué;* and the fortunate proprietor of a phaeton and four may fairly enter the lists with any man, except the half a million, or the second cousin of an English lord.

Thirdly. There is a class of beaux, who justly claim considerable consideration on the score of their costume. Dress being that which above all things distinguishes the man from the brute, it follows of course that the best-dressed man is the first man in the creation. Accordingly, the more accurate modern philosophers have rejected the definition of man given by Plato; to wit, "A two-legged animal without feathers": and substituted one much more applicable to his present state. They define him as, "An animal without legs, but with abundance of pantaloons — stitched, pressed, corseted — composition, regent's-cloth — makers, Scofield, Phelps, & Howard."* Well-dressed young men are therefore entitled to great consideration, and, if not of the first rank, assuredly deserve to come in immediately after the cavaliers and their horses, provided always they can show a receipt from the tailor.

Fourthly. Prize-poets, players on the piano, anniversary orators, and all that sort of thing, belong to the class of minor *distingués*, and are entitled to the notice of a fashionable young lady; for all fashionable young ladies ought to wear at least one blue stocking. They will answer, however, only for beaux in public and *en passant*. Never fall in love with them, as you value a coach, a Cashmere shawl, a soirée, or a three-story house with folding doors and marble mantel-pieces. If, indeed, the poet could build four-story fire-proof brick stores, or brokers' offices in Wall Street, as easily as he builds castles in the air; or the chemist transmute lead into gold; or the piano-hero erect walls by the magic of fingers, like Amphion; or the anniver-

[* Well-known tailors in New York, in 1828.]

sary orator coin bank-notes as he does words; then indeed they might be worthy the homage of your eyes and hearts;—as it is, they will do well enough to swell your train.

Fifthly. But, really, it is hardly worth while to notice such a miserable, obscure set of beings, who seem born for nothing else but to be useful. We mean the men who claim the attention of young ladies on the score of merit and an amiable disposition; who are not worth a plum; who drive no horses; who derive their being from no tailors; and who can neither write prize-poetry, turn lead into gold, fiddle sonatas, nor spout at anniversaries. We should like to know what such people were made for. Fortunately, however, there are now but few such scrubs; for it is not the fault of lexicons, catechisms, and compendiums, if every man, woman, and child, cannot know or do something to make himself or herself *distingué*. If nothing else, poetry can be written, that shall be excellent rhyme, however it may lack reason. Of the few scrubs, of whom the best that can be said is that they aspire to be *respectable* — (a word not to be found in the dictionary of fashion) — still fewer are to be met at the Springs, where neither the air nor the waters agree with them. They will much more likely be found attending to their paltry business, storing their minds with the lumber of antiquated knowledge, or enjoying the soporifics of the fireside — from which may all good stars deliver us! If, by any rare chance, one of these singular monsters should appear at the Springs, and peradventure make a demonstration towards a young lady aspiring to tournure, we would advise her to laugh him to death at once. Such men form a sort of icy atmosphere about a woman, in which dandies die, and affectation is irresistibly impelled into the vulgar ranks of nature and propriety.

CHAPTER V.

OF THE BEHAVIOUR PROPER FOR MARRIED LADIES AT THE SPRINGS.

1. A WELL-BRED wife should never take her husband to the Springs, unless she is afraid to leave him behind. If he is a stupid, plodding blockhead, he had better stay at home to make money while his wife is spending it. But if, on the contrary, he is a little gay, gallant, and frisky, she had better bring him with her, that she may have him under her eye, and justify her own little flirtations by his example.

2. In case they come together to the Springs, they should never be seen together while there, as it is considered indecent.

3. Married women should always single out old bachelors, whose whole business is to attend upon pretty women, as moths fly about candles, not to light a flame, but to be consumed in one. Or, in default of these, they should select young dandies, who lack a little fashionable impudence, if such can be found; or, in the last resort, the husbands of other ladies, who devote all their attention, as in duty bound, to the wives of other men. A married woman detected walking arm-in-arm with her own lawful husband, might better commit a *faux pas* at once — her reputation is irretrievably gone.

4. Never take children with you to the Springs. Leave them to the care of old nurse, at home, under the superintendence of Providence. They are perfect bores; and, besides, even the most gallant Lothario will hardly have the face to make love to a woman surrounded by her children.

5. Married ladies should never sit next their husbands at meals, as it might give rise to a suspicion that they could not get any body else to sit by them. Besides, the presence of a husband is sometimes a disagreeable check to the bachelor beaux, and spoils many a gallant speech.

6. Married ladies with grown-up daughters had better pass for their step-mothers, if possible; but if this is not possible, they should take every opportunity to observe that they were very young when they married.

7. Married ladies should forget they are married, as much as possible. The idea of a husband coming across the mind is apt to occasion low spirits, and put an awkward restraint on the behaviour.

8. Neither husband nor wife ought to say an ill-natured thing to each other in public, without prefacing it with, my dear Mr., or, my dear Mrs. In private it is no matter.

9. They should be particularly careful not to throw any thing at each other's heads at meal times; it is almost as bad as to be seen kissing in public. This accident however cannot occur, if due regard be paid to the first and second rules.

10. The primary object of a married lady at the Springs is, or ought to be, to be talked about. Whether it be for any thing commendable or praise-

worthy is a matter of not the least consequence. This *sine qua non* may be attained in various ways — by eccentricity in behaviour or dress; by making a fool of herself, in attempting to pass for a young woman; or by drinking such enormous quantities of the water, that people perplex themselves to death in guessing what becomes of it all. The best mode, however, of compassing the greatest of all possible pleasures, that of notoriety, is to encourage the attentions of some gay coxcomb, till all the world begins to talk about nothing else. This is the true eclat, without which it is not worth while to take the trouble of breathing in this world.

11. Mothers should never take grown-up daughters to the Springs; it makes them look so old.

12. There is, however, one exception to the foregoing rule: namely, when they wish to settle a young lady in life. In that case, they ought to be careful of seven things, to wit: —

To make them leave their hearts at home, lest they should give them away to young squires who can't pay value received.

To make them leave their feminine timidity, miscalled modesty, at home; otherwise, they may not have the face to make what is called at Almack's "a dead set", at the proper object.

To be sure to tell every-body in the most solemn manner, not more than twenty times a day, how fond Miss Angelina, or Miss Adeline, is of retirement, and how backward in showing off her accomplishments in public.

To ascertain the weight of a young gentleman's purse, or at least of that of his papa, before the young lady's heart is in danger. This is sometimes rather a difficult matter, as it is not uncommon, nowadays, for gentlemen to make a vast figure with other people's money. A copy of the will of the old gentleman is the best security for a matrimonial speculation. But even this is not infallible, for we ourselves once had a large landed estate left us, by an old bachelor who had feasted in our house for twenty years, which turned out to belong to another person.

Never to lose an opportunity, while condescending to accept the arm of the selected Adonis in a promenade around the drawing or dancing room, to repeat all the flattering things the young lady has not said in his praise. Where one man, ay, or one woman, is taken by the heart, a thousand are taken by this bait. We speak from long experience, having never yet been able to resist any woman who admired us, even though she might not have been handsome enough to make a song about.

If the mother of a young lady at the Springs has a hard character to deal with in her daughter, that is, one who cherishes certain pernicious and disobedient notions about loving, respecting, or, most of all, obeying, a husband, and prefers love to money, we know of no more hopeful plan for curing this romantic folly than to point out to her notice as many couples as may be, who have made love-matches. Ten to one, the contemplation of these will satisfy the young lady that money wears better than love.

Lastly, to consider merit, talents, amiability, and an attractive person and manner, as dust in the balance, when put in comparison with money. Money not only makes the mare go, but puts the horses to the coach; and, (what is the climax of human bliss), secures to the happy lady who don't mind how much she pays for it the first choice from a consignment of cast-off bonnets of an opera-dancer.

CHAPTER VI.

OF MARRIED MEN, AND THE BEHAVIOUR PROPER FOR THEM AT THE SPRINGS.

1. A MARRIED gentleman must never take an ugly wife to the Springs, lest he should have to wait upon her himself; nor a handsome one, lest she should be too much waited on by others. But if, as we are informed is sometimes the case, the lady's health absolutely requires it, and there is no help, the laws of fashion peremptorily prescribe to the husband a total oblivion of his wife in all public places, where she must be left to the exercise of her own powers of attraction upon other men, for obtaining the attentions necessary to her comfort and happiness. If she is handsome, she will be sure of these; if she is easy of access, and free from all vulgar airs of prudery, she will stand a fair chance of coming in for a due share; if she is neither one nor the other, she must fain take up with some forlorn bachelor in his grand climacteric.

2. Married gentlemen would do well to keep their marriage secret as long as possible, were it not for the great advantage it gives them in flirting with the young ladies.

3. Married gentlemen should be particular in reserving all their good-humour and spirits for public use. As to their private deportment, that is of no consequence, provided they have discreet wives, who are content to be a little miserable, provided everybody thinks them the happiest women in the world.

4. Married men should never forget, that it is better to be blamed for neglect and unkindness to their wives than to be quizzed for their attentions to them. It is better to commit sacrilege, than to be laughed at by people of fashion. We have known several persons of great sensibility who actually died in consequence.

5. It has been asserted by certain cynics and blockheads, that old married men who live in the country, and who have young, gay, and handsome wives, had better take them to Niagara, Montreal, Quebec, or — home, than to the Springs. Ballston and Saratoga, say they, are great places for scandal, and it is not absolutely out of nature for a lady to gain her health and lose her reputation, at one or other of these places. We hold these cautions in utter and prodigious contempt, maintaining in the very teeth of such heterodoxy in fashion, that an elderly gentleman, with a young, gay, frisky, handsome wife, cannot do half so well as to take her every season to the Springs. There she will be in her proper sphere — admired, followed, and caressed; and there, if there be any virtue in the waters, she will be in a good-humour with her husband, if it be only to repay him for the admiration of other men. There, if anywhere in the world, he will enjoy domestic felicity, and taste of that peace which surpasseth the understanding of all vulgar husbands. He ought to go as early, and stay as long, as

there is a sufficiency of admirers to keep his wife in fine spirits, for, ten to one — (we confess it, such is the instability of all sublunary happiness) — when they return to the quiet enjoyment of domestic bliss, in their solitary home, the recollection of past happiness will poison the enjoyment of the present, and smiles be turned to desperate frowns. For this, however, there is a sovereign remedy — a journey to town, and lodgings at a fashionable hotel.

6. For those wives that cannot be happy at home husbands are bound to find amusement abroad, just as they are bound to find them attendants, when they don't choose to act the part of *cavaliere servente* themselves.

7. As it is a received and inflexible law of the beau-monde here, to imitate all foreign fashions as a matter of course, we suggest to the fashionables who constitute good society, to mince matters no longer, and not to stand shilly-shally, like a horse with his forefeet in the water and his hind feet out. We would have them do exactly as the most elegant and fashionable models of Europe do — marry for money or rank; for, as to love, that can be got any where. We would have them consider marriage, not as tying them up, but as letting them loose. We would have them purchase their matrimonial freedom, by mutually conceding to each other the right of self-government in all matters whatever, except the enormity of being out of fashion. It is utterly inconceivable by those who have not had the advantage of an European tour, and of seeing people of the highest rank — in their carriages or at the theatres — it is utterly inconceivable how this mutual freedom conduces to the happiness of domes-

tic life. But, as example is said to be better than precept, we will record an instance that came under our observation, for the benefit of our fashionable readers, craving only leave to omit the real names.

Honorius and Honoria married for love: it was the mode then — at least it was the mode for people to persuade themselves they did so. The husband was a first-rate man of fashion; for he dined well, drove a handsome carriage, gave parties, and lived in a three-story house with folding doors and marble mantel-pieces. The wife was in like manner indubitably a fashionable lady; for she had a fashionable milliner, a fashionable air, a fashionable coach, a fashionable acquaintance, could not exist without silver forks, and her family was of the first respectability — for it could show more bankrupts than any in town. According to the most approved custom, Honorius gave punch, and Honoria saw company, in the first style, with eight grooms and groomesses of the highest ton. One of the former was a foreigner of great distinction, for he could play the piano divinely, and was third cousin to a principal tenant of an English prince of the blood — no, we mistake, of an English duke — the princes of the blood in England having no land to plague themselves with.

After seeing company, they moved into Broadway, or Hudson Square — it matters not — into a three-story house with folding doors and marble mantel-pieces, and for a time were as happy as the day is long, for the whole town visited them, and admired the folding doors, the marble mantel-pieces, the carpets, and the damask curtains of eight different colours. But, alas! the chase of happiness is nothing but the little boy running after the rainbow and falling into a ditch, unless people set out at first in the right path. The twenty-ninth evening after marriage, Honorius was detected in a yawn at the fireside — for Honoria had insisted, before marriage, that they should give up the world, and live to themselves in the pure enjoyment of quiet domestic bliss. A yawn *per se* is nothing; but with certain combinations and associations it becomes extremely formidable. Honoria was unfortunately sufficiently awake to see it, and it went nigh to break her heart. Still, as she was too proud to show her real feelings, she only exclaimed, a little sharply: "Lord, my dear — I wish you would leave off that practice of yawning, and showing off those great black teeth in the back part of your head." Honorius had wellnigh jumped out of his skin at this speech, so wanting in tournure, and had some trouble to answer mildly, "Really, I am so stultified with want of exercise and variety, that I am grown quite stupid." "You had better say at once you are tired of my company," cried Honoria, bursting into tears. Honorius assured her that he was not tired of her company — that he never was tired of her company — that he never would be tired of her company — and — here he was stopped by another yawn, that was absolutely irresistible.

That night neither party slept a wink, for the last yawn was followed by a keen encounter of wits, that ended in what might be called a matrimonial segregation. However, people must be very ill-tempered, if they can remain long on bad terms with their nearest connexions. A reconciliation soon took place, and

Honorius, to prove that he never was and never would be tired of his wife's company, staid at home all day, and all the evening, although his health suffered materially in the direful struggles to repress those violent impulses towards yawning which sometimes beset the animal man when he has nothing to say and nothing to think about. Too much fat puts out the candle, and too much ashes chokes the fire. Tedium is the mother of ill-nature, and testiness the offspring of ennui. Honorius did not go out, and consequently brought home no news, no topics of every-day gossip, no food for raillery, laughter, or ridicule; and thereupon it came to pass, that our young and faithful couple sometimes wanted themes for discussion, and took to disputing and contradicting, merely to pass the time.

Little by little — by those imperceptible snail's-paces, which so often lead from passion to indifference, from indifference to dislike, from dislike to antipathy, the good Honorius, who was a well-disposed man, and the amiable Honoria, who was really a reasonable woman as times go, came at length to quarrel once, twice, yea, thrice a day; nay, oftener, for, being always at home, they were continually coming in contact, and when married people have no other antagonist, they generally fall out with each other. It is indeed quite indispensable that we should have certain out-door acquaintance to criticise, for the security of peace within doors. This is considered by some sensible people as the principal use of intimate friends. In short, Honorius found fault with Honoria, and Honoria found fault with Honorius, even when they were both free from blame. They fell out about the baby

— they fell out about the servants, the inside of the house and the outside of the house, the stars, the planets, the twelve signs, and the weather, which never suited both at a time. In short, they fell out about every thing, and they fell out about nothing.

At length, after a severe brush, Honorius, in a fit of desperation, one day took his hat and actually sallied forth into the places where merchants most do congregate. There he heard the news of the day, the ups and downs of life, the whys and the wherefores, the fires and the murders, the marriages and the divorces, and all the items of the every-day drama of the busy world. He did not come home till dinner-time, and Honoria received him with as much kindness as if he were come off a long journey. They sat down, and she asked him the news. He told her all he had heard, and the dinner passed off without a single quarrel, although we are obliged to confess that Honoria once threw the gauntlet, by finding fault with his spilling the gravy on a clean damask table-cloth.

In the evening, however, there was another prolonged duet of yawning in andante, succeeded by a quick measure of altercation. Honorius took his hat again, and went to the theatre, whence he did not return till past twelve; for, what with horses, dogs, and devils, men made by nature's journeymen, spectacles, singing, dancing, tumbling, and the like, people now certainly get the worth of their money at the play, in quantity if not in quality. Poor Honoria was so alarmed at his long absence that she thought he had drowned himself, and was so glad to see him that she forgot to ask him where he had been, till the next morning at breakfast. He told all about the horses, the dancers, the devils, The Flying Dutchman, the flying Indians, the grins and the gauze, and the machinery and the pasteboard, till she laughed herself almost to death, and accused him of having been at a puppetshow. The breakfast went off charmingly, although Honorius broke a teacup belonging to a set that cost five hundred dollars, and Honoria put twice as much milk in his coffee as he liked.

By degrees, this habit of going out increased upon Honorius, so that, at length, he got to the other extreme, and Honoria was often left, day after day, evening after evening, in loneliness and solitude; for her children were yet too young for companions. She quarrelled a little with Honorius about it, who coolly answered, "My dear, why don't you go out too? nobody hinders you." "Where shall I go?— we have completely got out of society, by visiting nobody." "O, give a rout; I warrant you'll have company enough: every-body will be your acquaintance." It was decided; a rout was given, and every-body came. This of course entitled them to invitations from every-body, and, instead of spending every day and evening at home, they now spent every day and evening abroad. This again produced that desperate monotony, which, whether of company or solitude, excitement or stupidity, is equally tedious and unsatisfactory in the end. They began to dispute their way regularly to and from parties, and matters became worse than ever. Honorius was too polite to certain ladies whom Honoria particularly hated; and Honoria was too free with several gentlemen whom Honorius supremely despised.

"Alas!", said Honorius one day to himself, "is there no peace to be found in this world!" And Honoria repeated the same exclamation to herself, just at the same moment. A sudden ray of light broke in upon Honorius, as if in response to this pathetic appeal. If we cannot be happy together, is it not possible to be happy asunder? Honorius went out by himself the very next night, the night after, and the night after that. Honoria could hold out no longer, and reproached him bitterly. "My dear," answered Honorius, mildly, "why can't you go out by yourself, too?" The carriage was ordered on the instant by Honoria, who went to one party, while Honorius went in a hack to another. They both passed such a delightful evening, that they repeated the experiment again, and again. Each succeeded better and better, and the arrangement has subsisted ever since. Honorius is out all day, and, when he happens to be at home at night, Honoria is out at a party, or to the play. In the winter they are never seen together, except by accident at some public place, when you would take them for perfect strangers. In the summer, she goes to the Springs, he to Long Branch; the children are left at home with the nurses, to preserve peace and quiet in the family abroad. Honoria never gets up to breakfast with Honorius, and Honorius never is at home to dine with Honoria. She is at a ball till two in the morning; he, at the faro-table all night. They never meet — they never quarrel. Honoria is the delight of fashionable gentlemen; Honorius, the darling of fashionable ladies, who all envy Honoria the possession of such an agreeable, witty, polite husband. In short, they have discovered the grand secret of preserving domestic peace and tranquillity at home — never meeting there.

CHAPTER VII.

OF THE EXQUISITES, AND THE WHOLE DUTY OF MAN AT THE SPRINGS.

Happy the man who is born with whiskers, for he will not be under the necessity of buying a goodly pair. Without them, it is impossible to live. As the May-Fair poet, whom we have quoted heretofore with reprobation, most insolently sings: —

> "All now wear beards, or buy the beards they wear;
> The human face divine is lost in hair.
> While thus the mind so well the body suits,
> How wise to steal the livery of brutes!
> You think a warrior shoves you from the wall;
> 'Tis a meek creature, whom we prentice call,
> Bewhisker'd like crusader, or a Turk,
> In quick step marching homeward with his work,
> A pair of breeches, or a flannel gown,
> Looking the while as if he'd look you down —
> Pray don't be frighten'd, he'd not hurt a fly;
> His business in the world is but to lie."

Rule 1. Next to whiskers, dress is all important to the success of a young gentleman, at all places, especially at the Springs. Not manners, but tailors, make the man in the present improved state of the world, and nothing is more certain than that success in life mainly depends on the cut of the coat, the exuberance of the whiskers, and, above all, the tie of the cravat. We know several young fellows, who have carried off heiresses solely by virtue of preëminence in this last item.

2. Be sure you pay no attention to that musty old saw, about cutting your coat according to your cloth, except it be to reverse the ignoble maxim, by cutting it directly the contrary. N. B. For the cut of your coat, and for the most approved attitudes, see the figures in the windows of the men-milliners in Broadway.

3. Never get any article of dress from a cheap tailor, for he will be sure to make you pay for it; whereas a real fashionable, expensive tailor, always charges his good customers extortionately, to pay for his bad ones; for it would ruin him irretrievably, and frighten half his customers to the uttermost ends of the town, were he to be guilty of the ill-manners of suing one of them. He must never do this till he is about leaving off business.

4. Never stop to inquire whether you want a new coat, or whether you can pay for it. If the tailor trusts you, good — it is at his own risk, and if you don't pay him, somebody else must, after the manner hinted at in the preceding rule.

5. If you happen to see a wretch coming down the street, to whom you have been indebted three or four years, you have only to stop short, consider a moment, then turn suddenly around and trot off in a contrary direction. People will take it for granted you have forgot something.

6. Never pay any debts if you can help it, but debts of honour: such as tavern-bills, and, generally, all bills for superfluities. By the law of nature, man has a claim on society for the necessaries of life, and therefore is not bound to pay for them.

7. Never be deterred from going to the Springs by

any sordid motives of economy. All that is necessary is to pay your way till you get there. Once there, you have only to play at cards, pocketing your winnings and paying none of your losings, and it will go hard if you don't create a fund for necessaries. Failing in this, you have only to tell mine host, that you have been disappointed in remittances, and are going to Albany or New York to see about them. Never mind his blank looks, he won't dare to arrest you, for fear of losing one half of his lodgers, who would not fail to resent such an unfashionable procedure, not knowing how soon their turn might come, if such unheard-of enormities were tolerated in fashionable society.

8. Never pay any attention to the ladies, and they will be sure to pay attention to you: that is, if you have plenty of whiskers; plenty of cravats, and know how to tie them; plenty of coats; a curricle, or gig and tandem; and look grim. N. B. Heiresses are excepted; they expect to be sought after.

9. It is needless to caution you to avoid the desperate imprudence of falling in love with a lady who is poor in every thing except merit. Nobody commits such a folly nowadays, especially since the vast improvement in taste, and the prodigious advances made by the spirit of the age. Formerly, in the days of outer darkness, "when Adam delv'd and Eve span," poor people might marry without coming upon the parish. But it would be the extreme of folly to do it now, when it is impossible to fit out a wife of the least pretensions, for a walk in Broadway, under a sum that in those miserable days of delving and spinning would have purchased independence for life. Since

the age of paper-money, brokers, speculating, and breaking, and ever since the great encouragement of "domestic industry," women of decency never spin any thing but "street-yarn," a fashionable article, which has all the fashionable requisites to recommend it, being entirely useless. What would be the fate of an unfortunate youth, who is without a penny, and without the means or arts to gain one, who should marry a young lady who possesses but one single art, that of spending thousands? How would he get a three-story house with folding doors and marble mantel-pieces? how would he obtain the means of purchasing hats, at fifty dollars — pelisses, at a hundred — veils, at twice as much — and shawls, at ten times? How would he be able to keep a carriage, give parties, and drink Bingham, or Nabob, or Billy Ludlow? Without these things, what man or woman not quite insane will marry? And, then, the children! How are they to be furnished with artificial curls, and necklaces, and bracelets, and ear-rings, and pink hats of immeasurable size, and silken hose, and ruffles, and laces, and made to look like Lilliputian ladies? How are they to be taught the art of arts, the art worth all the arts, the indispensable art of spending money, unless there is money to spend? We know of but one way, and that is by running in debt and getting whitewashed. This can't be done above eight or ten times, without people beginning to grow shy of trusting you for any sum that will make it worth while to go into the limits. It is, however, hoped, that the wishes of the philanthropists will soon be realized, by the passage of a law to do away with this inhuman necessity; and that the time is not far distant, when the march of mind and the spirit of the age will lead to so pleasing a condition of things, that people may indulge in all the luxuries of life without money, and borrow, without the disagreeable alternative of paying or going into retirement. Then everybody will be rich — then every-body can reside in a three-story house with folding doors and marble mantel-pieces, give parties, live luxuriously, get the dyspepsia as well as messieurs the brokers, run in debt without the necessity of running away, get married, be happy, and dress his little girls as fine as a fiddle for a walk in Broadway! Until then, however, we repeat our caution not to marry any body that labours under even the suspicion of being poor, the worst of all possible disasters for a young lady, being enough to ruin her reputation past all recovery. Until then, the young gentlemen must be content with looking all the horrors of bachelorism in the face; and the young ladies riot in the anticipations of single blessedness, which, melancholy as it may be, is better than living in a house without folding doors and marble mantelpieces, and giving no balls. While the old gentleman lives, he must work, and shave, and speculate, and turn his pennies ten times a day, to keep the young ladies in the costume becoming the march of mind and the spirit of the age; and when he fails, or dies, they must trust to providence and the orphan societies. There is but one remedy for all this, and it is ten times worse than the disease — economy. As it is, bachelors will multiply prodigiously, marrying for love will go out of fashion, and there will not be a sufficiency of apes in all Africa, to supply the place of the dandies of this life, in the life to come.

10. After singling out the lady who possesses the needful, to wit, not less than a hundred thousand, it behooves the young gentleman to be particularly attentive to the — mother — if the young lady unfortunately has one at the Springs. Daughters are all so dutiful, that they never reject the recommendation of their parents in cases of this kind, especially if they threaten to disinherit them. He must be always on the alert; dip water for her, offer his arm, sit next her at table, run down all the rest of the married ladies, praise the daughter for looking so like the mother, perfume his whiskers, and take every opportunity of looking at the young lady tenderly, at the same time playing with his watch-chain, if he has one, or, in default, fiddling with his cravat — there is nothing like suiting the action to the look. He must be pensive, abstracted, and distracted; affect solitude, and drink enormously — we mean of the waters. He must wander in the woods, lose his appetite in public and make it up in private, bite his thumbs, chew his lips, knit his eyebrows, and grow as pale as he possibly can. Should all this fail, if he can afford it he must give a ball, or a collation, or a party on the lake, and upset the boat on purpose to have an opportunity of saving the lady's life. If even all these fail, he must resort to the desperate expedient of the hero who gave name to the famous rock, of eternal memory, near Ballston, known, and ever to be known, by the appellation of the LOVER'S ROCK. The story is as follows, on the best possible authority.

A young gentleman of good family, who could look back at least two generations without tracing his pedigree to a cobbler, or a shaver — we don't mean a barber — but whose fortune was in an inverse ratio to his birth, having the good-luck to raise the wind by a timely hit, visited the Springs in a gig and tandem. He had received the best education the country could afford; that is, he had learned enough Greek, and Latin, and natural philosophy, and mathematics, to forget it all in a year after leaving college. He had learned a profession which he did not practise, and he practised many things which he did not learn from his profession. He had a vast many wants without the means of supplying them, and professed as lofty a contempt for all useful occupations, as if he had been rich enough to pass for a fool. He was always well-dressed, well-mounted, and well-received, on the score of these recommendations added to that of his ancient descent; for, as we said before, he could trace back to a great-grandfather, whom nobody knew any thing about, so nobody could deny his having been a gentleman. Nothing is so clear a demonstration of ancient descent as the utter obscurity of the origin of a family.

Be this as it may, our hero was excessively fond of style, good living, and gentlemanly indulgences of all sorts; but his taste was cramped by the want of the one thing needful. 'Tis true, he got credit sometimes; but his genius was consequently rebuked by frequent dunnings of certain importunate people, who had the impudence to want their money sometimes. If it were not for this, living upon credit would be the happiest of all possible modes of life, except that of a beggar, which we consider surpassingly superlative. Beggars are the true patricians of the earth; they form the only privileged class, the real aristocracy of the land — they pay no taxes, obey no laws — they toil not, neither do they spin — serve not as jurymen, firemen, or militia-men — work not on the highways — have no country to serve, nor family to maintain — are not obliged to wash their hands and faces, or comb their hair every morning — fear nothing but the poor-house — love nothing so well as lying, except drinking — and eat what they please in Lent. In short, as the old song says: —

> "Each city, each town, and every village,
> Affords us either an alms or pillage;
> And if the weather be cold and raw,
> Then in the barn we tumble in straw;
> If warm and fair, by yea-cock and nay-cock,
> The fields will afford us a hedge or a hay-cock —
> A hay-cock — a hay-cock — and hay-cock —" &c.

Truly, it is a noble vocation; and nothing can afford a clearer proof of the march of mind and the improved spirit of the age than the multiplication and daily increase of this wise order of beggars, who have the good sense to know the difference between living by the sweat of their own brows and that of other people. Next to the wisdom of begging, is that of borrowing — or, as the cant phrase is, living upon *tick*.

The outward man of our hero was well to look at, especially as it was always clothed in the habiliments of fashion. He was tall, straight, stiff, and stately; his head resembled the classical model of a mop; and his whiskers would have delighted the good Lady Baussiere. The ladies approved of him; and, if he had only been able to achieve a three-story house in Hudson Square or Broadway, with mahogany folding doors and marble mantel-pieces, together with certain accompaniments of mirrors, sofas, pier-tables, carpets, &c., it was the general opinion that he might have carried a first-rate belle. But, alas! without these, what is man? Our hero felt this at every step, and his spirit rose manfully against the injustice of the world. At one time, he had actually resolved to devote himself to his profession, and, by persevering attention, amass a fortune that would supply the place of all the cardinal virtues. But the seductions of Broadway, and the soirées, and the sweet pretty belles with their big bonnets and bishops—there was no resisting them; and our hero abandoned his profession in despair. Finding he could not withstand the allurements of pleasure, he resolved within himself to kill two birds with one stone as it were—that is, to join profit and pleasure—and, while he was sporting the butterfly in Broadway, to have an eye to securing the main chance—a rich wife.

In pursuance of this gallant resolution, he made demonstrations towards every real or reputed heiress that fell in his way. Every Jack has his Gill—if one won't, another will—what's one man's meat, is another man's poison—there is no accounting for tastes—and he who never gets tired will come to the end of his journey at last—quoth our hero, and continued to persevere in the midst of continual disappointments. He might have succeeded in some instances, but for the sleepless vigilance of the mammas, who justly thought, that, having brought up their daughters to nothing but spending money, the least they could do was to provide them with rich husbands. Either the pursuit itself, or the frequent failures of our hero in running down his game, began to lower him in the estimation of the world — that is, the little world in which he flourished. Success only can sanctify any undertaking; and a thriving highwayman, or prosperous rogue, is often more admired than an unlucky dog who has nothing but his blundering honesty to recommend him. Besides, there is, we know not for what reason, a prejudice against gentlemen who pursue fortune in the shape of a young lady of a hundred thousand charms, — we mean, dollars. Men obtain a maintenance by divers means; some by handicraft trades — some by shaving beards, and some by shaving notes — some by long voyages, and others by perilous journeys on land. They spend the best part of their lives in these pursuits, and, at last, when worn with care, hardships, and anxieties, sit down in their old age, to nourish their infirmities, and pamper their appetites with luxuries that carry death in their train. Now, we would ask, is it not better to seize fortune by a coup-de-main and achieve an heiress off-hand, than to chase her all our lives, and only be in at our own death, instead of the death of our game? The prejudice against fortune-hunters, as they are called, is therefore unjust; and we advise all young fellows of spirit to hunt away bravely, rather than drudge through the desperate, lingering avenues of a profession.

Be this as it may, our hero began to be held rather cheap by the young ladies, who used to compare notes and find out that he had made the same demonstrations towards some score or two of them. It is observed by deep philosophers, that the last thing men or women will pardon in others is the fault of which they are most guilty themselves. All these pretty belle-butterflies had flirted with divers young men, and intended to do it again; but they were exceedingly indignant at our hero, and turned their backs to him on all public occasions. Some ignoble spirits would have sunk, in grovelling despair, into a profession, and have abandoned forever the pursuit of these fatal beauties. But our hero was not the man to give up. He mustered all his credit, and made a dead and successful set at his tailor, who furnished him with two full suits, the price of which that judicious tradesman apportioned equally among his punctual customers, who, he justly thought, ought to pay something for being in good credit. Our hero, moreover, blew a desperate blast, and raised the wind for a gig and tandem, which he obtained by means which have puzzled us more than any phenomenon we ever witnessed. He did all this, and he triumphantly departed for the Springs, where the fly-fisher's hook catches many an inexperienced belle and beau, and where the pretty rice-fed damsels of the south do congregate, whose empire extends not only over the whole region of beauty, but likewise over divers plantations of cotton, and divers scores of gentlemen, both of colour and no colour.

The arrival of our hero at the Springs occasioned quite a sensation. The young ladies inquired who he was, and their mammas what he was worth. The answer to this latter question was by no means satisfactory; although nothing absolutely certain could be gathered for some time, as to the precise state of his finances. Meanwhile he singled out a daughter of the sun, of whom fame reported that she was heiress to a rice-swamp and plantations of cotton, and feudal lady over hundreds of serfs, who bowed to her sway with absolute devotion. Our hero baited his hook, and angled for the fair lady of the rice-swamp, with more than the patience of a professor of what Isaac Walton calls the "gentle craft." The young lady was quite unknowing in the ways of bon-ton. She had been bred in the country, where she studied romance in books of religion, and religion in books of romance. She had never run the gauntlet through a phalanx of beaux, every one of whom gave her a wound; nor had she lost the sweetest inheritance of a woman — that willing, wilful credulity, which almost loves to be deluded, and which had rather be deceived into a conviction of worth than be obliged to believe it has been deceived. She was, in truth, deplorably unsophisticated in the ways of men and of the world. She did not even dream that money was actually necessary to supply our wants, much less did it enter into her innocent fancy that it was utterly impossible to be married, at present, without the indispensable adjuncts of mahogany folding doors and marble mantel-pieces, silver forks, satin curtains, Brussels carpets, and all those things which constitute the happiness of this life. In short, she had no tournure at all, and was moreover a little blue, having somehow imbibed a notion, that no man was worth a lady's eye unless he was distinguished by something of some sort or other — she hardly knew what. It never entered her head — and why should it?, for this is the result of experience alone — it never entered her head, that good sense, a good heart, and a good disposition, were far more important ingredients in the composition of wedded bliss, than a pretty turn for poetry, or a decided vocation to the fine arts.

But her lady-mother, under whose guardian wing our heroine now first expanded her pinions, was another sort of "animal," as the polite Johnnies say of a woman. She was perfectly familiar with the elements necessary to the proper constitution of a rational wedding. None knew better than herself, that money only becomes the brighter for wearing, and that a vast many other things especially esteemed by inexperienced young ladies, not only lose their lustre and value, but actually wear out entirely in the course of time. Experience had taught her, that Cupid was only the divinity of youth, whereas honest Plutus never lost his attractions, but only fascinated his votaries the more strongly as they grew in age and wisdom. In short, she had a great contempt for merit, and a much greater veneration for money.

Moved by these opposing influences, it is little to be wondered at if the old lady and the young one drew different ways. Our hero made daily progress with the daughter, but greater leeway with the mother. The old lady watched him closely, and always had something particular to say to her daughter, whenever he occupied her attention for a moment. She could not stir a step without the young lady, and grew so weak and infirm, that at length she could not walk across the room without the aid of her arm. Our hero entered the lists in the art of mining and countermining, but he was no match for the dowager, who, though she had but two eyes, and those none of the brightest, saw all that Argus could have seen with his fifty pairs. The opposition of currents is sure to raise the froth; and opposition in love hath the same effect on the imagination, which is Cupid's prime-minister, if not Cupid himself.

In this way things went on. Our hero was in the situation of a general with two frontiers to defend, and lost ground on one as fast as he gained it on the other. With the young lady he was better than well; with the old one, worse than bad. About this time, another pretender entered the lists against our hero, equally well-dressed, equal in whiskers, equal in intrepidity, and equally in want of the *sine qua non*. A rival is sure to bring matters to a crisis, except in the case of a young lady who knows and properly estimates the exquisite delights of flirtation. The good mother saw, pretty clearly, that this new candidate would infallibly, by the force of repulsion, drive her daughter to the opposite side — that is, into the arms of our hero. She therefore cut the matter short at once, and forbade the young lady to speak, walk, sit, ride, or exchange looks, with our hero. The young lady obeyed, except as to the last injunction; and, if the truth must be told, made up in looks for every thing else. The old lady saw it would not do, and, forthwith sending for our hero, peremptorily dismissed him, with the assurance that her daughter should never marry him — that if she did, she would never see or speak to her more, but hold her alien to her heart forever. She then quitted our hero with tears in her eyes, leaving him with his eyes wide open.

He took his hat and stick; paid his bill — no, I am wrong, he did not pay his bill — and, casting a look at the window of his "ladye love" that cracked six panes of glass, proceeded in a fit of desperation to the rock then without a name, but now immortalized as the **Lovers' Rock**. This crag frowns tremendously, as all crags do, and hangs in lowering majesty over the stream of Kayaderosseras — a name in itself sufficient to indicate the presence of something extraordinary, if not actually terrible. On arriving at this gloomy, savage, wild, and dreary spot, our hero took out a pocket-glass and adjusted his whiskers to the nicety of a hair. He then deliberately drew forth his penknife with a pearl handle and silver springs, and cleaned his nails. After this he pulled up his neck-cloth five or six times, and shook his head manfully; then he took off his coat, folded it up carefully, laid it down, took it up, kissed it, and shed some bitter tears over this object of his dearest cares: then, after a solemn and affecting pause, he tied a white pocket-handkerchief about his head, cast his eyes upwards, clasped his hands, took one farewell look at himself in the pocket-glass, and, dashing it into a thousand pieces, rushed furiously to the edge of the precipice. There, turning a somerset by mistake backwards, he fell flat on his bishops, on the hard rock, where he lay motionless for some time — doubtless as much surprised as was poor Gloucester, when he threw himself as he supposed from Dover Cliff, to find that he was not dead. The truth is, our hero could hardly believe himself alive; until at length he recognized, to his utter surprise and disappointment, that he had committed an egregious blunder, in throwing himself down on the top, instead of the bottom, of the rock.

He determined, in his own mind, to do the thing better next time, and was preparing to avoid a similar error, when, through the dim, enticing obscurity of the pine grove, he thought he saw a sylph-like figure, gliding — (not walking) — swiftly in the direction of the rock. He gazed again, and it assumed the port of a mortal woman. A little nearer, and it emerged from the glossy, silver foliage, in the form of the sovereign lady of his heart, the mistress of the rice-swamp. She had seen him depart with frenzy in his eye; she had heard from her mother of his summary dismissal; and had no doubt he had gone to that rock, where erewhile they had looked unutterable things, to kill himself as dead as a stone. Taking advantage of the interregnum of a nap, she escaped the maternal guardianship, and followed him at a distance. She had seen his preparations for self-immolation; she had seen the pathetic farewell between him and himself, the tying of the handkerchief, the pulling-off of the coat, the wringing of the hands, the rush towards the edge of the rock; and she had seen him disappear, just as, with a shriek which he heard not, she had fallen insensible to the ground. When she came to herself, and recalled what she had seen, she determined to follow her lover to the rock, and throw herself down after him, in the bitterness of her despair. But what can express her delight, when, on arriving at the fatal spot, she saw her true lover running towards her, apparently as well as ever he was in his life! An explanation took place, which was followed by words of sweet consolation on the part of the lady.

"I swear," said she, "by the genius which inhabits this rock, by the nymphs which sport in this babbling brook, by the dryads and hamadryads that live in these hollow pines, that I will not obey my cruel mother. I will marry thee, and, should my obdurate parent disinherit me and send me forth to beggary, I will share it with thee. Let her disinherit me if she will; what is fortune — what is — "

" Dis — dis — disin — disinherit, did you say?" interrupted our hero, staring in wild astonishment.

" Yes, disinherit," replied the young lady, enthusiastically; " I will brave disinheritance, poverty, exile, want, neglect, contempt, remorse, despair, death, all for you, so you don't kill yourself again."

" Dis — dis — disin — disinherit," repeated our hero, in a state of increasing perturbation: " pov—, ex—, wa—, neg—, con—, re—, des—, death! Why, what is all this, angel of my immortal soul?"

" O don't take on so — don't take on so, my own dear heart: I swear again, and again, a hundred, ay, ten hundred thousand million times, that I don't care if my mother cuts me off with a shilling — "

" Cut — cut — off — shilling — why, I thought — that is — I understood — that is, I was assured that — that — you had a fortune in your own right."

" No, not a penny, thank heaven; I can now show you the extent of my love, by sacrificing fortune — every thing for you. I'll follow you in beggary through the world."

" I'll be damned if you will," our hero was just going to say; but checked himself, and cried out in accents of despair — " And you have no fortune of your own?"

" No, thank heaven!"
" No rice-swamps?"
" No, thank heaven!"
" No cotton plantations?"
" No, thank heaven!"

"No uplands, nor lowlands, nor sea-island, nor long-staple, nor short-staple?"

"No, thank heaven!"

"Nor crops of corn?"

"No, thank heaven!"

"Nor neg — I mean gentlemen of colour?"

"Not one, thank heaven!"

"And you are entirely dependent on your mother?"

"Yes; and she has sworn to disinherit me if I marry you, thank heaven! You have now an opportunity of showing the disinterestedness of your affection."

"Our hero started up in a tumult of distraction — he rushed madly and impetuously to the edge of the precipice, and, avoiding a mistake similar to that he had just committed, threw himself headlong down into the terrible torrent with the terrible name, and floated none knew whither, for his body was never found. The young lady was turned into stone — don't be alarmed, gentle reader — only for a few minutes. These past, she bethought herself of following her lover; then, she bethought herself of considering the matter; and, finally, she fell into an inexplicable perplexity, as to what could have got into our hero, to drown himself in despair at the very moment she was promising to make him the happiest of men. She determined to live till she had solved this doubt, which, by the way, she never could do to the end of her life; and she died without being able to tell what it was that made her lover make away with himself at such an improper time. As for the rest, the landlord and the man-mercer, like the "devil and the king" in the affair of Sir Balaam, divided the prize; one taking the gig, the other the tandem. From that time the place has gone by the name of the LOVER'S ROCK, and not a true lover, or true-hearted lady, ever visits the Springs without spending many an hour of sentimental luxury on the spot where our hero could not survive the anguish of even anticipating that he should cause the lady of his heart to be disinherited for love of him.

CHAPTER VIII.

OF THE BEHAVIOUR PROPER FOR ELDERLY SINGLE GENTLEMEN AT THE SPRINGS.

IN days of yore, before the march of mind and the improvements in style and dress which distinguish the present happy age, old bachelors deserved no mercy, unless they came under the class of disappointed lovers, or proved to the satisfaction of the world, "they would if they could." But now, unless a man is born rich, he can't afford to marry till he grows rich, and in becoming so he is very apt to grow old. Hence the number of bachelors is sure to increase with the progress of refinement, which mainly consists in the invention or adoption of new modes of dress, new-fashioned furniture, and new ways of spending money. Bachelors have, for these reasons, become of late sufficiently numerous to constitute a class by themselves, and to merit a code designed especially for their use and government. At the same time we premise that, all things considered, we are of opinion that, since it is indecent for a man of any pretensions to get married until he can afford to live in a three-story house with mahogany folding doors and marble mantel-pieces, he ought not to be classed with old bachelors, till it can be proved he has been five years rich enough for matrimony, or till he is fully convicted of threescore, when he must give in, and take his place in the corps.

1. Bachelors, or, more politely, single gentlemen of a certain age, ought never to marry any but very young, sprightly belles, of the first fashion and pretensions. The true foundation of mutual affection is in the attraction, not of affinity, but of contrast. This contrast is perfect between a gentleman of fifty and a young lady of sixteen, and nothing can come of such a union but mutual love and perfect obedience on the part of the lady, who, ten to one, will look up to him as a father.

2. Single gentlemen of a certain age, who are rich enough to afford a curricle, together with a three-story house with folding doors and marble mantel-pieces, need not be under any apprehensions of being rejected by a young lady, brought up as she ought to be, with a proper insight into the relative value of men and things. But they should not be more than ten years making up their minds, remembering the fowler, who was so long taking aim that the bird flew away before he drew the trigger.

3. Single gentlemen of a certain age should never play a double part, or sport with the hearts of inexperienced young ladies.

4. Single gentlemen of a certain age should beware of the widowers, who are always in a hurry. We

have known a bachelor cut out by a brisk widower, before he knew where he was.

5. Single gentlemen of a certain age should never plead guilty to the least ache or pain, except growing pains. They should never remember any thing that happened more than ten years back. To recollect past times is a melancholy proof of old age.

6. Single gentlemen of a certain age should never attempt a cotillon, or try to cut a caper, except they are sure of going through with it. If they are once laughed at in public, it is all over with them. They had better be poor.

7. Single gentlemen of a certain age should beware how they " buck up " to widows, unless they have previously brought themselves, as Lady Macbeth (who was undoubtedly a widow when Macbeth married her) says, " to the sticking place," that is, to the resolution of committing matrimony at a moment's warning. Your widows, if they mean to marry again at all, never like to linger on the funeral pyre of a bachelor's indecision.

8. Single gentlemen of a certain age should never marry, except they have proof positive of the disinterested affection of the young lady. In order to ascertain this, it would be well to circulate a rumour of great losses, or actual bankruptcy, and put down the equipage.

9. Single gentlemen of a certain age ought never to have more than two ladies in prospect at one time — one for each eye — else they may chance to lose both. The prevailing offence of bachelors is that of ill-bred pointers: you cannot bring them to a dead point, although they will be popping their noses everywhere.

10. Single gentlemen of a certain age, being always young, should never keep company with old people, for fear the stale proverb, about birds of a feather, should be fired at their heads. They should now and then commit a gentlemanly excess, such as drinking six bottles at a sitting, or playing cards all night, though it might be expedient not to appear in public till the effects are gone off. An old field is not easily renovated.

11. Single gentlemen of a certain age, who are well-to-do in the world, when inspired with a desire to appropriate young ladies, ought to make the first advances to the mothers. The latter know the value of money better than the former, and a well-bred daughter will think it indelicate to pretend to know any difference between one man and another, except as respects his fortune. For, as the great poet says, "*worth* makes the man," that is, the money he is worth.

12. Single gentlemen of a certain age — (which phrase we ought before this to have explained, as indicating gentlemen whose ages are altogether uncertain) — ought never to deceive the young ladies in any thing but their years and their money. A desire to appear young and to be thought rich is so natural and amiable, that none but a cynic would ascribe it to a bad motive.

13. Very old single gentlemen of a certain age should be careful how they marry in the month of January, for reasons which shall be nameless; or in February, for reasons which will readily present themselves; or in March, for reasons we do not think proper to specify; or in April, for reasons best known to our-

selves; or in May, for reasons of the first magnitude; or in June, for reasons which cannot be obviated; or in July, for reasons which no one will venture to to controvert; or in August, for reasons which every body will understand; or in September, for reasons which to be ignorant of would impeach the reader's understanding; or in October, for reasons highly appropriate; or in November, for reasons deep and profound; or in December, for reasons as plain as the nose on our face. There are, moreover, seven days of the week on which very old single gentlemen of a certain age ought not to think of being married. Monday, because that is washing-day. Tuesday, or *Twosday* as it was originally written, because it suggests that, "man and wife will be *two*", before the end of the week. Wednesday, or Wedding-day, as is the true orthography, for that is generally the day of all others an old single gentleman of a certain age recollects with the least satisfaction. Thursday, or Thorsday, because it was christened after the Pagan deity, *Thor*, and marriage is a Christian ceremony. Friday, because it is hanging-day, and he might be tempted to turn himself off. Saturday, because that is too far from the middle of the week. Above all, Sunday, for that is *dies non*, and no moneyed transactions, or purchases and sales, are lawful on that day. Any other day in the week, it is perfectly safe for them to marry.

CHAPTER IX.

OF MATRIMONY, AND OF THE BEST MODE OF INSURING HAPPINESS IN THE STATE, BY A DISCREET CHOICE OF A HELPMATE.

In the present improved system of society, when the young ladies wear spatterdashes and the young gentlemen corsets, money is absolutely essential to the patient endurance of the married state. The choice of a rich husband or wife supersedes, therefore, the necessity of all rules, as wealth secures to the successful adventurer all the happiness this world can give, so long as it lasts. But as every one is not so fortunate as to achieve a rich heir or heiress, the following hints may enable even the tyro to make a choice that will in some measure supply the absence of cash.

1. Beauty is a principal ingredient of happiness in the married state, and it is scarcely ever observed that a handsome couple is otherwise than truly happy. If it be objected that beauty is but a fading flower, we answer, that, when it is faded, all that the parties have to do is to *think* each other beautiful. If such an effort of the imagination is beyond them, they must do the best they can, and admire each other for their good qualities.

2. Next in value to beauty is the capacity of cutting a dash at all public places, by dressing well, dancing well, and making one's self agreeable to every-body. Nobody, except the person that has experienced it, can conceive the happiness of having one's wife, or husband, admired by all the world. As to how people conduct themselves in private, and in the domestic *tête-à-tête*, that is a matter of very little

consequence, so long as they have sufficient discretion to keep their own secrets, and sufficient good-breeding not to quarrel before the public.

3. As nothing is so outrageously vulgar as the idea of not spending money because one has not got it to spend, the next best thing to having a rich or handsome wife is having a wife that knows how to feign a fortune. This is an infallible proof of high-breeding, and great cleverness withal. Any fool can make a figure with money, but to make an equal figure without it is an invaluable qualification in a wife.

4. Never marry any body you have ever heard or seen laughed at by people of fashion, unless he or she is rich; nor any body who does not always follow the recent fashions in every thing. A bonnet or a coat out of fashion infallibly degrades people from their station in society, whether they are young or old, and a person that leads the ton is almost an equal prize with an heiress or a beauty.

5. Never marry a lady who appears unconscious of her beauty or accomplishments, except she is an heiress; for this presupposes a degree of blindness and stupidity truly deplorable. How can you expect a woman to see the good qualities of her husband, when she is blind to her own?

6. Never marry a woman of prudence, good-sense, good-temper, and piety, excepting always she is rich; for, if you happen to turn out an indifferent husband, all the world will blame you: whereas if she be as bad as, or worse than, yourself, you will have the best possible excuse.

7. Never marry a woman who is particularly retiring in her disposition and habits. This bespeaks

shyness, and shyness indicates slyness, and slyness, hypocrisy. Your bold-faced, harum-scarum women, who show all, and disguise nothing, are the best. There is no deception about them, and it is a proof that they have nothing to hide, when they hide nothing. Ladies that eat nothing in public generally make it up in the pantry, and, to quote a saying fashionable at Almack's, "The still sow", &c. &c.

8. Beware of that terrible monster, a woman that affects to have a will of her own before marriage, and to act up to certain old-fashioned notions of propriety and decorum; one who refuses to make herself ridiculous, despite of the fashion; who will not waltz in public with a perfect stranger, despite of the fashion; who will not flirt with any-body that comes in her way, despite of the fashion; and who absolutely refuses to act and look like a fool, though every body else sets her the example. Such a woman will trouble you exceedingly, and, ten to one, never let you rest till you become as preposterous as herself.

9. Beware also of a woman who had rather stay at home and read Paradise Lost, than walk up and down the Paradise of Broadway in a high wind and a cloud of dust, holding her hat with one hand, and her cloak with the other. Such a woman decidedly prefers exercise of mind to exercise of limbs, and will never make a good waltzer.

10. Beware of blue-stockings, for they are abroad.

11. Beware of bishops and hoop-petticoats, for they are abroad.

12. Beware — we now address ourselves particularly to the ladies — beware of all men that aspire to be useful in their generation, except they be rich; be-

ware of all men who look as if nature had any hand in their composition, except they be rich; beware of all that aspire to be better and wiser than their neighbours, except they be rich; beware of young lawyers, who think of nothing but estates and entails; beware of young physicians, whose knowledge of anatomy and craniology enables them to dive into all your secrets; beware of the young parsons in spectacles, who look through and through your hearts; beware of all manner of men who look at bills before paying them; beware of all sorts of handicraft men, except Monsieur Manuel, the barber, and Monsieur Simon, the cook; and, above all, beware of your stiff, starched fellows that aspire to the *cardinal* virtues, for that smacks of *Popery*.

We had thoughts of following up these rules for entering the happy state of matrimony, with some general directions for preserving harmony after marriage. But, upon the whole, it is scarcely worth while. The great thing, after all, is to be fairly and honestly married, and what happens afterwards is of minor consequence. If you have money, you cannot be otherwise than happy; if you have beauty, fashion and good dancing, it is your own fault if you are not happy; and if you have none of these, you have no right to expect happiness. If you are only contented and comfortable, that is all you can hope for in this world, without riches, beauty, or fashion; and that is more than you deserve for marrying only a discreet, prudent, sensible, amiable, tolerable-looking dowdy of a man or woman. We shall therefore conclude this portion of our undertaking, by cordially wishing all our fashionable readers, well, that is, richly, married — a wish which includes all sublunary blessings.

CHAPTER X.

OF THE BEST MODES OF KILLING THE GRAND ENEMY OF THE FASHIONABLE HUMAN RACE, WHO HAVE NOTHING TO DO IN THIS WORLD — BUT TO BE HAPPY.

Of all the various modes and inventions devised since the creation of the world, for passing the time, none can compare with EATING; and nothing appears wanting to human happiness, but the capacity of eating on without stopping, from the cradle to the grave. But, alas!, people cannot gormandize forever! and all they can do, after one meal, is to anticipate the delights of another. When we can feed no more, the best possible substitute is to think of feeding. Such are the glorious effects of the waters at the springs, that they would constitute the best substitute for Nectar, or Bingham, or Nabob, to be found upon this earth, if the good things to be eaten were only in proportion to our appetite to eat them. But, alas! truth obliges us to confess, this is not the case. No canvas-backs, no oysters, no turtle, but will cloy at last! — no Goose and Gridiron, no Drozé, no Pardessus, no Sykes, can stimulate the appetite for ever! — Nay, no Niblo, high-priest and caterer of the gourmands of New York! Here we would say, caterer of the gods themselves, were we not of opinion that they knew little of the importance of the grand science, as appears from their omitting to ennoble one of their number, by installing him god of eating, and thus placing him above the great Bacchus himself. But, on second thoughts, this might have arisen from the jealousy of Jove, who doubtless foresaw that such a deity would monopolize the incense of mankind, and leave his shrine without a votary.

Well, therefore, might the great philosopher lay it down as the grand secret of human happiness, that "we should live to eat, and not eat to live," since in this is contained the true secret of the *summum bonum*, which so puzzled all antiquity. Previous to those prodigious steps in the march of mind, which have ennobled the present age beyond all others that preceded or that will succeed it, the gentler sex were unhappily precluded, in some degree, from eating more than was absolutely necessary. Nay, some of the most approved models of heroines of romance, so far as we are without any authority from the authors of these works to the contrary, never ate at all. It used to be considered indelicate for women of fashion to eat as if they cared any thing about it; and there is good authority for saying, that a great match was once broken off, in consequence of the lady being detected by her lover in eating raw oysters. But the world, of late years, grows wiser much faster than it grows older — thanks be to the steam-engines for it! The interdict against female eating is withdrawn, and it does one's heart good to see how the ladies enjoy themselves at the Springs, and at parties in town. They eat like so many beautiful little pigeons, till their beautiful little craws seem, as if they might, peradventure, burst their corsets; and foul befall those egregious innovators, who, as we hear, are attempting to revive the fashion of giving soirées, without the accompaniments of oysters, porter, and champagne. May they be condemned to sponge-cake and lemonade all their lives, and be "at home" to nobody, till they learn how to treat their friends.

One of the phenomena which has puzzled us more than almost any thing in this world is, that people who meet together solely for pleasure should ever get tired of themselves or their company. But so it is; those who live only for amusement, more than any other class, find time hanging on their hands. Hence it is that rich and fashionable people are so frequently dull, out of humour, and splenetic; while the labouring classes, and those who ought in reason and propriety to be miserable, enjoy an unaccountable hilarity of spirits, and actually seem to crowd into one hour more real enjoyment than a man of pleasure, whose sole business is to be happy, gathers in a whole life of uninterrupted pursuit. How provoking it is to see a miserable linsey-woolsey villain, without a solitary requisite for comfort in high life, laughing, and dancing, and revelling in an exuberance of spirits, while a company of people of pleasure, who have nothing to do but be happy, will sit enveloped in gloom, dance as if they were following a funeral, and laugh, if they laugh at all, with a melancholy indifference truly depressing. Is it possible that labour, or at least employment of some kind, is necessary to the enjoyment of ease, and to the vivacity of the animal spirits? Certainly it would seem so. Nobody laughs with such glee as the chimney-sweep, and the negro slave of the south, whom we are always pitying; and of all the grave people on the face of the earth, the

North-American Indian, who despises work, and lives a life of indolence, is the gravest; while his wife, who carries the burdens, cultivates the corn, and performs all the domestic labours, is observed to be gay and cheerful. It is certainly passing strange, though it would appear to be true, that the people we most envy, namely the rich and the idle, enjoy the least of life's sunshine, though they seem to be always basking in it. The old Indian affirmed, that, among the white men, "the hog was the only gentleman," for he never worked, was fed upon the best corn, and at last grew so fat he could not walk. Verily, the comparison is not far from odious; but there are, nevertheless, certain mortifying points of resemblance between the quadruped and the biped gentleman.

Be this as it may, such being the difficulty which besets the hapless beings who in their chase of pleasure at length run it down at the Springs and know not what to do with themselves afterwards, we hold him a great public benefactor, equal to the father of a canal or a rail-road or a cotton-manufactory, who shall devise ways and means to rid these unfortunate beings — unfortunate in having too much time and money on their hands — at least of a portion of the former. After much deep and intense cogitation, we have devised a series of amusements, which, if followed up with proper industry, will seldom, if ever, fail of the desired end.

The first and best preservative against ennui is falling in love. If you are successful, that cures all evils for the time being; while, if otherwise, the disappointment is a specific for this disease, which never troubles people who have any thing else to trouble them.

Dressing is no bad preventive, provided you are long enough about it, and take a proper interest in looking well. We have known a dishabille give a tone of dejection for an entire day; and could tell of more than one person, cured of a serious indisposition by resolutely getting up, changing his linen, displaying a new suit, shaving his beard, and perfuming his whiskers. Many ladies also have been rescued from profound melancholy, by putting on a brilliant dress, with ear-rings and bracelets which proved remarkably becoming. The oftener you dress, the better; for, besides the manual exercise, the frequent change produces a corresponding succession of ideas, and a consequent gentle exercise of the animal spirits which is highly salutary. Gay colours are best, as they make people look cheerful, which is the next thing to being cheerful. After all, we are but chameleons, and owe the colour of our minds to outward objects.

Gentlemen have a great resource in the reading-room, provided they have a literary turn, and are reduced to great extremity to pass the morning. We recollect a literary character at the Springs, who spent three hours over the newspapers every day, yet could never tell the news, nor the day of the week. Ladies must, however, be careful to read nothing but romances, lest they should pass for blue-stockings, which, among the fashionables, are considered synonymous with blue-devils.

Music and reading-parties are not bad in a rainy day. A little music, provided it is not out of tune or time, will while away the leaden hours of pleasure wonderfully, when there are admiring beaux, who can relish pure Italian, to listen and applaud. Beware however of *di tanti palpiti*, which is grown so common that the very sweeps whistle it while making their way up chimney. When any thing gets so common with the vulgar, it is beneath the notice or patronage of people of fashion, however beautiful it may be. The greatest, and at the same time the sole, objection to eating, drinking, sleeping and breathing, is, that we enjoy them in common with the brutes, and the vulgar who are little better. Moore's songs ought always to be preferred on these occasions, because they are altogether sentimental, or sensual, which is quite synonymous nowadays. Next to actual kissings, embracings, palpitations, honeyed meetings, and heart-rending adieus, is the description of these things in luscious verse, aided by the magic strains of melting melody. It almost makes one feel as if really going through these delightful evolutions. It is not worth while to mind what stiff people, who affect decorum of speech, say on the subject. There are many matters that may be sung, but not said. One may sing about things which it would be thought rather critical to talk about.

In respect to reading, it is much to be regretted that we have nothing new of Lord Byron, but his helmet. This, we understand, is to be exhibited at the Springs, the present season, provided it is not disposed of to a valiant militia officer, who is said to be in treaty for the same. Formerly the literary society of the Springs could calculate upon a new canto of Don Juan every month, redolent with the inspiration of misanthrophy and "gin and water;"* but now, at

* See Leigh Hunt's notice of Lord Byron's life and habits.

least with the exception of this present work, unless a **Waverley** or a **Cooper** tumbles down from the summit of Parnassus, there is scarcely any thing worth reading but **Souvenirs,** which unluckily appear so out of season, that they are a hundred years old before the spring, that is, the spring of fashionable life at the Springs, arrives, with all the birds of passage in its train. In this dilemma, the choice must be left to the judgment of the party, with this solemn caution, to select no work that is more than a month old.

People who are not addicted to deep studies may manage to get through a long storm pretty tolerably, by looking out at a window, and wondering when it will clear off. A north-east storm of two or three days is the most trying time; for, as nobody thinks of a fire in summer though it be never so cold, the votaries of pleasure have no other resource than going to bed to keep themselves from an ague. Gentlemen who play have a never-failing panacea for all vicissitudes of the weather, which pass unfelt and unnoticed, in the delightful excitement of winning and losing. The best way to guard against these storms is to shut the windows, lock the doors, light candles, and turn day into night, as there are certain amusements which are only proper for darkness and obscurity.

In addition to these domestic enjoyments, pastime may be found without doors in pleasant weather. For example, there is the excursion to Saratoga Lake, to ramble along its banks, or fish, or flirt, or do any other fashionable thing. The water of the lake is so pure and transparent, that people with tolerable eyes may see their faces in it. Hence arises a great advantage; for young persons, who don't care to contemplate any beauties but their own, may thus behold them in the greatest perfection. More than one Narcissus hath admired himself there, and pined to death for love of his own image; and many a fair and unsuspecting damsel, that never saw herself in gilded mirror, has here, for the first time, become conscious of her charms. So vivid are the pictures thus displayed, and so true to nature, that a young fellow of our intimate acquaintance, who had somewhat spoiled a pair of good eyes by eternally squinting through a glass because it was the fashion, once actually mistook the shadow of a young heiress in the lake for the young heiress herself, and jumped in to save her from drowning. The lady was so touched by this gallant mistake, that she took the will for the deed, and the young man into the bargain. N. B. The fish are not worth the trouble of catching; but the men that go there, are — sometimes: so with the ladies.

There are fine trout in Barheit's Pond, to which there is a pleasant ride through the pine woods; at least they say there are fine trout, if one could only catch them with any thing but a silver hook. But such is the staid allegiance of these loyal fishes, that they will not suffer themselves to be hooked by any body but their sovereign lord, the proprietor of the waters. We ourselves have fished in this famous pool, till a great spider came and wove his web, from the tip of our nose to the tip-end of our fishing-rod, and caught several flies. But we caught no fish, nor would St. Anthony himself, we verily believe, had he preached ever such sound doctrines. N. B. Mine host may possibly *bite*, though the trout won't.

For a longer excursion, seek the famous field of Saratoga, on which the key-stone of the arch of our independence was raised. There, six thousand English invaders laid down their arms, and there a pillar ought to be erected to commemorate the triumph of free soldiers. Lake George, the masterpiece of nature, and Hadley's Falls, will richly repay a visit, and charmingly occupy a day. There is also a pleasant ride, which we ourselves discovered, due North of Saratoga, along an excellent road, skirted on one hand by rich meadows, on the other by a rugged, rocky hill, from which, ever and anon, pours down a little brawling stream, that loses itself among the high green grass of the lowland. Of a fine afternoon towards sunset, when the slanting beams of the sun leave the eastern side of the hills enveloped in cooling shades, it is pleasant to ride along and taste the charms of nature, after revelling in those of art at the Springs. But what are we talking about?— we have forgotten ourselves. Such matters are unworthy our book, and those to whom it is addressed.

Who indeed would waste his time in loitering about these ignoble scenes, unsaid and unsung by names of fashionable note, when he can walk back and forth on the long piazzas at the Springs, where ladies bright are sitting in the windows, ready to talk and be talked to, to exchange smile for smile, and to accompany any body in this charming promenade, if they are only asked? And, as for the ladies, why should *they*, when they can take a ride to Ballston if they are at Saratoga, or to Saratoga if they are at Ballston, all the way through the beautiful pine woods; show off their airs— we mean graces; display their fashionable dresses; spy into the enemy's camp at Sans Souci or Congress Hall; criticise rival belles, rival houses, rival waters; and bring home matter for at least one day's conversation?—which last is no trifling affair let us tell them.

We have mentioned Sans Souci and Congress Hall. Dire is the hostility between these rival houses, the Montagues and Capulets of modern days; dire are the conflicts between the votaries of the diuretic and cathartic nymphs of the Springs; and dire the scandals they utter of each other, when under the influence of the inspiring draughts. Not rival cities, such as Athens and Sparta, Rome and Carthage, London and Paris, New York and Philadelphia; not rival belles, rival poets, rival reviews, rival players, potentates, or politicians, ever breathed such defiances as Congress Hall and Sans Souci. As sings the prize-poet,—

> "Not vast Achille,* the greatest of the name,
> (Not e'en excepting him of Grecian fame),
> Not vast Achille, such pedal wars did wage
> Against the mimic monarch of the stage,
> Whom, with his hard invulnerable heel,
> He laid all prostrate, quick as flint and steel;
> Nor e'er did soda, iron, or fixed air,
> So play the mischief with the rival fair," &c.

No vulgar mind can possibly comprehend the exquisite excitement of this civil warfare of fashion, and what a capital resource it is to the votaries of pleasure at the Springs, especially on a stormy day. In

[* Monsieur and Madame Achille, with other dancers, were imported by Charles Gilfert, lessee and manager of the new (and first) Bowery theatre, for the season of 1826-7, to compete with "the legitimate" drama under "King Stephen" Price and Edward Simpson, at the Park. Achille was ballet-master; and it appears that heels carried the day triumphantly over heads.]

vain hath Professor Silliman essayed to *neutralize* these conflicting and angry waters, by impartially bearing testimony to the unequalled merits of both, unknowing that there exist antipathies which are not dreamt of in his chemistry. The war still rages, and will continue to rage till Ballston and Saratoga, like Babylon and Nineveh, are no more, and their sweet waters, for the sins of the people, turned into Dead Seas and lakes of sulphur.

It may however happen, since all things are possible in this wonderful age, that, notwithstanding all these expedients, these varied and never-ending delights, people may be at last overtaken, even here, by the fiend ennui, which seems to have been created on purpose to confound the rich and happy. In that case, they may as well give up the pursuit of happiness at once, as desperate. There is nothing beyond the SPRINGS; they are the *ultima Thule* of the fashionable world, and those who find not pleasure there may as well die at once — or go home. In vain will they toil on to "Old Ti," the Plains of Abraham, the Falls of Montmorenci, and the Lord knows where — in vain fly from Ballston to Saratoga, from Saratoga to Ballston, from Ballston to Lebanon, from Lebanon to Rockaway, and from Rockaway to Long Branch, where they may have the satisfaction of bathing in the same ocean with people of the first fashion. It is all useless. Let them despair, and go home; and, as a last forlorn hope, endeavour to find happiness in administering to the welfare of those around them, an expedient we have actually known to be successful in more than one instance. Let the young ladies devote themselves to working caps for a time of need;

their mothers devote themselves to their household gods; their husbands, to planting trees, breeding merinos, and cultivating politics and ruta-bagas; the brokers, to shaving closer than ever, to make up for lost time; the dandy, to the limits; and his spruce rival, the shop-keeper, to his counter. We have said.

And now, gentle tourist!, having conducted thee safely, (and, we hope, pleasantly), to the sanctuary, where if thou findest not happiness it is not our fault, (since we have shown thee where she dwells and how to woo her), we bid thee an affectionate farewell, cautioning thee, as a last proof of our solicitude for thy welfare, not to go to Niagara, lest, peradventure, thou shouldest fall into the hands of the "Morgan Committee." Mayest thou — to include all in one consummate wish — mayest thou pass thy whole life in travelling for pleasure, meeting with glorious entertainment by the way, and, at length, find peace and repose at that inn where, sooner or later, all mankind take up their last night's lodging.

THE

NYMPH OF THE MOUNTAIN.

THE NYMPH OF THE MOUNTAIN.

In a certain corner of The Bay State there once stood, and we hope will continue to flourish long and happily, a snug town, now promoted to be a city, the name of which is not material to our purpose. Here, in a great shingle palace, which would have been a very comfortable edifice had it only been finished, lived a reputable widow, well to do in the world, and the happy mother of a promising lad, a wonderful clever boy, as might be expected. In fact, Shearjashub (that was his name) was no bad specimen of the country lad. He was hardy, abstemious, independent, and *cute* withal; and, before he was a man grown, made a great bargain once out of a travelling merchant, a Scotchman, who chanced that way. Besides this, he was a mechanical genius; and, though far from being lazy, delighted in the invention of labour-saving machines, some of which were odd enough. He peeled all his mother's pumpkins by water, and spun her flax with a windmill. Nay, it was reported of him that he once invented a machine for digging graves upon speculation, by which he calculated he should certainly have made his fortune, had not the people of the village all with one accord taken it into their heads to live for ever. The name of the family was Yankee, they having been the first that had intercourse with the Indians, who called them Yankee, because they could not say English.

The Widow Yankee was a right pious, meeting-going woman, who held it to be a great want of faith not to believe in everything; especially everything out of the way and impossible. She was a special amateur of demonology and witchcraft. Moreover, she was gifted with a reasonable share of curiosity, though it is recorded that once she came very near missing to get at the bottom of a secret. The story ran as follows:—

One day, as she was sitting at her window, which had a happy aspect for overlooking the affairs of the village, she saw a man of mysterious mien, with a stick in his hand and a pipe in his mouth, walking exactly three feet behind a white cow. The same thing happened precisely at the same hour in the same manner the next day, and so continued for some time. The first week, the widow began to think it rather odd; the second, she thought it quite strange; the third, it became altogether incomprehensible; and the fourth, the poor woman took to her bed, of the disease of the man and the cow.

Doctor Calomel undertook the cure in a new and original manner, to wit, without the use of medicine. He wrought upon the mysterious cow-driver to come to the widow's house, and tell her the whole secret of the business. When he came into the room the sick woman raised herself up, and in a faint voice addressed him as follows:—

"Inscrutable man! I conjure thee to tell me what under the sun makes thee always follow that cow about every day at the same hour, and at the same distance from her tail?"

"Because the cow always goes before me", replied he.

Upon which the widow jumped out of her sick bed, seized an old shoe, flung it at his head, and was miraculously cured from that moment. Doctor Calomel got into great practice thereupon.

Shearjashub inherited a considerable share of his mother's inquiring disposition, and was very inquisitive about the affairs of other people; but, to do him justice, he took pretty good care to keep his own to himself, like a discreet lad as he was. Having invented so many labour-saving machines, Jashub, as he was usually called by the neighbours, thought it was great nonsense to work, himself; so he set his machines going, and took to the amusement of killing time, which, in a country village, is no such easy matter. It requires a considerable share of ingenuity. His favourite mode of doing this was taking his gun on his shoulder, and sallying forth into the fields and woods, followed by a cur, whose genealogy was perfectly abstruse. Nobody could tell to what family he belonged; though certain it was, that he was neither "mongrel, puppy, whelp, nor hound," but a cur of low degree, whose delight was to bask in the sun, when he was not out with his young master.

In this way Jashub would pass day after day, in what he called sporting; that is to say, toiling through tangled woods and rough bog-meadows and swamps, that quivered like a jelly at every step, and returning home at night hungry as well as tired. Report said that he never was known to shoot anything; and thus far his time was spent innocently, if not improvingly.

One fast-day, early in the spring of 1776, Jashub went forth as usual, with his gun on his shoulder, and little Snap, (such was the name of the dog), at his heels. The early May had put on all her charms; a thousand little patches of wild violets were peeping forth with deep blue eyes; a thousand, yea, tens of thousands of buds were expanding into leaves, apace; and crowds of chirping birds were singing a hymn to ever-gracious Spring. Jashub could not find it in his heart to fire at them; and if he had fired, there would have been no danger, except of frightening the little warblers, and arresting their song.

Beguiled by the beauties of Nature and her charming music, Jashub almost unconsciously wandered on until he came to the opening of a deep glen in the mountain, which rose at some miles distance, west of the village. It was formed by the passage of a pure crystal stream, which, in the course of ages, or perhaps by a single effort, had made a cleft in the mountain, about twenty yards wide, ten of which were occupied by the brook, which silently wound its way along the base of steep and rocky precipices several hundred feet high, that formed the barriers of the glen on either side. These towering masses of gray eternity were here and there green with the adventurous laurel, which, fastening its roots in the crevices, nodded over the dizzy steep; and at intervals a little spring stole forth, high up among the lichen-covered rocks, and trickled down their sides in threads of silvery brightness. In other places patches of isinglass appeared, sparkling against the sober masses, and communicating a singularly lustrous character to the scene, which had otherwise been all grim and disheartening.

Jashub gazed a while in apprehensive wonder, as he stood at the entrance of these everlasting gates. Curiosity prompted him to enter and explore the recesses within, while a certain vague unwillingness deterred him. At length curiosity, or perhaps fate, which had decreed that he should become the instrument of her great designs, prevailed against all opposition, and he entered the portals of this majestic palace of nature. He slowly advanced — sometimes arrested by a certain feeling of mysterious awe, and again driven on by the power which had assumed the direction of his conduct. At length he arrived at the centre of the hallowed solitude. Not a living thing breathed around him, except his little dog; and his gun trembled in his hand. All was gloom, silence, isolation. The brook poured forth no murmurs; the birds and insects seemed to have avoided the unsunned region, where everlasting twilight reigned; and the scream of the hawks, pursuing their way across the deep chasm, was hushed as they passed.

Jashub was arrested by the melancholy grandeur of the scene, and his dog looked wistfully in his face, as if he wanted to go home. As he stood thus lingering, leaning on his gun, a merry strain broke forth upon the terrible silence, and echoed through the glen. The sound made him suddenly start, in doing which his foot somehow or other caught in the lock of his gun, which he had forgot to uncock, as was usual with him, and caused it to go off. The explosion rang through the recesses of the glen in a hundred repetitions, which were answered by the howlings of the little dog. As the echoes gradually subsided, and the smoke cleared away, the tune again commenced. It was a careless, lively air, such as suited the taste of the young man, and he forgot his fears in his love of music.

As he stood thus entranced, he heard a voice, sweet, yet animating as the clear sound of a trumpet, exclaim,

"Shearjashub! Shearjashub!"

Jashub's heart bounded into his throat, and prevented his answering. He loaded his gun, and stood on the defensive.

In a moment after, the same trumpet-voice repeated the same words,

"Shearjashub! Shearjashub!"

"What d'ye want, you tarnal critter?" at length the young man answered, with a degree of courage that afterwards astonished him.

"Listen — and look!"

He listened and looked, but saw nothing, until a little flourish of the same sprightly tune directed his attention to the spot whence it came.

High on the summit of the highest perpendicular cliff, which shone gorgeously with sparkling isinglass, seated under the shade of a tuft of laurels, he beheld a female figure, holding a little flageolet, and playing the lively air which he had just heard. Her height, notwithstanding the distance, appeared majestic; the flash of her bright beaming eyes illumined the depths of the gloom, and her bearing was that of a goddess. She was dressed in simple robes of virgin white, and on her head she wore a cap, such as has since been consecrated to Liberty by my gallant countrymen.

Shearjashub looked, trembled, and was silent. In a few minutes, however, his recollection returned.

"Shearjashub!" exclaimed the lady of the rock, "listen!"

But Shearjashub had given leg-bail. Both he and his faithful friend, little Snap, had left the haunted glen as fast as their feet would carry them.

He told the story when he got home, with some venial exaggeration. Nobody believed him except the widow, his honoured mother, who had faith to swallow a camel. All the rest laughed at him, and the wicked damsels of the village were always joking about his mountain sweetheart.

At last he got out of patience, and one day demanded of those who were bantering him what proof they would have of the truth of his story.

"Why," said old Deacon Mayhew, "I guess I should be considerably particular satisfied, if you would bring us hum that same fife you heard the gal play on so finely."

"And I," said another, "will believe the young squire, if he'll play the same tune on it he heard yonder in the mountain."

Shearjashub was so pestered and provoked at last, that he determined to put his courage to the proof, and see whether it would bear him out in another visit to the chasm in the mountain. He thought he might as well be dead as have no comfort of his life.

"I'll be darned if I don't go," said he; and away he went, with no other company than his little dog. It was on the fourth day of July, 1776, that Shearjashub wrought himself up to a second visit.

"I'm just come of age this very day," said he, "and I'll show the critters I'm not made a man for nothing."

He certainly felt, as he afterwards confessed, a little skittish on this occasion, and his dog seemed not much to relish the excursion. Shearjashub had his gun, but had not the heart to fire at any of the birds that flitted about and seemed as if they were not afraid of coming nigh him. His mind ran upon other matters entirely. He was a long while on his way. Sometimes he would stop to rest, as he said to himself, though he was not in the least tired; sometimes he found himself standing still, admiring nothing; and once or twice actually detected his feet moving on the route home, instead of towards the mountain.

On arriving at the vast gates that, as it were, guarded the entrance to the glen, he halted to consider the matter. All was quietude, and sublimity. His spirit at first sunk under the majesty of nature, but at length became gradually inspired by the scene before him with something of a kindred dignity. He marched forward with a vigorous step and firm heart, rendered the more firm by hearing and seeing nothing of the white nymph of the rock or her gay music. He hardly knew whether he wished to see her or not, thinking, if she appeared, he might be tempted to run away again; and if she did not, the deacon and the girls would laugh at him worse than ever.

With these conflicting thoughts he arrived at the very centre of the gloomy solitude, where he stood a few moments, expecting to hear the music. All was loneliness. Repose lay sleeping on his bed of rocks, and Silence reigned in her chosen retreat.

"Is it possible that I was dreaming the other day,

when I was here, as those tarnal critters twitted me I was?" asked the young man of himself.

He was answered by the voice of the white girl of the mountain, exclaiming, in the same sweet yet clear, animating, trumpet-tones,

"Shearjashub! Shearjashub! listen."

Jashub's legs felt some little inclination to run away; but this time he kept his ground like a brave fellow.

Again the same cheerful air echoed through the silence of the deep profound, in strains of attractive yet simple, careless vivacity. Shearjashub began to feel himself inspired. He bobbed his head from side to side to suit the notes, and was once or twice on the point of cutting a caper.

He felt his bosom thrill with unwonted energies, and a new vigour animate his frame as he contemplated the glorious figure of the mountain nymph, and listened to her sprightly flageolet.

"Shearjashub!" cried the nymph, after finishing her strain of music, "listen!"

"Speak — I hear," said the young man.

"My name is Liberty: dost thou know me?"

"I have heard my father and grandfather speak of thee, and say they came to the New World to seek thee."

"Well, I am found at last. Listen to me."

"Speak on."

"Your country has just devoted herself for ever to me and my glory. Your countrymen have this day pronounced themselves freemen, and they shall be what they have willed, in spite of fate or fortune. But my blessings are never thrown away on cowards; they are to be gained by toil, suffering, hunger, wounds, and death; by courage and perseverance; by virtue and patriotism. The wrath and the mighty energies of the oppressor are now directed against your people; hunger assails them; force overmatches them; and their spirits begin to fail. Take this pipe," — and she flung him the little flageolet, which he caught in his hand. "Canst thou play on it? Try."

He put it to his lips, and, to his surprise, produced the same animating strain he had heard from the nymph of the mountain.

"Now go forth among the people and their armies, and inspire them for battle. Wherever thou goest with thy pipe, and whenever thou playest that air, I will be with thee and thy countrymen. Go, fear not; those who deserve me shall always win me. Farewell — we shall meet again."

So saying, she vanished behind a tuft of laurels.

Shearjashub marched straight home with his pipe, and somehow or other felt he did not quite know how; he felt as if he could eat gunpowder, and snap his fingers at the minister.

"What the dickens has got in the critter?" said the deacon, when he saw him strutting along like a captain of militia.

"I declare, Jashub looks like a continental," exclaimed the girls.

Just then Shearjashub put his pipe to his mouth, and played the tune he had learned, as if by magic, from the mountain nymph; whereat Deacon Mayhew made for the meeting-house, (whither all the villagers followed him), and preached a sermon, calling on the people to rise and fight for liberty, in such stirring strains that forthwith all the men, young and old, took their muskets and went out in defence of their country, under the command of Shearjashub. Wherever he came he played the magic tune on his pipe, and the men, like those of his native village, took to their arms, and went forth to meet the oppressor, like little David against Goliath.

They joined the army of Liberty, which they found dispirited with defeat, and weak with suffering and want. They scarcely dared hope for success to their cause, and a general gloom depressed the hearts of all the true friends of freedom. In this state the enemy attacked them, and threw them into confusion, when Shearjashub came on at the head of his troops, playing his inspiring music with might and main. And, as he came, the sounds seemed to awaken the spirit of heroism in every breast. Those who were retreating rallied; and those who stood their ground maintained it more stoutly than ever. The victory remained with the sons of Liberty, and Shearjashub celebrated it with the marvellous air, which echoed through the whole land, and wakened it to new triumphs.

After a hard and bloody struggle, in which the pipe of Shearjashub animated the very clods of the valley wherever he went, the promise of the nymph of the mountain was fulfilled. The countrymen of Shearjashub were free and independent. They were about to repose under the laurels they had reaped, and to wear what they had so dearly won.

Shearjashub also departed for his native village with his pipe, which had so materially assisted in the attainment of the blessings of freedom. His way lay through the chasm in the mountain, where he first encountered the nymph with the cap and snow-white robe. He was anticipating the happiness of seeing his aged mother, who had lived through the long war, principally on the excitement of news, and the still more near and dear happiness of taking to his bosom the girl of his heart, Miss Prudence Worthy, as fair a maid as ever raised a sigh in the bosom of lusty youth.

He had got to the centre of the glen when he was roused from his sweet anticipations by the well-remembered voice of the nymph of the mountain, who sat on the same inaccessible rock, under the same tuft of laurel, where he had first seen her, with an eagle at her side.

"Shearjashub!" cried she, in a voice which made the echoes of the rocks mad with ecstasy, — "Shearjashub! thou hast done well, and deserved nobly of thy country. The thought of that is, in itself, a glorious reward for toil, danger, and suffering. But thou shalt have one as dear, if not dearer than even this. Look, where it comes."

Shearjashub looked, and beheld afar off a figure all in white coming towards him, at the entrance of the glen. It approached nearer, and it was a woman; nearer yet, and it was a young woman; still nearer, and Shearjashub rushed towards it, and kissed its blushing cheek. It was the girl of his heart, Miss Prudence Worthy.

"This is thy other blessing," exclaimed the mountain nymph, the sight of whom made Miss Prudence a little jealous; "a richer reward for noble exertions than a virtuous woman I know not of. Live free, live righteously, and then thou wilt be happy. I shall be with thee, an invisible witness, an invisible protector; but, in the mean while, should the spirit of the people ever flag, and their hearts fail them in time of peril, go forth among them as thou didst before, and rouse them with thy pipe and thy music. Farewell, and be happy!"

The nymph disappeared, and the brief jealous pang felt by Miss Prudence melted away in measureless confidence and love. The tune of the mountain nymph was played over and over again at Shearjashub's wedding, and became known ever afterwards by the name of YANKEE DOODLE.

JONATHAN'S VISIT

TO

THE CELESTIAL EMPIRE.

JONATHAN'S VISIT

TO

THE CELESTIAL EMPIRE.

Somewhere about the year 1783, Jonathan, a young fellow who lived away down East, took it into his head to make a voyage to Canton. Accordingly, he fitted out his sloop, a tarnation clever vessel of about eighty tons, and, taking a crazy old compass for his guide, his two cousins (one a lad about sixteen) and a great Newfoundland dog for his crew, and a couple of rusty Revolutionary swords for an armament, boldly set forth on a voyage to the Celestial Empire.

Jonathan was a mighty cute lad, and had read a little or so about the great devotion of the Chinese to the herb called ginseng, which every-body knows is a remedy for all things. He happened one day to hear an Indian doctor give it as his opinion, that a certain plant which grew in the neighbourhood of Jonathan's birthplace was very much like the famous Chinese panacea, as he had seen it described. He took a hint from this, and rather guessed he would carry a good parcel along with him, on speculation. Accordingly, he gathered a few hundred pounds, which he dried, and stowed away in one of his lockers under the cabin floor.

Providence, which seems to take special care of such droll fellows as Jonathan, who calculate pretty considerably on their native energies, blessed him with fair winds and good weather; his old compass behaved to admiration; his old chart, which had been torn into fifty thousand pieces and pasted on a bit of tarpauling, proved an infallible guide; and, somehow or other, he could not exactly tell how, he plumped his sloop right into Table Bay, just as if the old fellow had been there a hundred times before.

The Dutch harbour-master was sitting under his hat on his piazza, when he beheld, through the smoke of his pipe, this strange apparition of a vessel scudding like a bird into the bay. He took it for the famous Flying Dutchman, and such was his trepidation, that he stuck his pipe into his button-hole without knocking out the ashes, whereby he burned a hole in his waistcoat. When Jonathan rounded to, and came to anchor, the harbour-master ventured to go on board to get information concerning this strange little bark. He could talk English, Dutch fashion, for indeed he had been promoted to the office on account of his skill in languages.

"Where did you gome from, mynheer?" quoth he.

"Right off the reel from old Salem, I guess," replied Jonathan.

"Old Salem — whereabout is dat den? I ton't know any sich blashe about here."

"I guess not. What's your name, squire?"

"Hans Ollenbockenoffenhaffengraphensteiner ish my name."

" Whew! why, it's as long as a pumpkin vine — now a'n't it?"

" But whereabout ish dish blashe you speague of?" reiterated the harbour-master.

" Oh, it's some way off — about six or eight thousand miles down West there."

" Six tousand duyvels!" muttered Hans with the long name. " Do you tink I vill pelieve such a cog and pull shtory as dat, mynheer?"

" If you don't believe me, ask my two cousins there — and, if you don't believe them, ask my dog. I tell you I come right straight from old Salem, in the United States of Amerrykey."

" United Shtaites of vat? I never heart of any United Shtaites but de Shtaites of Hollant."

" Ah — I suppose not — they've jist been christened. I s'pose, now, likely you've never heard of the New World neither, have you, mister — what's your name?"

" Hans Ollenbockenoffenhaffengraphensteiner I tolt you zo pefore."

" Maybe you'll have to tell me again before I know it by heart, I calculate. But did you never hear of the New World, squire?"

" Not I — ant if I hat, I vouldn't hafe pelieved it. Tare ish no new worlt zinze de tiscovery of de Cabe of Goot Hoop dat I know. Put, gome along, you must co vid me to de gubernador."

Jonathan puzzled the governor about as much as he had done the harbour-master. But his papers were all fair and above board, and the governor had heard not only of the New World but of the United States of Amerrykey, as Jonathan called them. Accordingly, he was permitted to enjoy all the privileges of the port.

Nothing could exceed the curiosity and wonder excited by the vessel among the people at the Cape. That she should have made a voyage of so many thousand miles with such a crew and such an outfit was, in their opinion, little less than miraculous, and the worthy governor could only account for it by the aid of witchcraft, which he had somewhere heard abounded in the New World. Jonathan was the greatest man, and his dog the greatest dog, at the Cape. He dined with the governor and the burgomasters, cracked his jokes with their wives and daughters, danced with the Hottentots, and might have married a Dutch damsel of five hundred weight and five thousand ducats a year, provided he would have given up old Salem for ever.

After partaking of the hospitalities of the Cape a few days, Jonathan began to be in a hurry to prosecute his voyage. He knew the value of time as well as of money. On the sixth day he accordingly set sail amid the acclamations of the inhabitants, taking with him a hippopotamus, an orang-outang, and six ring-tailed monkeys, all of which he had bought on speculation. One of his cousins had, however, been so smitten with the country about the Cape, or with the charms of a little Dutch maiden, that he determined to stay behind, marry, and improve the inhabitants — on speculation. A Dutch sailor offered to supply his place, but Jonathan declined, saying he guessed his other cousin and the Newfoundland dog, who was a pretty particular cute critter, could sail his sloop quite round the world and back again.

Not much of interest occurred during the voyage until he arrived at Macao, where he excited the same astonishment, underwent the same scrutiny, returned the same satisfactory answers, and came off as triumphantly as he did at the Cape of Good Hope. While here, he saw everything, inquired about everything, and went everywhere. Among other adventures, he one day accompanied his cousin in a fishing-boat, to see if they fished as the people did on the banks of Newfoundland. Unfortunately, a violent storm came on; some of the boats were lost and their crews drowned. The survivors went and offered up some of their paddles at the great temple of Neang-ma-ko. Those that were able added some matches and gilt paper. At Macao, it occurred to Jonathan's other cousin that he might make a speculation by curing the fish after the manner of mackerel: so he determined to stay there. Jonathan did not much like this, but he said, " Never mind, I partly guess I can do without him."

Jonathan had now no one but his Newfoundland dog to assist in the navigation of his sloop. But he thought to himself that his voyage was almost at an end, and, at all events, if he hired any of the Macao people, they would be offering up matches and gilt paper to Neang-ma-ko, instead of minding their business. So he set sail for Canton, the Chinese prognosticating he would go to the bottom, because he did not make an offering to Neang-ma-ko, and the Portuguese prophesying that he would go to the devil, because he did not pay his devoirs to the Virgin.

At Lin-tin he was taken for a smuggler of opium by some, and for a magician by others, when they saw his vessel, heard where he hailed from, and became convinced that his whole crew consisted of a Newfoundland dog. The commander of the fleet of ships of war stationed at Lin-tin, to prevent the smuggling of opium into the Celestial Empire, seized the sloop, and devoted its brave commander to the indignation of the mighty emperor, who is brother to the sun and moon. Hereupon Jonathan bethought himself of a piece of the herb he had brought with him and had in his pocket. "It is a mighty good chance," thought he, "to try if it's the identical thing." Accordingly, he took a convenient opportunity of presenting to the valiant commander a bit about as big as his finger. The admiral, whose name was Tizzy-Wizzy-Twang-Lang, stared at him at first with astonishment, then at the present with almost dismay, and, thrusting it into his pocket, immediately caused it to be proclaimed that the "foreign barbarian" was innocent of the crime, or the intention, of smuggling opium, and might go anywhere he pleased. Tizzy-Wizzy-Twang-Lang then sat down and wrote a despatch to the Governor of Canton, stating that he had routed the "foreign barbarians," destroyed their fleet, and thrown all their opium overboard. After which he shut himself up in his cabin, and took a morsel of the treasure Jonathan had presented him, about as large as the head of a pin. It is astonishing how much better he felt afterwards.

In the mean while Jonathan had set sail, and was ploughing his way towards Canton, with a fair wind and a good prospect of making a great speculation, for he had ascertained to a certainty that the article he had brought with him was the real ginseng, which was worth five times its weight in gold. He went ashore at the village of Ho-tun, where he saw the people catching wild ducks and geese, which they fatten by feeding in the dark. "That's a good hint," said Jonathan, shutting one eye, "and I'll tell the folks at old Salem." While he was walking about, looking into everything, he was unexpectedly saluted by a shower of stones from a parcel of children with their hair sticking up behind like two horns. Jonathan thought this tarnation ungenteel, but he prudently suppressed his anger, considering he was in a strange country, and was come to try his fortune.

"May I be buttered," quoth Jonathan, as he approached Canton, and saw the countless boats—"may I be buttered, if here isn't a city all afloat. This beats all nater!"

And, sure enough, here was a scene that might have made one of our Indians wonder. The whole world seemed on the water. Junks with two eyes staring at the bows, canal-boats, flower-boats, pleasure-boats, and boats of all sizes and descriptions, filled with all sorts of people, lay moored in regular streets, or were moving about to and fro in every direction, painted in all the colours of the rainbow, and ornamented with gold leaf and grinning monsters having no prototypes in nature, or anywhere else but in the grotesque imagination of the artists of the Celestial Empire.

The busy activity of some of these boats was singularly contrasted with the luxurious ease of others, in which might be seen a couple of Chinese dandies reclining on mats and resting their heads on bamboo pillows, with pipes in their mouths, either listlessly contemplating the scene before them, or gazing with lack-lustre eye on the picture of some favourite beauty with pencilled eyebrows, nails like a tiger, and feet almost invisible. Others were performing the ceremony of chin-chin-joss, which consists in throwing bits of burning paper into the water, while the din of innumerable gongs contributed to the scene a species of music that made honest Jonathan stop his ears in reverential dismay.

When our adventurer moored his sloop at Whampoa, in the midst of a fleet of vast ships of almost all the nations of Europe, they did not know what to make of her. All he could say failed in convincing them that he had come from such a long distance, in such a vessel, navigated by such a crew. Besides, what could have brought him to Canton? He had neither money to purchase, nor cargo to exchange for, Chinese commodities, except it might be his river-horse, his orang-outang, and his monkeys.

Jonathan kept his own secret. He had heard that the Chinese were as sharp as "the leetle end of nothing whittled down," and determined to be as keen as the best of them. Accordingly, nothing could be got out of him, except that he had come on his own bottom, and meant to turn a penny one way or another. He said nothing about his ginseng, which he had, as I before stated, stowed away in a secret locker.

The story of the strange man and the strange vessel that had been navigated from the New World by a man and a dog made a great noise, and thousands flocked to see them. The gentleman who officiated as American consul, without, however, having a regular appointment, behaved in the most kind and friendly manner to Jonathan, and introduced him to a hong, or, as our hero called him, a *hung*, merchant, who undertook to do his business for him, that is, if he had any to do, which seemed rather doubtful.

"I chin-chin you," said Fat-qua, the hong-man.

"You don't now, do you?" quoth Jonathan. "Well, then, I chin-chin you, and so we are even, I guess."

Fat-qua was very anxious to know all about Jonathan's business; but the Chinese were such plaguy slippery fellows, that he was afraid to trust him with his secret. He therefore, very gravely, and with infinite simplicity, commended to him his cargo of live stock, begging that he would dispose of them to the best advantage and invest the proceeds in a lading of notions. Fat-qua did not know whether to laugh or be angry — however, he concluded by laughing and promising to do his best.

The trifle which Jonathan brought with him had been all expended in maintaining himself and his dog, and Fat-qua did not feel inclined to advance any money on the security of his odd wares. This being the case, Jonathan one day brought a pound or two of his ginseng, and asked him, carelessly, what it might likely be worth in these parts.

"Hi yah!" exclaimed the hong merchant in astonishment. "No have got some more of he — hi yah!"

"Some small matter — not much," said Jonathan, who was of opinion that if he displayed the whole parcel at once it might lower the price, and injure his speculation.

Fat-qua disposed of the two pounds of ginseng for a thumping sum, which Jonathan pocketed in less than no time, and chuckled in his sleeve, as he thought of the means to get rid of the whole at the same rate.

A day or two after, he delivered the hong merchant a few pounds more, which he said he had accidentally found in a place where he had stowed it away and forgotten it.

"Hi yah! Missee Joe Notting, I chin-chin you." And he began to have a great respect for Missee Joe Notting.

In this way, by degrees, did friend Jonathan bring forth his hoard of hidden treasure, till it was all disposed of, and he found himself in possession of almost half a million of dollars; for, it is to be recollected, this happened long before the value of ginseng was brought down to almost nothing, by the large quantities carried to China in consequence of the successful venture of Jonathan.

Every time he produced a new lot, he declared it was all he had left, and, consequently, to the last moment, the price was kept up. Fat-qua began to believe that Joe Notting had discovered some hidden place where it grew, in the neighbourhood of Canton, or that he dealt with the prince of darkness. He accordingly caused him to be watched, but our hero was too wide-awake for the hong merchant.

"Hi yah! Missee Joe Notting — some yet more — when you shall think shall you no more have — hey? Every day here come you — say the last is he — hi yah! I think no last come for ever."

"I ha'n't another stick to save my gizzard," said Jonathan; and, this time, he spoke like a man of honour. He had at last sold out his hoard, with the exception of a small parcel for presents, and to use on an emergency.

Jonathan was now thinking he would gather himself together, and point his bowsprit straight towards home. But he determined to see about him first, for he expected to be asked a heap of questions when he got among his old neighbours; and not be able to tell them all about the Celestial Empire would be to show he had little or no gumption.

He accordingly visited the famous flower-garden of Fa-Tee, where he saw a fine collection of the most beautiful flowers, and roses of all colours. Returning, he passed through the suburb of Ho-Nam, where he was called Fan-kwei, which means "foreign devil," and pelted handsomely with stones, according to the hospitable custom of the inhabitants.

Jonathan was now so rich, that he felt himself a different man from what he was when the boys stoned him at the village of Ho-tun. He had, moreover, seen the bamboo so liberally employed on the backs of the Chinese by their own officers and magistrates, that he thought he might make use himself of this universal panacea for all offences in the Celestial Empire. Accordingly, he sallied forth among these inhospitable rogues, and plied his stick so vigorously that the rabble fled before him, crying out, "Fan-kwei!", and making motions significant of cutting off the head, as much as to say that would be his end at last. The reader must know that beheading is considered the most disgraceful of all punishments in the Celestial Empire, where they do everything differently from the rest of the world.

A formal complaint was laid before the *Gan-chat-sze*, a minister of justice at Canton, against the Fan-kwei, who had feloniously bambooed the mob of Ho-Nam. Fat-qua, one of our hero's securities, was taken into custody till his appearance, and an express was sent off to Pekin to announce to the brother of the sun and moon that a Fan-kwei had beaten at least two hundred of his valiant and invincible subjects, who could not bring themselves to soil their fingers by touching even the clothes of a foreign barbarian.

Jonathan was soon arrested, and, being carried before the illustrious *Gan-chat-sze*, was astonished at seeing the infinite mischief he had done. There was one poor man who had had his eye put out; another, his head fractured; a third, his arm broken; and, what was worse than all this, three children were so disabled that they could not stand; — all by Jonathan's bamboo, which was about as thick as your finger.

This was a serious business for a Fan-kwei. But his friend Fat-qua whispered in his ear —

"Hi yah — Missee Joe Notting — you some more have got of that grand — hi yah! You stand under me — hey?"

Jonathan tipped him a knowing wink, and Fat-qua then crept close to the ear of the incorruptible *Gan-chat-sze*, and whispered him in like manner; but what he said, being only intended for the ear of justice, must not be disclosed. The effect, however, was miraculous; the *Gan-chat-sze* forthwith started up in a mighty passion, and, seizing his bamboo, attacked the complainants in the suit with such wonderful vigour, that he actually performed a miracle, and restored every one of them to the use of their limbs. After this, he discharged the offender with a caution, which Fat-qua translated into excellent English; and the next day Jonathan sent him, by the hands of the same discreet friend, a pound of ginseng.

"Hi yah! Missee Joe — more some yet, hey? Believe him make him as him go along. Hi yah! Chin-chin you, Missee Joe Notting."

Fat-qua was determined to signalize this triumph of Chinese justice over prejudice against foreigners by a great feast of bears' claws, birds' nests, and all the delicacies of the East. He therefore invited a number of the Fan-kweis about the factory to meet Jonathan at his country-seat, near the gardens of Fa-Tee, and they had a jolly time of it. Our hero was complimented with a pair of chopsticks of the most elegant construction and materials, which he managed with such skill, that, by the time the dinner was over, he was wellnigh starved to death.

The "hung merchant", Fat-qua, was a jolly little fellow, "about knee-high to a toad," as Jonathan used to say, and fond of a good glass of wine. He plied his guests pretty neatly, until they began to feel a little top-heavy and rolled away one by one under rather high steam, leaving Jonathan alone with his friend, the latter fast asleep. Jonathan was by this time in high feather, and thought this would be a good time to take a peep at the establishment of his friend, that he might know something of these matters when he got home.

He arose without disturbing the little fat gentleman, and proceeded to penetrate into the interior of the house, until he came to the female apartments, in one of which he saw a young lady smoking, to whom he paid his compliments with a low bow. Her pipe was formed of slender pieces of bamboo, highly polished, with a bowl of silver and a mouth-piece of amber. Her hair was beautifully long and tastefully dressed with flowers and gold and silver bodkins, and the whole atmosphere of the room was perfumed with jasmine and other odoriferous plants and shrubs. By her side lay a guitar, on which she seemed to have been playing.

The entrance of Jonathan threw her into great confusion, and she uttered several violent screams, which, however, brought no one to her assistance. The illustrious Fat-qua was still sleeping in his seat, and the servants making merry, as usual, with the remains of the feast. Jonathan attempted an apology for his intrusion, but the more he apologized the louder the young lady shrieked. Jonathan wondered what could be the matter with her.

"Well, I never saw anything like this growing among corn — what's come over the gal? May I be chiselled if I don't think she's afeard I'll eat her. But, why the dickens, if she's frightened, don't she scamper off, that being the most nat'ral way of getting out of danger?" Jonathan did not know the feet of the screeching damsel were not more than two inches and a half long, and that she could no more run than fly. They were what the Chinese poets call a couple of "golden lilies."

Encouraged by this notion, that her pretending to be frightened was all sheer affectation, he approached her still nearer, took up the guitar, and begged her to play him a tune, such as "Yankee Doodle," or anything of the sort that was pretty easily managed, for he did not much admire any of your fine fashionable whimseys. Jonathan was a plaguy neat kind of a chap — as handsome a lad as might be seen; tall, and straight, with blue eyes, white forehead, and red cheeks, a little rusted, to be sure, with the voyage.

The pretty creature with the little feet, whose name was Shangtshee, ventured at last to look at this impudent intruder, and, sooth to say, he did not appear so terrible at the second glance as at the first. She smiled, and put out one small foot for Jonathan to admire. She then took her guitar, and played him a tune — it was not "Yankee Doodle" to be sure, but it rather pleased Jonathan, for he declared it beat all, he'd be switched if it didn't. Shangtshee seemed to understand the compliment, for she smiled, and put out her other golden lily, I suppose to show Jonathan she had a pair of them. Jonathan admired the pipe; she handed it to him, he put it to his lips, and, on receiving it again, she put it to her lips, which our hero finally concluded came as near to kissing as twopence to a groat.

"How the critter blushes," thought Jonathan. He did not know she was painted half an inch thick, after the fashion of the Chinese ladies. As they sat thus exchanging pleasant little civilities, which, innocent as they were, endangered both their lives, they were alarmed — at least the lady was, (for Jonathan had never particularly studied Chinese customs) — by the sound of a guitar in the garden. It approached, and, in a few minutes, seemed directly under the window of the apartment. Shangtshee appeared greatly agitated, and begged Jonathan, by signs, to depart, the way he came. But Jonathan had no notion of being scared by a tune, and declined to budge an inch. It was a nice tune, and he didn't much mind if he heard another just like it.

Presently the music ceased, and all at once the young Shangtshee screamed a scream almost as loud as the former ones. "What can have got into the curious varmint, now, I wonder?" quoth Jonathan. He little suspected she had caught a glimpse of the face of her lover through the blinds. This young man was called Yu-min-hoo, which signifies feathered, because he was a great poet, and took such high flights that his meaning was sometimes quite out of sight. He always carried an ink-bottle suspended to his button, a bamboo pen stuck behind his ear, and a book under his arm, in which he wrote down his thoughts, that none might escape him. He made verses upon Shangtshee, in which he compared her to a dish of bears' claws, since her nails were at least six inches long, and she was a delicacy which the epicure might admire every day in the year. It was this sentiment which he had set to music, and sung on this eventful evening under the window of his mistress.

Yu-min-hoo was petrified when he saw his Shangtshee sitting so cosily by the side of a Fan-kwei, which, as I said before, means foreign devil. His indignation was terrible, and his jealousy prodigious. He had thoughts of sitting down by the light of the moon and writing a furious ode, consigning the Fan-kwei to all the Chinese devils, which are the ugliest in the world. Even their gods are monsters; what, then, must the others be? On second thoughts, however, Yu-min-hoo restrained his muse, and in a moment or two they heard the clatter of his wooden shoes gradually receding. Shangtshee again entreated with her eyes, her hands, nay, her very feet, that Jonathan would make himself scarce. The tears ran down her cheeks, and, like torrents of rain, wore deep channels in them that almost spoiled their beauty.

Jonathan tried all he could to comfort her, when,— (imagine his surprise and indignation at her base ingratitude!) — he was greeted with a scratch of those long nails that constitute the most unequivocal claim of a Chinese lady to rank. It was a scratch so emphatic and well directed, that every nail, and most especially the little finger nail, left its mark on his cheek, and it was preceded and followed by a scream of the highest pretensions.

Our hero was astounded at this salutation. He had heard of love-taps, but never of such as these. But he soon understood the whole squinting of the business as slick as a whistle, when he saw little Fat-qua standing before him, breathing fire, and looking fury with his dark sharp-cornered eyes.

"Hi yah! Missee Joe Notting — s'pose tink you daughter my one flower-woman — hey?"

Jonathan endeavoured to convince Fat-qua that there was not the least harm in sitting by the side of a young woman in a civil way — that it was done in his country every day in the year, particularly on Sundays — and that the women there were quite as good as in China, though they did not wear wooden shoes and nails six inches long.

Fat-qua was wroth at this indecorous comparison of the Fan-kwei ladies with those of the Celestial Empire, and ordered his servants to seize Jonathan, as a violator of Chinese etiquette, and a calumniator of wooden shoes and long nails. He determined, in the bitterness of his heart, to have him immediately before the worshipful *Gan-chat-sze*, who would not fail to squeeze some of his dollars out of him.

But further reflection induced him to abandon this course. He recollected, when the fumes of the wine were somewhat dissipated, that both himself and his daughter would be disgraced and dishonoured if it were publicly known that she had been in company with a Fan-kwei, a stain of the deepest dye, according to the statutes of the Celestial Empire, in any but the common women. The only way, therefore, was to make the best of a bad business. Accordingly, he bribed his servants to secrecy — married his daughter to the poet — and swore never to invite another Missee Joe Notting to dine with him so long as there was a woman in his house. He had never, he said, met with a fellow of this *chop* before.

Various were the other adventures of our hero, which are recorded in the annals of the Celestial Empire, where he figures as "The Great Fan-kwei, Joe Notting." My limits will not suffice to particularize them all, else would I relate how he was fined a thousand dollars by his old friend, the *Gan-chat-sze,* for bambooing a valiant sentinel who refused to let him enter the gates of Canton without a bribe; and how his river-horse, being tired of confinement, took an opportunity to jump overboard, whereby he upset a boat, and came nigh drowning the passengers. This cost him three thousand dollars more. His next adventure was picking up the body of a drowned man in the river one evening, in passing between his sloop and the shore, whose murder he was found guilty of before the *Gan-chat-sze,* who kindly let him off for ten thousand dollars, advising him, at the same time, through the hong merchant, Fat-qua, to take the earliest opportunity of making himself invisible within the precincts of the Celestial Empire.

"I partly guess I'll take his advice, and pull up stakes," said Jonathan. "I never saw such a tarnal place. It beats everything, I swow. Why, Squire Fat-qua, I'll tell you what — if you'll only come to our parts, you may go jist where you please — do jist as you please — and talk to the gals as much as you please: I'll be choked if it isn't true, by the living hokey."

"Hi yah! Missee Joe Notting," replied Fat-qua, "she must be some very fine place, dat Merrykey."

"There you are right, squire. But, good-by; I conclude it's best to cut stick. They're plaguy slippery fellows here: if they a'n't, may I be licked by a chap under size."

Jonathan received the remainder of his money, which he was then earnestly advised to invest in bills, and at the same to sell his vessel, and embark for home in a safer conveyance.

"D'ye think I'm a fellow of no more gumption than that?" said he. "I'll be darned if there's a tighter, safer thing than my sloop ever sailed across the salt sea; and, as for your paper-money, I've had enough of that in my own country in my time."

He declined shipping a crew, for he said he must trust, in that case, to strangers; and he thought to himself that he could easily induce his two cousins to go home with him, now he was so rich. It happened as he had anticipated: both gladly rejoined him, each having failed in his speculation. The Dutchmen at the Cape prohibited the one from using a machine he had invented for saving labour, lest it might lower the price of their negroes; and the Portuguese and Chinese refused to eat the fish of the other, because he neither crossed himself before the picture of the Virgin, nor burned gilt paper to the image of Neang-ma-ko.

A prosperous voyage ended in Jonathan's happy return to Salem, where he became a great man, even to the extent of being yclept honourable. He lived long and happily, and his chief boast to the end of his life was, that he had been the first of his countrymen to visit the Celestial Empire, and the only man that navigated with a Newfoundland dog for an officer.

THE HISTORY

OF

UNCLE SAM AND HIS BOYS.

THE HISTORY

OF

UNCLE SAM AND HIS BOYS.

ONCE upon a time there lived, and lives still, in a country lying far to the West, a famous squire, rich in lands and paper-money. Report made him out to be the son of John Bull, who, as every one knows, has children in all parts of the world. But, if the truth were told, I believe he had a great many fathers, though his mother was a very honest woman, for he looked like as many people as there were hairs on his chin. But old Squire Bull had the credit of being his father, and truly there was a great likeness between them. Like Bull, he was somewhat given to boasting, tippling, fighting, and sailing boats; and was apt to hold his neighbors in contempt, dubbing them a pack of snivelling, pitiful rascals, that did not dare to call their souls their own, or look their king in the face, as every cat had a right to do. He took after his father in another respect; that is to say, nobody could tell which he was most fond of, making money like a horse, or spending it like an ass. But, for all this, he did not so much favour John Bull but that you could now and then catch an expression in his face that put you in mind of every-body you had ever seen in the world.

John Bull had christened this son of his by the name of Jonathan; but, by and by, when he became a man grown, being a good hearty fellow, about half horse half alligator, his friends and neighbors gave him the title of Uncle Sam; a sure sign that they liked him, for I never in my life knew a respectable nickname given to a scurvy fellow. Be this as it may, his family and all his acquaintances at last came to call him nothing but Uncle Sam; and all his beef, pork, and flour, in fact everything that belonged to him, was marked with a huge U. S., six inches long.

As I have a great respect for universal example, I shall give him this name in the sequel of my history, which I hereby commend to the special attention of all wise men, more especially the wise men of the East. As to the fools, every body knows they are so scarce nowadays, that I hereby snap my fingers at and defy them.

I flatter myself no man living is better qualified for this piece of biography. Uncle Sam and I have been hand and glove these fifty years. Many are the bouts we have had together when boys; many the frolics we have kicked up among the buxom young hussies, who now are all honest, sober, mothers of families; and many the bottles we have cracked together at sundry times and on divers occasions, during the good old days when, if a man did not choose to be merry sometimes himself, he did not cry out against those who did. Uncle Sam was a sad fellow at raccoon-hunting, and a barbecue was his delight, until it got to be the custom to talk politics and make long speeches at them.

Uncle Sam, in early life, gave some offence to his father, about going to the meeting-house instead of the church. One word brought on another, until John Bull at length took to beating the poor fellow into conformity with his notions. He was a lad of spirit, that would put up with this from no man, not even his father; and, accordingly, without saying a word to any body, he packed up his all and marched off into the wide world, to seek his fortune.

As you may suppose, Uncle Sam had little to begin with; but he was a stirring blade, who did not mind trouble at first, if he could only see his way clear to something better in the end. He set himself to the business of clearing and selling new lands. As fast as he became pretty comfortable on one farm, he sold out at a profit and set off for another; so that he was seldom more than two or three years in the same place. But, for all this, he never lost sight of the main chance; since there was nothing on the face of the earth he loved so dearly as a bargain or a profitable speculation. By good management and good luck he at last came to have a vast property in lands, which he was every day adding to, by buying out the Indians, or taking farms for debts that were owing him. In short, he prospered in all his undertakings, and became, in process of time, a great man among his neighbours. But, to my mind, he was not above half as clever a fellow as when he was poor. Then he was a jolly, careless, high-minded dog — generous as a prince, and hospitable as a Turk. Though he would swear a little at times, he never meant any harm by it. But, as he got rich, he aspired to be mighty genteel; aped the manners of all the would-be fashionable stragglers that came along; never invited any body to his house except to show off his new finery, and left off all his honest old habits by little and little.

The fact is, he took to canting, and turned the embroidered side of his jacket outward, as a Turk does when he goes to court. Many people doubted whether he was anything the better for this; and, if I must speak my mind, I think he lost more than he gained; for, as respects myself, I had rather a man should rip out and drink punch a little, than pick my pocket while he is prating about brotherly love and good-will to all men. If Uncle Sam is angry at this, let him scratch his back and get pleased again.

As Uncle Sam got rich, and withal stout, and lusty as a young giant, the neighboring gentry, who called him an upstart, and looked askance at his prosperity, would shake their heads very wisely, and cry out, "Ah! poor man, to be sure he looks well and hearty; but any body can see with half an eye he is not long for this world." And then they would sigh, and take a pinch of snuff to the success of their prognostications. But it happened, somehow or other, that every attack he had, and every rub he met with, only served to show the strength of his constitution, and make it still stronger, until at last these false prophets began to say to themselves, "The rogue will last forever."

Now, I don't pretend to say this would be the case, seeing there is an end to all things; but I verily believe he would have lived to a happy and green old age, had it not been for the undutiful behaviour of his children, which made his latter days one scene of trouble and turmoil.

You must know that, as soon as Uncle Sam thought himself able to maintain a family comfortably, he got him a wife, who proved an excellent house-keeper, and, in the course of years, his children amounted to I am afraid to say how many; all jolly, strapping, roistering blades, with the exception of two or three, that were rather stinted in the growth, or, as Uncle Sam used to say in joke, "shrunk in the boiling." These last were rather conceited and jealous, as I suspect most little people are.

As fast as these lads grew up, Uncle Sam portioned them off on his farms, which they were to pay for when they were able, at very low prices. They all turned out pretty industrious fellows, with the exception of here and there one who got all his work done by negroes. They differed in some respects; but there was a family likeness among them — all took after the mother, who was a pretty considerable particular talker. One was a famous fellow for cod-fishing; another a great hand at splitting shingles; a third was an amateur of road-making and ditching; a fourth was mighty fond of barbecues, taking after his father in that respect; a fifth dealt largely in wooden bowls and onions; a sixth was a great cultivator of rice and cotton; a seventh was a pretty high-handed fellow, fond of a good horse, and of an independent, open-hearted spirit: — and so on. They all lived together like loving brothers, having a rich father who could do what he pleased with his money — that is to say, they were as jealous of each other as two cocks running in the same yard.

If Uncle Sam made a Christmas present to one, or conferred a special kindness on another, there was the deuse to pay among the rest. They accused the old man of being partial, and allowed him no rest until he put them all on a level; which he had no sooner done, than they, one and all, began to grumble and find fault, saying the poor man was in his dotage, only because he had not given each one a preference over his brother. Uncle Sam sometimes said to himself, "Happy is the man who has nothing, for his children won't quarrel about his estate."

But this was not the worst of it. The old Harry got into them about improving their farms, which they all swore was Uncle Sam's business; he was devouring all the money they could rake and scrape together to settle for the lands he had sold them. They said it was a sin and a shame for him to make them pay everything, seeing they were his natural-born children, entitled to bed, board, education, and an outfit. Besides, daddy was now become so rich he did not know what to do with his money, and it was actually a kindness to rid him of its management in his old age.

Thus these cunning varlets agreed in the propriety of sharing Uncle Sam's money, but they fell out about the manner of dividing it, like a parcel of undutiful rogues as they were. The big fellows argued that they ought to share according to weight, and insisted they should all go down to the mill and be weighed. But the little fellows who had been "shrunk in the boiling" demurred to this, and swore it was all in my eye, Betty Martin. They were as much the lawful sons of Uncle Sam as the best and biggest of them, and were determined to have their share at the point of the bayonet. There was one, particularly, who lived on an island about as big as my thumb-nail, who talked like a giant, and threatened to dissolve the family union and set up for himself if they did not treat him like a full-grown man. They had a great many hard bouts at words, and some of the neighbours feared they would come together by the ears. But though they quarrelled like so many old women, like old women, they seldom came to blows. They had a sort of sneaking kindness for one another at the bottom, which always prevented their proceeding to extremities.

At the same time they were forever falling out about nothing, or some trifle next to nothing, and never gave each other a good word except when they all put their heads together, as they often did, to diddle Uncle Sam out of a few thousands for the improvement of their farms. Fortunately, however, for his pocket, it was seldom they could agree about the division of the spoils, or it would not have been long before he was as poor as a rat.

Be this as it may, the good man had no peace of his life, and was several times on the point of making over all his property to build meeting-houses and educate the children of other people. Certain it is, he had good reason to do so, for these undutiful boys left him no rest day or night, on account of his money. Not being able to agree to the plan of dividing Uncle Sam's surplus income according to weight, it was proposed to do it by measure; but here again the little fellows that were "shrunk in the boiling" made a most infernal rout, and opposed it tooth and nail.

They swore they were as good as the big fellows, any day in the week; and they insisted that the apportionment should be made according to merit — not weight or size. All agreed to this, and the matter was just on the point of being amicably settled, when a trifling difficulty occurred in adjusting the scale of desert. The roistering barbecue fellow swore he was equal to any man you could shake a stick at; the splitter of shingles maintained the superiority of his art; the young squire, who was fond of riding a fine horse and doing nothing, declared he considered himself the most of a gentleman; the raisers of rice and cotton claimed precedence on the score of administering both to the back and stomach; and the little fellow that lived on his island put in his claim on the score of morality. This would not do, and so the old man escaped being plundered that time.

But these fine boys had another iron in the fire, which they heated till it was red-hot. Quoth one of the rascallions — I believe it was the barbecue chap —

"Let us set about improving our farms, and make the old boy pay the piper."

Upon this scheme they agreed, and set up a hurrah about internal improvement, which means digging ditches, pulling up snags, and making roads through the desert.

Upon this one of them went and set up a loom in his back building, for the encouragement of domestic industry, as he said, and hired other people to come and tend it. When he had done this, he went to Uncle Sam, and insisted on a handful or two of money, to encourage him in such patriotic and praiseworthy undertakings.

"Stop, there, my little fellow," cried the biggest brother of all, who had a fist like a sledge-hammer; "stop, if you please — I have set up my looms at my own expense, and I'll be switched if the old man is going to pay you for doing what I have done for myself."

Then another started a blacksmith shop for making hobnails, and advanced the same claim to touch a few thousands of the old gentleman's money for the encouragement of domestic industry, which about this time began to be very low-spirited, and wanted a little patting.

"Avast, there, you landlubber," exclaimed one of the brothers, a bold, hearty Jack tar, who had sailed round and round the world, and was a mighty navigator. "Avast, there; none of your fresh-water gabble. I should like to know the reason why you should be paid for making hobnails, any more than I am for building ships. Avast, there, I say, you lubber, or I'll be foul of your dead-lights."

Next came another brother, who was a great hand at raising sheep, which he called being a wool-grower, to demand that, as people could not exist without clothes, Uncle Sam should shell out a few dollars to reward him for being a great public benefactor.

"Fudge!" exclaimed the cotton-growing brother, — "where one man is clothed in wool, a thousand wear cotton. Why not encourage me, then, instead of this woolly fellow? Away with your bleating, or I'll be into your mutton before you can say Jack Robinson."

Next came a sober, sedate, economical brother, who had set up a shoe-shop, and wanted Uncle Sam's protection — that is to say, some of his money.

"Rot your sole," cried the high-handed gentleman, who despised hard work, and had rather ride a blood-horse than make his own shoes, a thousand times — "What are you talking about, there? It's mighty natural, to be sure, that you should be asking encouragement for making shoes. If it were horseshoes, now, I'd talk to you."

So saying, he mounted his steed, and challenged Uncle Sam to run a race for a thousand dollars.

After this — (there was no end to their persecution of the poor old man) — after this came another brother, a great mechanical genius, who had invented a machine for peeling apples, and wanted encouragement of Uncle Sam for the great saving of time and labour in making apple-pies.

"Whoo! whoo! whoop!" cried the wild, harum-scarum, barbecue boy, one of Uncle Sam's youngest sons, who had just settled a town away off West, and had not yet cast his moccasons; "whoop! mister, mind which way you point your rifle there — I can turn a flip-flap somerset, grease your head with bear's meat, and swallow you whole without a pang. You'd better take keer how you steer your steam-boat, or you'll run foul of a snag."

By and by came another of this hopeful family, with a long story of the great advantage Uncle Sam would derive from clearing out a ditch, at his own expense, for the benefit of other people.

Here the great big fellow mentioned before, who was the richest of the brothers, put in his oar and cried out : —

"None of that fun, Brother Jonathan; I've done all my own ditching myself, and I'll be teetotally rumswizzled if I am going to let daddy pay you for just the same sort of work. Dig your own ditches, my boy, as I dug mine."

Then came a fine fellow, one of the young fry, who wanted to persuade Uncle Sam to pony up for a lane he was about making from his barn to his bog-meadow, which he assured the old man would be a vast public improvement; for that, whereas his carts stuck in the mud now, they would be able to get along like a streak of lightning as soon as it was done.

"Thunder and blarney!" exclaimed three or four of the elder brothers all at once, "haven't we made our own roads at our own cost, and without asking daddy for a cent; and do you think, you snivelling blockhead, we'll stand by and see the old man cheated out of what belongs to us?"

"Goody gracious!" at length cried Uncle Sam, throwing up his eyes — "goody gracious, what can be the matter with these boys! I believe they mean to eat me up alive. I wish — I wish I was as poor as Job's turkey."

Now, all that was required for Uncle Sam to be just as he wished was to let the boys have all his money, as they desired. But, what is a little odd, he never thought of this, and continued wishing himself poor, without once hitting on the best possible way of becoming so.

Things went on, getting worse and worse, for some time afterward. Uncle Sam was almost every day pestered for money to pay for some improvement or other in the boys' farms. He kept an account of these, and the amount they would cost, and found that it would take all he was worth in the world, and more besides, to get through with half of them. So, one day, he put his hands in his breeches' pockets, and swore roundly they were a brood of ungrateful rogues that wanted to get him on the parish, and not another penny would he fork out for man or beast.

This raised a terrible hue and cry among the boys, who threatened to disinherit the old man, and set up for themselves. But he was a pretty stiff blade when his pluck was up, and he thought himself in the right. You might as well try to move a mountain as Uncle Sam, when he put his foot down and toed the mark. He told the boys he had honest debts, and meant to pay every penny he owed in the world before he began to talk about laying out money in improvements.

These graceless young scamps were a little stumped at the stand Uncle Sam had taken, and began to plot together to turn the old man out of house and home and take possession of all his estate, as soon as they could bring matters to bear. Accordingly, they went about among their neighbours, insinuating that he was incompetent to manage his affairs any longer. It was high time, they said, that he should give up his estates into their hands, and set about preparing for a better world. They raised all sorts of stories against him, — how he did not care any more about the law or the gospel than a pagan; how he tucked up people just for the pleasure of seeing them kick their heels in the air; and how he threatened to cut off the ears of a member of Congress, only because he told stories about him.

In this way these roistering boys raised a great

clamor against Uncle Sam, which emboldened them at last to hatch a diabolical plan for taking away all his lands at one blow. They were not content with getting them by degrees, to pay for building schoolhouses, teaching dumb people philosophy, and a thousand other things; but they now determined to make one business of it, and strip the old gentleman as bare as my hand.

Not finding any law for this, they determined to get one passed for the purpose; to pave the way for which, they spread abroad a hundred cock-and-bull stories about this, that, and the other thing. They swore the land of right belonged to them when they came of age, according to an old settlement, which declared that Uncle Sam's children should all share his estates equally after his death. But they kept the latter part to themselves, as you may suppose, and pretended that they had a right to take the old man's property while he was alive. Besides, they would say, the poor gentleman don't know what to do with so much land; half of it lies waste for want of proper attention, and, if we only had it, we would make it ten times more valuable, and pay the taxes, which he is exempted from by virtue of an ancient charter.

The notion of getting money by taxation is a bait which generally takes with people whose business consists in law-making and not in tax-paying, as I have always heard. So the legislators who had authority where Uncle Sam's property lay rubbed their hands, and were mightily tickled with the notion of being able to squeeze a little money from his new lands. Perceiving that this argument told, the boys devised another complaint, about Uncle Sam's receiving all the money for the lands he sold, and then forcing those who bought them to work their fingers to the bone to make themselves whole again, as if this were not the way all over the world.

Uncle Sam defended his bacon to the last, like a stout old hero as he was; but by degrees the influence of these twopenny varlets prevailed, and a law was passed, taking away all his property and dividing it equally among the boys, so that those who were "shrunk in the boiling" got the same portion as the big roistering blades, who, rather than not come in for a slice, consented at last to share, and share equally. They were all specially enjoined to take care of Uncle Sam, and see that he wanted for nothing; but the poor old man fared pretty much as people generally do who make over all their property to their children in their lifetime. At first they treated him pretty well, for decency's sake; but gradually deprived him of all his usual comforts. First, they took away his pipe, because the young madams the sons had married could not bear tobacco-smoke. Then, the eldest boy seized possession of his arm-chair and his seat in the chimney-corner. Next, they removed the blankets from his bed, on the ground that it would injure his health to lie too warm; and next, nearly starved him to death, for fear he should die of apoplexy. Finally, losing all respect for the ties of blood, and all recollection of the early benefits they had derived from the good old man, they fairly turned him out of doors. The last I heard of Uncle Sam, he was in the poor-house.

THE HISTORY

OF

UNCLE SAM AND HIS WOMANKIND.

THE HISTORY

OF

UNCLE SAM AND HIS WOMANKIND.

I TOLD you, some time ago, about the unseemly behaviour of UNCLE SAM'S BOYS: how they wanted to divide his new lands among themselves; and how they quarreled about the old man's not doing his duty by them, in the way of protection. But, as it did not concern my business at that time, I said nothing of his daughters, of whom he had a goodly family, all buxom, industrious damsels; nor of his wife, who, as all the world knows, talked and scolded by the hour, and was never quiet in the house five minutes at a time; so that, what between the boys, the girls, and the old woman, Uncle Sam had a time of it — especially during the winter season, when they had nothing to do but sit disputing in the chimney-corner from morning till night.

The old lady, Uncle Sam's wife, according to the marriage-contract, had a HOUSE and establishment of her own, where she played the mistress finely, and bit her thumb at him, as if he had been nobody, instead of her wedded husband. Report said, and I believe it spoke truth this time, that she was a mighty capricious body, that hardly ever knew her own mind; and, instead of treating her children on all occasions alike, had ever some pet or other among them, on whom she lavished her favours, to the exclusion of the rest, for the time being. But, on the whole, she made Uncle Sam a tolerable wife, as times go, and took special good care of his money, except when it was to be spent on her own back. She always made out to have plenty of cash for her household expenses, and never wanted pin-money, though the rest of the family might be destitute enough. She was exceedingly jealous of her dignity, and never would let Uncle Sam have a finger in any pie of hers; though, sometimes, when the worthy old gentleman put his arms a-kimbo, and plucked up courage to say NO to some of her extravagant schemes of domestic improvement, she made a great to-do, and cackled about the house for all the world like an old hen that has lost her last chicken.

The daughters were, in the main, honest, industrious, good girls; but they took after the old lady, in being most mighty talkers; and, beside this, had a pestilent notion that Uncle Sam did not do by one as he did by the other. He never patted one on the cheek, or kissed her rosy lip, that the rest did not pout in a corner for a whole day; and, if he happened to give one of them a new gown or a pair of ear-rings or any such matter, the others would spit fire at him, like so many mad pussy-cats, and raise a fine dust in his chimney-corner. But, notwithstanding these kick-ups, they were a very *united* family, and prided themselves on having a common interest in everything. In truth, the little bickerings they sometimes had were nothing but April showers, that, as it were, cleared the air, and produced a fresh crop of good-will and sisterly affection. One thing was repeatedly observed of them, that let them be quarreling never so hard, they almost always pulled together against a common enemy.

But, after living in this way, sometimes falling out, and invariably making friends again, until many of them had grown up, a bone of contention was somehow thrown in among them, which, it was feared, would at length dissolve the family union, that, notwithstanding these little squalls, had furnished an example of prosperity and happiness to the whole country round, insomuch that the neighbours looked up to it with equal envy and admiration. It seems that some of the girls, being, as I said before, naturally given to industrious habits, and fond of making a trifle of pocket-money for themselves, had set up various little domestic manufactures within doors, such as spinning, weaving, making straw-bonnets, and the like; which the others, being inclined to different occupations, such as cultivating the garden, attending to the dairy, and, it may be, sometimes reading romances and poetry, did hold in great contempt, and take every opportunity to laugh at incontinently. This by degrees bred a terrible hubbub in Uncle Sam's family, insomuch that the worthy patriarch had no rest night or day, and at divers times applied to the old lady to interfere. But he only burnt his fingers, for every-body said she generally made matters ten times worse by trying to mend them.

Things went on at this rate for some time, and

Uncle Sam was privately heard to declare, that he most devoutly wished all the young baggages fairly married and settled off; "though," added the good simple soul, "heaven help the man that undertakes to manage them." At length, step by step, by little and little, a habit of contention grew up among them, so that they never met without having a fling at each other. One party became perfectly idle, out of pure spite; and the other spent all their time in huddling together, scolding and talking, and coming to resolutions to play the deuse, and turn up jack in the HOUSE, if something was not done to quiet the idle jades who did nothing but skim novels and write verses.

By the marriage-compact between Uncle Sam and his wife, it was agreed that matters of import in the family affairs should be talked over and settled in the old lady's premises, and under her special sanction. All the privilege reserved to the old gentleman was that of saying YES and NO; with a special injunction, that he should avoid the latter on all occasions, on penalty of a good scolding from his wife and short commons at dinner. The old gentleman, after casting about, and turning the matter this way and that, inside and out, upsidedown and topsy-turvy, and cudgelling his brains till they foamed up like whip-syllabub, at length determined to call these refractory damsels before the old lady in her own house, and leave it to her to settle the matter. At the same time he could not help laughing in his sleeve at what a devil of a job he had bequeathed her. "Let them scold it out," thought he; "I wash my hands of it." So he sat himself down and smoked his pipe, like a hearty old cock as he was.

Now the obstreperous damsels were accordingly called together before the old lady, who had a hot cup of strong tea ready for them, and, having initiated each into a little gentle excitement by plying her with the cooling beverage, desired them to tell what they had to say in as few words as possible; for the old lady loved to hear herself talk a great deal better than she did any body else, you may depend upon it.

The first that spoke was one of the elder sisters, the eldest but one, who was called Miss Massy Twoshoes, a notable, clever, sensible, well-educated, girl, a great lover of cucumbers and dumb-fish; (but she was a pretty particular loud talker, for all she liked dumbfish). She stated to the old lady, in as many words as possible, what I shall not repeat, for the special reason that I will not be accessory to increasing the burthens of posterity, which will be condemned to bear enough without my aid, provided it is obliged to read all that has already been spoken and written on the subject. Suffice it to say, that Miss Massy made out a tolerably clear case, and proved, to the satisfaction of every-body that was of the same opinion before, that domestic industry consisted entirely of work done in manufactories, two or three miles from home; that spinning-jennies were the corner-stones of national prosperity; and weaver's-beams the best of all possible weapons of defence against a foreign enemy.

The next sister that spoke was Miss Carolina, who was reckoned one of the genteelest of the family, though her complexion was a little bronzed, on account of sleeping in a room that fronted the South, where she was rather too much exposed to the sun. Whether this southern aspect affected her temper or not, I can't tell, but she was a high-spirited little body, and had lately given the old woman, and Uncle Sam too, a great deal of uneasiness, by threatening to marry against their consent, and set up for herself under his very nose. She was a fine girl, but rather fond of show, and somewhat extravagant with her allowance, in consequence of which she was sometimes short of money. All this she laid at the door of Uncle Sam's partiality for some of the other sisters, though it was shrewdly suspected that her being so often out of pocket was partly owing to her having such a fierce hankering after travelling and junketing about all summer, that, the moment the birds began to sing and the flowers to bloom at home, neither the old man nor the old Harry could keep her within doors. Like the wild ducks and geese, she was seen flying North as soon as the rivers and lakes were clear of ice. But for all this I can't help saying that, if I were a bachelor, I should like to have such a baggage for a wife, though she is so great an enemy to union that I fear I should have some trouble to keep her in order.

Be this as it may, Miss Carry made a considerable long talk, in which she clearly showed, to the satisfaction of those who did not disagree with her, that domestic industry was occupying one's self abroad instead of at home; that spinning-jennies were the foundation of all abominations, and not the pillars of independence; and that she herself would undertake, with a sling and a stone, to discomfit all the weaver's-beams in the universe, with Goliath at their head. How she proved all this I can't explain; for, may I be "eternally onswoggled," as they say in Kentucky, if I am not so utterly confounded with elucidations, vindications, declamations, and observations on this horrible subject, that if I do not lose my wits before it is finally settled, I shall certainly, in pure gratitude, found an hospital for politicians who have lost their reason by reasoning.

Miss Massy and Miss Carry, being the antipodes or extremes in this case, like the blades of a pair of shears, got all the other sisters crimped up between them, and, as it were, almost cut them in two. There was Miss Pen, a bouncing girl in a Quaker bonnet, a plain industrious creature, but a great belle just about this time, because she had a big voice, held the purse-strings, and carried mighty sway in the family, insomuch that the rest of the sisters complained that for several years past Uncle Sam and his wife had spent more money on her than on all the rest of the girls put together. Pen had a charming face, and an agreeable aspect; but, if you looked at her back, she was rather Dutch-built, as they say.

Then there was Miss Virginia, the eldest of the girls, who, I confess, was a great favorite of mine, though a little proud, and on the shady side of thirty. She was an independent damsel, who always thought for herself and acted for herself. She took her own way in every thing, and went quietly to work, without scolding or making a hubbub in the family, except on very special occasions. I always thought her a girl of excellent principles, and looked upon her as one of the main-stays of Uncle Sam's family, which she often presided over with dignity and discretion. Virginia was no great hand at the spinning-jenny and weaver's-beam, but she was fond of rural economy, and delighted in the innocent and gentle excitements of a country life. Above all, she knew her own mind, which is an excellent thing in man or woman; and, it was said correctly, you always knew where to find her, to wit, at home.

There was also Miss York, as she was called; for I ought to have observed before, that Uncle Sam and his old woman had a queer notion of naming many of their daughters after a parcel of sixteenth cousins beyond sea. Miss York was the largest of the family, a buxom, easy-tempered creature, who had so many employments about the house, that she did not fly into a passion when one of them was interfered with. If she had any fault, it was that of not knowing her own mind for half an hour together; though, in justice to her, I must observe that she accounted for these frequent changes from north to south, and from east to west, very ingeniously. She was perfectly independent, she said; and girls that could do as they pleased had a right to change their opinions as often as they pleased, or where was the use of being one's own mistress? The rest of the girls often taunted her with this, but she got off very well by saying it was better to be a feather, blown about by the wind, than an old, rusty weathercock, which, if it once got wrong, remained so to the end of time. Probably one reason why Miss York seemed sometimes to float about, as it were, without rudder or compass, was, that she grew so very large that when a notion sprung up in one end of her head it had so far to travel to reach the other that it died of old age before it arrived there; and so, when an impulse waked up in her heart, body o' me! if I don't suspect it fell fast asleep before it arrived at the extremities. While it was glowing in one place, the other remained quite cool; and it seldom or never happened, that every part of this stout spinster was under the same impression at one and the same time. Now your little people, like Miss Rhoda, another of Uncle Sam's daughters, are not subject to such contingencies. A spark will set them on fire from the roof to the cellar, and the smallest atom of a little local interest, like a stone thrown into a puddle, will agitate them from the centre to the circumference. It is next to impossible to make a very large person angry all over at once, while the prick of a pin will convulse a little contentious body like Miss Rhoda. I thought it meet to say thus much in behalf of a young woman with whom I have long kept company, and for whom, I confess between ourselves, I have a bashful predilection, especially as some certain persons, who owe all their consequence to her patronage and good-will, have lately taken upon themselves to disparage her before Uncle Sam and the old woman, more than once. I maintain that she can hold up her head on every occasion and everywhere, with any of Uncle Sam's girls, and snap her fingers at her detractors, who are no better than they should be; and, indeed, not half so good, for that matter.

On one side of Miss York sat a sly little toad, Miss Connecticut — a hard name for a spinster; (but, never mind, young ladies always live in hopes of getting rid of such incumbrances;) and on the other, a tight, small affair of a damsel, known among the family as little Jersey Blue, from her having a couple of as beautiful blue eyes as ever looked through a pair of spectacles. Little Conn, as she was called, was a mighty snug, steady-going girl; a trifle prinky, but not averse to a training or a thanksgiving-frolic. There was nothing she loved like sparking it of a Saturday night; and nothing she abominated like travelling on Sundays, unless to church to be married. She had several sweethearts in her day; but, somehow or other, lost them all. However, she did very well by the matter, for she prosecuted them for a breach of promise, and recovered damages sufficient to console the most inconsolable damsel that ever died of a broken heart. She was an industrious, pains-taking body, and the best hand at house-keeping among Uncle Sam's daughters. She saved all the goose-feathers, and could make wooden nutmegs that would deceive any of the Coenties Slip grocers.

Little Jersey Blue and Miss York slept in the same room, together; but, as frequently happens, they did not agree the better for that. It seems that an old gentleman, called in the family Uncle Charles, had, a great many years ago, when they were very young, bequeathed them each a piece of land, which when they grew up they cultivated as garden-plots. A creek ran between them, which abounded in fish and oysters, of which the girls were excessively fond; and they were eternally disputing about this matter, though every body said there was quite enough for both of them. Miss York claimed the whole creek, because, she said, her piece of land was six times as large as the other; but little Jersey Blue, who had a tongue and a temper of her own, flouted such notions. She said, that if Uncle Charles was such a fool as to give her sister all the land, she was not such a fool as to give up all the water, and therefore she was re-solved to have her full share of the oysters. This bred great contentions between them, insomuch that I am sorry to say they at last got to pulling caps over a fine oyster-bed. Hereupon the friends of the family interfered, and advised them, as they were both of age, to go to law about the matter, which many people thought was getting out of the frying-pan into the fire. However, Miss York, being, as I said, a good-natured, fat, spinster, consented to waive her rights, and both sides referred the matter to the justice, each secretly determining in her own mind to submit quietly to his decision, provided it was in her own favour: and thus the affair stood at the period of which I speak.

But it is high time I say something of Uncle Sam's youngest daughter, who, because she slept in the west chamber of the house, which was very large, went by the name of the Great West; for she was quite stout of her age, and had grown up, like Jack's bean-stalk, in a single night, and presumed not a little on her great size. Some people said she had rather outgrown her discretion, but it was behind her back, for if she had heard it, I warrant you she would have given them a sound box on the ear. She was a wild, graceful hoyden, that cared nothing for dress, and was all the while riding on horseback; that is when she could get a horse to ride, for Uncle Sam was very much afraid she would meet with some accident, she rode at such a rate. But she was a fine, high-spirited girl, an honour to the family, and one who would make an excellent wife to a man that carried a tight rein and sat stiff in the saddle. There were several other daughters, whose names I shall not particularize in this place, but who, (some of them at least), will be noticed by and by.

The time being come, they all appeared in their best bibs and tuckers, in the presence of the old lady, who had thrown open the great hall of the HOUSE, and made up her mind, for the first time since she was married, to listen instead of talk. Uncle Sam kept at an awful distance, for he had heard enough about this business to serve him all the rest of his life. Being requested to speak according to their respective ages, and not to interrupt each other, Miss Virginia opened the case.

She was moderate, didactic, and metaphysical; but, on the whole, made a very respectable figure on the occasion; and, as she had a right to do, (being the eldest), treated the younger girls to a weary deal of good advice about obeying their parents, loving each other with a sisterly affection, and preserving the family union. When she came to this part of her speech, little Carry could stand it no longer, but interrupted her in a great passion.

"Union!" said she — "marry, come up! I should like to know what I get by the family union, but cuffs, instead of coppers? See here, I have calculated the value of the union to a fraction, and find that I have lost at least six and eightpence of my pocket-money by it, already."

Then she showed her calculation, which would have puzzled Mr. Bowditch himself, for she knew no more about ciphering than the man in the moon.

"Well, my dear Carry," said Miss York, with her usual good-nature, "suppose you *have* lost six and eightpence — what then? You have only to stay at home next summer, instead of travelling about as you do every season, and you'll save ten times as much.

Now do be a good girl, do Carry, and mind what your parents say to you."

"I'll tell you what, sister," replied Miss Carry, "you'd better go and look to your oyster-beds, and let me alone."

And then she fell to calculating the value of the family union, again; but, happening to miss a figure or two, she made out her losses to be so great, that she almost fell into hysterics. I ought to have mentioned, in the beginning of this true history, that, after Uncle Sam had been argued out of his lands in the manner I formerly stated, he grew so poor, that each of the girls who had come in for a share of the family spoils was obliged to pay her proportion of the expenses of house-keeping.

When Miss Virginia had got through, Miss Massy Twoshoes replied, and talked a great deal about the old story of spinning-jennies and weaver's-beams. But as this is a worn-out topic, I shall refer to the seventeen thousand volumes of documents, reports, addresses, speeches, &c., that have been perpetrated on the subject. She concluded by giving poor little Carry a lecture on disobedience to her parents; but she got as good as she gave, for the peppery brunette cut her short.

"The less you say about that matter, Miss Goody Twoshoes, the better," said she. "I suppose you have forgot, for it is very convenient to have a short memory sometimes — I suppose you have forgot, when daddy was fighting, not long ago, with old John Bull, in defence of his bacon, how you sneaked away, and said John was in the right, and that your poor old father deserved a good beating! And don't you remember how you threw up your eyes, like a great hypocritical old maid as you are, and refused to rejoice, when he at last got the better of his antagonist? Ha! hah! Miss Goody Twoshoes, I've not lost my memory, though it seems you have."

Miss Massy did not pretend to deny this, but flung up her hands, and exclaimed, " what a little vixen!"

Miss Virginia, and Miss Pen, and Miss Georgiana the next sister to little Carry, and the Great West, all called out shame on her, for treating her elder sister in this manner; but as for Miss York, she had got such a wipe about her oyster war, that she sat with folded arms, as quiet as a lamb. But little Carry was a match for them all. She turned to Virginia, and exclaimed,

" *You* needn't talk, madam : — how long is it since you wrote a saucy letter to our father, telling him as much as that he was an old fool, and didn't know his own rights, or those of his daughters? If I don't mistake, you were very obedient then, for you threatened, if he didn't mind his p's and q's, you'd quit his house and kill your own mutton. As for *you*, Miss Pen, with your Quaker bonnet and smooth face — how I *do* hate hypocritical faces! — as for you, Miss — I am almost ashamed to talk about such a filthy subject — but didn't you once fly in the face of our good father, (at least I thought him so then), because — because — pshaw! it makes me sick to think of it — because he raised the price of his whiskey? And as for *you*, Miss Georgiana, you'd better go home and take care of the poor old Cherokee Indian you want to turn out of the farm old uncle Charles left you, like a great oaf as he was; and you'd better go and settle that matter about the parson — you understand me, sister. Marry, come up! instead of lecturing and lecturing one in this manner, I tell you again, I've calculated the value of the family union to a fraction, and settled the balance by Cocker's Arithmetic, and there's an end of it."

Then she turned round to the Great West : —

" As for you, you great overgrown awkward thing, you'd better go home too, and put on your moccasons. Only look at the creature, in her homespun frock, stitched with bark, and pinned with great thorns! What a pretty figure you'd make in a drawing-room — and who's your mantua-maker, pray? I suppose *you* don't remember either, when you threatened the old gentleman, to run away, the Lord knows where, because he did not choose to go to loggerheads with one of his neighbors, about a mill-stream he would not let you sail bark-boats on? Once for all, I tell you, you're all as deep in the mud as I am in the mire, and had better be quiet about the family union. There isn't one of you that has not deserved to be well switched, half a dozen times."

This broadside pretty conclusively silenced Miss Massy Twoshoes and the rest of them, and almost overawed the old lady, who could not help in her heart, however, being proud of a daughter so much like herself, in the matter of having a tongue in her head. After considering a short time, she looked round, and fixed her attention on Miss York, whose good-temper and discretion she looked to, in a great measure, for settling all the family feuds. She accordingly called upon her for an opinion on the best mode of bringing about so desirable a consummation.

The good spinster was somewhat puzzled. The truth is, her head had one opinion, and her heels another; the heart was pretty decided, but the ends of the fingers and toes, being, as I observed before, such a great way off, had each a different bias, and could by no means be brought to a proper understanding with each other. The consequence was, the poor girl was pulled so many different ways, that she could hardly hold together, and spoke first on one side of the question, then on the other, until Satan himself would have been puzzled to tell her real opinion, if she had any, which was doubtful.

Now, if I had been the old lady, I should have made something like the following speech.

"Sit down, you overgrown goose, sit down till you can make up your mind to say something a body can understand. And now hear me, young ladies. Touching the blessings and advantages of the family union, which I hope none of you doubt or disparage, except Miss Carry, who I advise to stay where she is, for nobody else will take in such a little vixen — touching the family union, I say, I trust there is no necessity for me to point out its benefits and blessings. Miss Carry may calculate them if she pleases, but I can't help laughing to think of her pretending to cipher, when I remember she never could tell the amount of three yards of calico at sixpence a yard. But, as I was saying — what was I saying? — O!, you will never agree, if you continue to differ in this way all your lives: at least, that is my present opinion. The best manner of settling this question will be, to think of the manifold advantages of sisterly and domestic union — the strength, the wealth, the dignity and happiness it communicates to all — and not, like Carry there, calculate the six and eightpence it costs to keep the pot boiling and the chimney-corner warm. And then, how unseemly and wicked it is, for sisters to be always squabbling and fighting, and calling each other names, and falling into fits of envy and jealousy, because one outgrows the other, or is a little handsomer; or because their parents give one a ring, another a new gown, another a pair of silk stockings. Such carryings-on disgrace a family, let it be never so prosperous, and prevent its members ever being happy or respectable. I'll tell you what, girls, you will become the laughing-stock of the neighbourhood, and not one of the young men will ever cast a sheep's-eye at you. You'll never be married if you go on in this way; and as for Carry, I pity the poor man, if there be any such desperate character in the world, who should undertake her guidance. She'll lead him a dance, I'll be bound. My dear daughters, I beg of you now, join hands, be friends, sisters, again, and each follow your own tastes, inclinations, and employments, without interfering with those of the others. Massy, and the rest of you that like, can spin and weave, while you, Virginia, and those that choose, may cultivate your fruits and vegetables and garden-flowers, and milk the cows, in peace and quiet. All these employments are equally useful in their proper sphere, and under proper discipline, and all essential to the welfare of your father's house. Come now, be good girls — kiss, and be friends — and may heaven bless you all, my dear daughters."

But, instead of making such a discreet commonplace speech as this, the old lady talked all round the compass ten times worse than Miss York. She declaimed and flourished away, first lauding the spinning-jenny and weaver's-beam, then denouncing them as pestilent innovations and praising the simplicity of a country life and rural occupations, until neither she herself, her daughters, nor any body else, could tell what her opinion on the subject was. In short, after talking herself dry, and tiring her hearers to death, she concluded by coming to no conclusion, at the same time beseeching the girls to have patience, keep their tempers, shake hands, and be friends.

"Well, for my part," said Miss Massy Twoshoes, "I have not the least objection, provided I can have my will in one thing."

"Nor I," said Miss Carry, "on the same condition."

"Nor I," echoed all the others in chorus.

"My dear children," cried the old lady, with tears in her eyes, "how your poor old father will be delighted with your dutiful submission. And what is it my darlings would have? What is this condition?"

"That we each of us have our own way in everything," cried the sisters, in full chorus.

The old lady was struck dumb at this new mode of preserving the family union.

"Go," said she at length, "go to your old father, receive his blessing, and quit our presence forever, if such is your wicked will."

The refractory baggages obeyed her for once in their lives, and departed, crying out together, "Divided we stand, united we fall."

Thus was the great union of Uncle Sam's family dissolved forever. But the vengeance of heaven overtook these unnatural children. Wherever they went, people pointed their fingers at them, and cried out, in their hearing, "here are the foolish virgins, that calculated the value of a family union by pounds, shillings, and pence, and left the house of their father because they could not have their own way in every thing." Nobody would receive them, nobody would associate with them, and they wandered about in rags and beggary, a prey to each other, a scoff to the virtuous, a mark for the finger of scorn. They lived, and died, miserably. Poor Carry, the ringleader in this monstrous affair, was inveigled into the arms of a wily stranger, who, after robbing her of all she had, honour, virtue, reputation, and fortune, "flung her like a worthless weed away," and left her to perish by the roadside.

HASCHBASCH,

THE PEARL-DIVER.

HASCHBASCH,

THE PEARL-DIVER.

Haschbasch was held, by general consent, the best diver in all the Gulf of Ormuz. He would plunge deeper, stay longer, and come up drier than any half-horse-half-alligator in the whole western hemisphere. But, somehow or other, he was always unsuccessful; if he brought up both hands full of oysters, ten to one they did not contain a pearl; so that at last he got to be a byword among his fellows, who used to call an oyster without a pearl, "one of Haschbasch's oysters."

One day, after frequent disappointments in diving, he, in a fit of despair, threw an oyster, which he knew was too plump and healthy to have any pearls in it, so violently against a rock hard by, that it broke the shell; whereupon he was not only astonished, but alarmed, to see a volume of smoke ascending from the fragments. As it gradually cleared away, he beheld a little squab genius, with an oyster knife in his hand, and so fat that he might well have passed for the personification of a veritable Blue-Pointer.

Haschbasch contemplated the droll figure till he recovered from his terror, and fell to laughing with all his might. At length he exclaimed,

"Who art thou, and whence didst thou come?"

"I am the Genius of Oysters," replied the strange little man, "and I came from the bottom of the sea. How daredst thou break my palace in this rude manner?"

Haschbasch apologized very respectfully, and explained the cause of his violence, at the same time appealing to his compassion for pardon.

"Thou lookest so round and jolly," said he, "I am sure thou must be good-natured. I never heard of such a person that was otherwise."

"Well," said the placable genius, "I will not be an exception. I forgive thee; nay, I will reward thee; for, between ourselves, I was a prisoner when thou didst release me. I was shut up by a tyrannical necromancer of an alderman, for eating oysters in a month that had no *r* in it. I owe thee a good turn — dive just where I throw this."

So saying, he flung a chip into the sea, and Haschbasch obeyed his commands. The queer genius swallowed the contents of the broken oyster at one gulp, and, waddling down to the wave, disappeared in its blue bosom.

In a few minutes Haschbasch came up with both hands full of oysters, each of which, on being opened, was found to contain a pearl as big as a pigeon's egg.

At that moment the genius emerged from the waters, and, after puffing like a porpoise, exclaimed, "Go to Ispahan;" and again vanished, having only come up to take a mouthful of air.

Haschbasch concealed his prize from every eye, and shut his lips on the subject as close as an oyster. He took leave of little Flimflam, the black-eyed daughter of the collector of the schah's tribute, (who, if he had dreamed of the large pearls, would have had his head off in less than no time), and, promising soon to return, departed for the renowned city of Ispahan, where Schah Hussein, who called himself the "king of kings," then reigned, if not in the affections, at least in the fears of his people.

Haschbasch, after considering a day or two concerning the best manner of disposing of his treasure on his arrival at Ispahan, at length determined upon going to the fountain-head at once. We know not where he got his experience, but he had somehow found out that in matters of business it was always best to deal with principals.

Accordingly, one day when the great "king of kings" was amusing his people with the royal farce of, "pride in the garb of humility," and listening very condescendingly to petitions he forgot the next moment, Haschbasch threw himself on his face, licked a reasonable quantity of dust, and in tones and words of genuine Eastern humility begged an audience of, the vicegerent of Allah, the master of the universe, and the example of the angels.

Schah Hussein was tickled at these new and illustrious titles, which he thought were peculiarly applicable to him, above all his predecessors, not excepting the great Rustan himself, who is celebrated in the "Epic of Ferdousi," which contains twenty thousand bad verses. He ordered Haschbasch to wait the conclusion of the farce, and then attend him at the palace.

The diver crawled after him to his royal residence,

and, being admitted on all fours, most submissively petitioned for a private interview, on a matter of the utmost consequence. He did not forget to conclude by calling the schah, as before, "vicegerent of Allah, master of the universe, and example of the angels." The schah was melted into compliance, and beckoned him to follow to his private apartment.

When there, Haschbasch prostrated himself three hundred and sixty-five times, the vicegerent counting all the while with his fingers.

"Well, slave," cried the schah, "what would thy insolent presumption have? Take notice, if thy business is not of sufficient moment to excuse thy bold request, thou art as dead as the man who offended me yesterday by sneezing in the midst of a speech I was making to the representative of the Giaours, who came to offer me tribute."

Haschbasch thought he had got himself into a pretty predicament, and trembled so that he could scarcely find the pearl as big as a pigeon's egg, which he had brought with him. The schah began to be alarmed, lest he should be fumbling for a dagger to despatch him; and was just on the point of calling for help, when he was struck almost dumb by the sight of the magnificent bawble.

"Allah!" cried he, snatching it out of the hands of the shivering diver—"Allah! can I believe my eyes! Is it not the ghost, the shadow, the counterfeit of a real pearl? If it be, slave, tremble! for thy life shall pay the forfeit of my disappointment. Hast thou any more like this?"

Haschbasch assured him there was not such another in the world, and that it was genuine.

The schah, on comparing it with some which he wore about him, became satisfied. He debated in his own mind whether to purchase it at any price, or make short work of the affair, by cutting off Haschbasch's head and becoming his heir according to the laws and customs of Persia, that is to say, the will of the "king of kings."

Justice, however, prevailed. He recollected the charming titles Haschbach had bestowed upon him, and that he had thus enabled him to triumph over his barbarian neighbour, the Giaour of Russia, who had just drubbed him soundly, and possessed himself of two or three of his finest provinces.

"He has not such a pearl in his diadem!" exclaimed he, mentally. — "What is thy price for this treasure? Quick — tell me this instant, or —"

"Example of the angels!", cried Haschbasch, "a mere trifle — nothing but to make me governor of the city, with the title of prince, and appoint a deputy to do the drudgery, while I pocket the honours and the money."

"Thou art the most reasonable of slaves," cried the schah in transport; "I would have given thee the city, and all the inhabitants for slaves, rather than have missed this opportunity to eclipse the barbarian Giaour. Give me the pearl, and take thy wish."

The bargain was struck, and Haschbasch departed, governor of Ispahan, and a prince. The next day he took possession of his post, and appeared in a turban as large as a small balloon. The people neither missed their old governor, who had met the destiny of the bowstring, nor wondered at their new. They were used to such matters.

Haschbasch was a tolerable ruler, as times go. He made a number of wise regulations, which he forgot to see put into execution; and issued a vast quantity of proclamations, to which nobody paid the least attention. However, he boasted of the reformation he had brought about, and smoked a golden pipe, eighteen feet long, with entire satisfaction. His deputy was a capital fellow: according to contract, he did all his excellency's work for him — but he did not give him all the money. He thought he had a right to a trifle of sly bribery and extortion, on his own proper account — and what deputy can blame him?

Haschbasch for a while was as happy as a little king; nay, much happier than a little king in these degenerate days. Nobody troubled him with protocols, and non-intervention. He had his dancing-girls, his story-tellers, his poets, and his parasites, who swore by Allah he was fit to be Schah of Persia. He ate hugely of the richest viands; he drank, under the rose, wine dearer than Chateau Margaux; he sung odes of Hafiz, till he could neither see nor hear; and, in time, he waxed as fat as the Genius of Oysters.

But — alas! that mortal man cannot enjoy all these things without paying more for them than they are worth! — Haschbasch began to be sleepy all day, and wakeful all night. His deputy took upon him all the duties of his principal, and Haschbasch could not eat, and drink, and sing odes, and admire the dancing-girls for ever. He sometimes longed for a dive, by way of variety, even though he should bring up nothing but oysters without any pearls.

One hot, debilitating day, he sat in a listless, tedious, laborious sort of apathy, in a cool gallery that overlooked the street. He yawned once, twice, thrice, and at length exclaimed, audibly, though almost unconsciously, to himself,

"Oh, Allah! if I only had SOMETHING to do!"

"Oh, Mohammed! if I only had NOTHING to do!" answered a voice in the street, directly under the gallery.

He looked down, and beheld a diminutive hunchback of a fellow, about four feet high, and as crooked as a ram's horn, bending under two heavy buckets.

"Who art thou? cried Haschbasch, rubbing his eyes.

"Buzbuz, the water-carrier," replied the other.

"What wouldst thou?"

"I should like to be a governor. Thou saidst just now, thou didst want something to do, and I want nothing to do. Let us exchange, and each will have his wish."

"Thou art a merry slave. I cannot give thee my office, but I constitute thee my jester. Thou shalt make me laugh, and I will make a man of thee. Come hither."

"Thou must add a cubit to my stature before thou canst do that; however, I accept thy offer, and, if thou only knewest how lazy I am, thou wouldst pity me."

Buzbuz proved an invaluable auxiliary in assisting Haschbasch to kill time. His spirits were inexhaustible; and, if not always witty, he never lacked impudence, which sometimes does just as well. At length Haschbasch willed him to give some account of himself.

"I was born crooked, as thou seest me now," said he, "which was a great happiness; for I never knew what it was to be straight, and therefore escaped the curse of being miserable by comparison. I was apprenticed to a water-carrier, who made me carry twice as much as other people, because, as he wisely said, there was no danger of spoiling my shape; and I was just on the point of trying to better my fortune, by making the most of my figure in a matrimonial speculation, when your highness had the good-fortune to take me into your service. Such is my history; now, tell me thine. I bet my old buckets against thy turban, thou hast been a diver in thy time."

"Why so?" said Haschbasch, somewhat startled.

"Why, because thou art always bobbing thy head, as if thou wast going to plunge into the water."

"Thou art a sage," said the governor, and related his story, substituting a single pearl for the handful he had acquired through the favour of the Genius of Oysters.

"Oh Prophet!" exclaimed Buzbuz, "what is the difference between a pearl-diver and a water-carrier, that thou shouldst make a governor of the one and a jester of the other? Destiny, destiny, thou art more blind than a bat — she at least sees in the dark."

Haschbasch laughed at this sally; but he soon had cause to repent of the disclosure of his early life. Buzbuz was continually joking about his former calling; and, though he always did it when they were alone together, it was not relished. Haschbasch loved to hear others made game of, but to be made game of himself was quite a different affair.

On one occasion, the great mufti of Ispahan, a sort of Mohammedan archbishop, came to visit Haschbasch in state, to negotiate a marriage between the governor and his niece, who was a first-rate beauty, and very fond of hearing the odes of Hafiz. There was any quantity of ceremony between them, and the matter was finally settled.

"Thou didst bow to the great mufti just as if thou wert going to take a dive for pearls," said Buzbuz when he was gone, laughing ready to kill himself. But he soon laughed on the wrong side of his mouth. The governor became wroth at length, at being so frequently reminded of his profession, and turned his jester neck and heels into the street.

"Never mind," quoth Buzbuz, as he took up his old buckets — "never mind; from the capital jester to a dull governor, I am become a poor water-carrier, once more; who knows but, from a stupid governor, thou mayst become a half-starved pearl-diver again."

"Off with his head!" cried Haschbasch, like King Dick in the tragedy. But the carrier disappeared in a twinkling, and he never laid eyes on him again.

The marriage of Haschbasch and the niece of the great mufti took place shortly afterwards; and, for a few days, he was the happiest of all governors, except the governor of one of the "old thirteen." But his wife, whose name was Fatima, was a perfect Mrs. Bluebeard for curiosity. She ransacked every hole and corner of the house, to see what was in it; and nothing baffled her but a small box of gold, so massy she could not break it open, and so fastened that she could not come at the secret.

The next day, the next, and the next, she was observed to be low-spirited, and her low-spirits increased with every passing hour. Haschbasch sometimes found her in tears, which he kissed away; but, though this act of kindness ought to have stopped the tears of any reasonable woman, those of Fatima only flowed the faster. Haschbasch conjured her to tell him the cause of her sorrows; but she shook her head mournfully, and sobbed out,

"Thou-ou-ou — do-do-dost not — lo-v-v-e — me — ech!" — and her heart seemed almost ready to break.

The governor swore by the sacred camel of Mohammed, and by the white beard of her uncle the mufti which was not half so white as her fair neck, that he loved her better than his office. But even this did not satisfy her, and in less than a week she took to her bed.

Poor Haschbasch was almost distracted. He went to her, and, kneeling at her bedside, or rather — to be orientally orthodox and particular — at the side of her couch, swore by the Prophet, that there was nothing on the face of the earth he would not do to convince her of his affection.

"Tell me, tell me," said Fatima, in a weak and plaintive voice, — "what is contained in the little gold box thou keepest so carefully closed from thy devoted wife?"

"Beard of the Prophet!" exclaimed the husband, "how didst thou come to know of that box?"

"By accident, lord of my soul," said Fatima; "but thou hast sworn, and here I promise to be a happy and obedient slave to thee if thou wilt open it in my presence."

Haschbasch dared not break his oath. Turning all the attendants out of the room, he proceeded to the secret depository, brought back the box, and touched the unseen spring. His wife shrieked, clasped her hands, and almost fainted at the sight of a dozen pearls as large as pigeons' eggs. She was never tired of handling and admiring them; and the governor was at length obliged to force them from her, which occasioned a paroxysm of her old disorder.

Her illness increased every hour, until Haschbasch again became alarmed, and was wrought upon to make her the same rash promise, and with the same rash sanction, as before.

The lady took him at his word, and demanded her choice of the beautiful pearls. Haschbasch trembled, and obeyed; but, ere he did so, he related the history of the bargain with the schah, to whom he had sold a similar pearl, under a solemn assurance that it was the only one of its kind in the universe.

"My office, nay, my head, will pay the forfeit of the discovery of this falsehood. Take thy choice; but, before thou dost so, promise to me, on thy duty as a wife, thy faith as a true believer, that thou wilt never wear this bawble, nor disclose to any living being that it is in thy possession."

Fatima complied, the pearl became her own, and her health was restored, as if by miracle. The old mufti ascribed it to his prayers and a vow to get up a grand pilgrimage to Mecca if his niece recovered. Nothing could equal the childish delight of the governor's lady, in the possession of a pearl as large and as perfect as that of the great schah himself. She looked at it ten hours every day, and it seemed as if she would never be tired of admiring it. The thought, however, at last struck her, on a sudden, that there was little pleasure in its possession so long as nobody knew of it. She might as well not have it at all.

From that moment she began to be unhappy. One day, the dearest friend she had in the world called to see her, wearing a beautiful amethyst her husband had just presented her.

"If I could only show her my pearl, as large as a pigeon's egg and as white as the beard of the mufti, how blue she would look," thought Fatima.

The temptation was irresistible. After exacting a solemn pledge of secrecy, she exhibited the inestimable treasure to her friend, who almost fainted at the sight.

"She will tell some of her acquaintances," thought Fatima, "who will tell it to others; and it will soon be known, I hope. A fig for the schah, and the terrors of the governor."

But her friend was faithful to her word, and poor Fatima was sorely disappointed. A grand festival was now at hand, and she determined, at all risks, to exhibit her pearl to the eyes of all but the schah, who would thus, in all probability, remain ignorant of the deception practised by Haschbasch. On that unlucky day the governor was somewhat indisposed, and did not attend the ceremony, at which the schah himself officiated. Fatima, thus freed from the controlling eye of her husband, dressed herself in all the splendours of Eastern vanity, and placed the pearl in the centre of a turban, glittering with gold and precious stones.

Great was the envy and admiration excited by the jewel, and millions of questions were asked of Fatima concerning its origin and history; but she kept the secret, and her imprudence might possibly have passed without any serious consequences, had not the whispers of admiration reached the ears of the schah, who demanded a sight of the wonderful bawble. Fatima advanced, trembling like an aspen leaf, and the schah turned pale with rage. He snatched the pearl from her turban, and compared it with his own. It was equally large and equally beautiful, and the passion of the schah persuaded him it was actually superior in both respects.

"Slave!" cried he, most ungallantly,—"slave! whence came this pearl?"

"My husband gave it me," answered she, sinking at his feet.

"And where is the slave, the traitor? why is he not here?"

"He is gone to fulfil a vow at the mosque, without the city, for the recovery of his health," said the poor wife, resolved to make one effort for the safety of the governor.

"Follow him, and drag him hither alive, to answer for deceiving the vicegerent of Allah," exclaimed the schah.

The unhappy Fatima was permitted to go home, which she did as fast as possible. In agitated haste she met her husband, bidding him fly for his life without further explanation, for not a moment was to be lost. Disguising themselves, they mounted a pair of swift horses, and, taking an opposite direction from the mosque whither the guards of the sultan had gone in search of Haschbasch, fled towards Ormuz like chaff before the wind. Fatima, in the midst of her troubles, did not forget to secure the gold box and the beautiful pearls.

Favoured by their disguise and a series of lucky

accidents, they arrived in safety at the Gulf of Ormuz, among the old friends and associates of the diver.

"Welcome, Haschbasch!", exclaimed they.

"And welcome poverty!", cried Haschbasch, as he entered his native cottage, now somewhat out of repair; "I will be a diver for pearls, again."

"A diver for nonsense!" cried Fatima. "Look here!"—and she produced the golden box containing the pearls as big as pigeons' eggs.

"Curse them!" cried he, snatching it out of her hand, and fleeing towards the shores of the gulf so swiftly, that Fatima, who was a Mohammedan beauty, and somewhat lusty, could not overtake him. He arrived at the spot where he had seen the genius, and, opening the box, threw the pearls, one by one, against the same rock on which he had broken the oyster, so violently that they were all dashed to pieces.

He had no sooner finished the last than a smoke, such as he had formerly seen, rose in the same spot, and, as it slowly dissipated, he again recognised the little fat Genius of Oysters, as jolly and round as ever; for, be it remembered, it was now the month of October, and his old enemy, the necromantic alderman, could not prevent his eating his fill according to law.

"Thou seest I am better lodged than I was, the last time we met. But what is the matter, and what brings thee here?" said the genius.

Haschbasch told the whole story, and concluded by reproaching the genius for sending him to Ispahan with such a fatal gift.

"I have scarcely had a comfortable moment," said he, "since I possessed those accursed pearls."

"I can only give the means of happiness," answered the genius, "not happiness itself; that depends upon thyself. Go, and be a diver again; and, if thou art content with thy lot, thou mayst be happy." So saying, he disappeared for ever in the blue waters, and Haschbasch returned home.

Fatima scolded him for destroying the pearls, but she was a good-natured soul, and soon forgave him, and loved him better than when he was a governor and a prince.

On the return of Haschbasch with a wife, his old sweetheart had murmured a little. He took her to himself as a second helpmate, and Fatima and little Flimflam lived together in perfect harmony. What a peace-making religion is that of Mohammed!

KILLING, NO MURDER.

KILLING, NO MURDER.

A TRUE STORY.

I AM a sober, middle-aged, married gentleman, of a moderate size; with moderate wishes, moderate means, a moderate family, and everything moderate about me, except my house, which is too large for my means, or my family. It is, however, or rather, alas! it was, an old family mansion, full of old things of no value but to the owner, as connected with early associations and ancient friends, and I did not like the idea of converting it into a tavern or boarding-house, as is the fashion with the young heirs of the present day. Such as it was, however, although I sometimes felt a little like the ambitious snail who once crept into a lobster's shell and came near perishing in a hard winter, I managed for ten or twelve years to live in it very comfortably, and to make both ends meet. My furniture, to be sure, was a little out of fashion, and here and there a little out at the elbows; but I always persuaded myself that it was respectable to be out of fashion, and that new things smacked of new men, and were, therefore, rather vulgar. Under this impression, I lived in my old house, with my old-fashioned furniture, moderate-sized family, and moderate means, envying nobody and indebted to no one in the world. I had neither gilded furniture, nor grand mantel-glasses, nor superb chandeliers; but then I had a few fine pictures and busts, and flattered myself they were much more genteel than gilded furniture, grand mantel-glasses, and superb chandeliers. In truth, I looked down with contempt not only on these, but on all those who did not agree with me in opinion. I never asked a person to dinner a second time who did not admire my busts and pictures, considering him a vulgar fellow and an admirer of ostentatious trumpery.

But let no man presume, after reading my story, to flatter himself he is out of the reach of the infection of fashion and fashionable opinions. He may hold out for a certain time, perhaps, but human nature can't stand forever on the defensive. The example of all around us is irresistible, sooner or later. The first shock given to my attachment to respectable old-fashioned furniture and a respectable old foursquare double house was received from the elbow of a modern worthy, who had grown rich, nobody knew how, by presiding over the drawing of lotteries, and who came and built himself a narrow four-story house right at the side of my honest foursquare double mansion. It had white marble steps, white marble door and window sills, folding doors and marble mantel-pieces, and was as fine as a fiddle, within and without. It put my rusty old mansion quite out of countenance, as everybody told me, though I assure my readers I thought it excessively tawdry and in bad taste.

But, alas! — such is the stupidity of mankind — I could get nobody to agree with me.

"What has come over your house, lately?" cried one good-natured visitor; "somehow or other it don't look as it used to do."

"What makes your house seem so rusty and old-fashioned?" said another good-natured visitor.

"Mr. Blankprize has taken the shine off of you," said Mrs. Sowerby; "HE HAS KILLED YOUR HOUSE!"

Hereupon the spirit moved me to go out and reconnoitre the venerable mansion. It certainly did look a little like a chubby, rusty, old-fashioned Quaker by the side of a first-rate dandy. I picked a quarrel with it outright, which, by the way, was a very unlucky quarrel. I was not rich enough to pull it down and build a new one; and it is great folly to quarrel with an old house until you can get a better. But if I can't build, I can paint, thought I, and put at least as good a *face* on the matter as this opulent lottery-man, my next-door neighbour. Accordingly, I consulted my wife on the subject, who, whether from a spirit of contradiction, or, to do her justice, I believe from a correct and rational view of the subject, discouraged my project. I was only the more determined. So I caused my honest old house to be painted a bright cream color, that it might hold up its head against the scurvy lottery-man.

"Bless me!" quoth Mrs. Smith; "what is the matter with this room? It don't look as it used to do."

"Why, what under the sun have you done to this room?" cried Mrs. Brown.

"Protect me!" exclaimed Mrs. White; "why, I

seem to have got into a strange room. What is the matter?"

"You've killed the inside of your house," said Mrs. Sowerby, "by painting the outside such a bright color."

It was too true; this was my first crime. Would I had stopped here!—but destiny determined otherwise. It happened, unfortunately, that my front parlour carpet was of a yellow ground. It was, to be sure, somewhat faded by time and use; but it comported very well with the unpretending sobriety of the outside of my house, under the old *régime*. But the case was altered now, and the bright cream color of the outside "*killed*" the dingy yellow carpet within. So I bought a new carpet, of a fine orange ground, determined that this should not be killed. It looked very fine, and I was satisfied. I had done the business effectually.

"Bless my soul!" cried Mrs. Smith; "what a sweet pretty carpet!"

"Save us!" exclaimed Mrs. Brown; "why, you look as fine as twopence!"

"Protect us!" cried Mrs. Sowerby; "what a fashionable affair!" Then, casting a knowing look around the room, she added, in a tone of hesitating candor, "But, don't you think, somehow or other, it kills the curtains?"

Another murder! thought I;—wretch that I am, what have I done? What is done cannot be undone; but I can remedy the affair. So I bought a new suit of yellow curtains. I thought I had 'em now.

Mrs. Sowerby came the very next day.

"Well, I declare, now this *is* charming! I never

saw more *tasty* curtains. But, my dear Mr. Sobersides, somehow or other, don't you think they KILL THE WALLS?"

Murder again! Killed, four lath-and-plaster walls! But I'll get the better of Mrs. Sowerby yet. So I got the walls colored as bright as the curtains, and bade her defiance in my heart the next time she came.

Mrs. Sowerby arrived as usual. Her whole life was spent in visiting about everywhere, and putting people out of conceit with themselves.

She threw up her eyes and hands. "Well, I declare, Mr. Sobersides, you have done wonders. This is the real French-white" — which, by the way, my unlearned readers should know, is yellow. "But," continued this pestilent woman, "don't you think that these bright-colored walls KILL THE CHAIRS?"

Worse and worse! Here were twelve innocent old arm-chairs, with yellow satin bottoms and backs, murdered in cold blood, by four unfeeling French-white shiny walls! But there is a remedy for all things but death. I forthwith procured a new set of chairs as yellow as custard, and snapped my fingers in triumph at Mrs. Sowerby the next time she came.

But, alas! what are all the towering hopes of man? Dust, ashes, emptiness, nothing. Mrs. Sowerby was not yet satisfied. She thought the chairs beautiful: —

"But, then, my dear friend," said she, after a solemn and appalling pause, "my dear friend, these bright yellow satin chairs HAVE KILLED THE PICTURE-FRAMES."

And so they had, as dead as Julius Cæsar; the picture-frames looked like old lumber in the midst of all my improvements. There was no help for it, and away went the frames to Messrs. Parker and Clover. In good time they came back, "redeemed, regenerated, and disenthralled." I was so satisfied now that there was nothing left in my parlour to be killed, that I could hardly sleep that night, so impatient was I to see Mrs. Sowerby.

That baleful creature, when she came next day, looked round in evident disappointment, but exclaimed, with great appearance of cordiality,

"Well, now I declare, it's all perfect; there is not a handsomer room in town."

Thank heaven! thought I, I have committed no more murders. But I reckoned without my host. I was destined to go on murdering, in spite of me. The spring was now coming on, and, the weather being mild, the folding doors had been thrown open between the front and back parlours. This latter was furnished with green, somewhat faded I confess. I had heretofore considered it the *sanctum sanctorum* of the establishment. It was only used on extraordinary occasions, such as Christmas and New-Year days, when all the family dined with me, bringing their little children with them to gormandize themselves sick. The room looked very well by itself; but, alas! the moment Mrs. Sowerby caught sight of it, her eye brightened — fatal omen!

"Why, my dear Mr. Sobersides, what has got into your back parlour? It used to be so genteel and smart. Why, I believe I'm losing my eyesight. The green carpet and curtains look quite yellow, I think. O, I see it now — THE FRONT PARLOUR HAS KILLED THE BACK ONE!"

The dickens! Here was another pretty piece of business. I must either keep the door shut all summer and be roasted, or be charged with killing a whole parlour — carpet, curtains, chairs, sofas, walls, and all.

It would be a mere repetition to relate how this wicked woman again led me on from one murder to another. First the new carpet "killed" the curtains; then the new curtains "killed" the walls; the new painted walls "killed" the old satin chairs; and so, by little and little, all my honest old green furniture went the way of the honest old yellow.

"The spell is broken at last," cried I, rubbing my hands in ecstasy. Neither my front nor back parlour can commit any more assassinations. Elated with the idea, I was waiting on Mrs. Sowerby to the front door, when suddenly she stopped short at the foot of the old-fashioned winding staircase, the carpet of which, I confess, was here and there infested with that modern abomination — a darn. It was, moreover, rather dingy and faded.

"Your back parlour HAS KILLED YOUR HALL," said Mrs. Sowerby.

And so it had. Coming out of the splendour of the former, the latter had the same effect on the beholder as a bad set of teeth in a fine face, or an old rusty iron grate in a handsome room.

I began to be desperate. I had been accessory to so many cruel murders that my conscience became seared, and I went on, led by the wiles of this daughter of Satan, to murder my way from the ground-floor to the cockloft, without sparing a single soul. Nothing escaped but the garret, which, having been for half a century the depository of all our broken or banished household gods, resembled Hogarth's picture of the "End of the World," and defied the arts of that mischievous monster, Mrs. Sowerby.

My house was now fairly revolutionized, or rather, reformed, after the French mode, by a process of indiscriminate destruction.

I did not, like Alexander, after having thus conquered one world, sigh for another to conquer. I sat down to enjoy my victory under the shade of my laurels. But, alas!, disappointment ever follows at the heels of fruition. It is pleasant to dance, until we come to pay the piper. By the time custom had familiarized me to my new glories, and they had become somewhat indifferent, bills came pouring in by dozens, and it was impossible to kill my duns as I had done my old furniture, except by paying them, a mode of destroying these troublesome vermin not always convenient or agreeable. From the period of commencing housekeeping until now, I had never once had occasion to put off the payment of a bill. I prided myself on always paying ready money for everything, and it was an honest pride. I can hardly express the mortification I felt at being now occasionally under the necessity of giving excuses instead of money. I had a miserable invention at this sort of work of imagination, and sometimes, when more than usually barren, I got into a passion, which is a common shift of people when they don't know what else to do. More than once I found myself suddenly turning a corner in a great hurry, or planting myself before the window of a picture-shop, studying it very attentively, so as not to notice certain persons, the very sight of whom is always painful to people of nice sensibility.

Not being hardened to such trifles by long use, I felt rather sore and irritable. Under the old *régime* it had always been a pleasure to me to hear a ring at the door, because it was the signal for an agreeable visitor; but now it excited disagreeable apprehensions, and sounded like the knell of a dun. In short, I grew crusty and fidgety by degrees, insomuch that Mrs. Sowerby often exclaimed:—

"Why, what has come over you, Mr. Sobersides? Why, I declare, somehow or other you don't seem the same man you used to be."

I could have answered, "The new Mr. Sobersides has killed the old Mr. Sobersides." But I said nothing, and only wished her up in the garret, among the old furniture.

My system of reform produced another source of worrying. Hitherto my old furniture and myself had been so long acquainted, that I could take all sorts of liberties with it. I could recline on the sofas of an evening, or sit on one of the old chairs and cross my legs on another, without the least ceremony. But now, forsooth!, it is as much as I dare do to sit down upon one of my new acquaintance; and as for a lounge on the sofa, which was the Cleopatra for which I would have lost the world, I should as soon think of taking a nap in a fine lady's sleeve. As to my little rantipole boys, who had hitherto feared neither carpet, chair, nor sofa, they have at length been schooled into such awe of finery, that they walk about the parlour on tiptoe, sit on the edge of a chair with trepidation, and contemplate the sofas at a distance with the most profound veneration, as unapproachable divinities. To cap the climax of my ill-starred follies, my easy-old-shoe friends, who came to see me without ceremony because they felt comfortable and welcome, have gradually become shy of my novel magnificence; and the last of them was the other evening fairly *looked* out of the house by a certain person, for spitting accidentally upon a new brass fender, that shone like the sun at noonday.

I might hope that in the course of time these evils would be mitigated by the furniture growing old and sociable by degrees, but there is little prospect of this, because it is too fine for common use. The carpet is always protected by a worn crum-cloth, full of holes and stains; the sofas and chairs are in dingy coversluts, except on extraordinary occasions, and I fear they will last forever — at least, longer than I shall. I sometimes solace myself with the anticipation that my children may live long enough to sit on the sofas with impunity, and walk on the carpet without going on tiptoe.

There would be some consolation in the midst of these sore evils if I could only fix the reproach of them on my wife. Many philosophers are of opinion, that this single privilege of matrimony is more than equivalent to all the rubs and disappointments of life; and I have heard a very wise person affirm, that he would not mind being ruined, at all, if he could only blame his wife for it. But I must do mine the justice to say, that she combated Mrs. Sowerby gallantly, and threw every obstacle in the way of my rash improvements, advocating the cause of every piece of old furniture with a zeal worthy of better success. I alone am to blame in having yielded to the temptations of that wicked woman, Mrs. Sowerby; and, as a man who has ruined himself by his own imprudence is the better qualified for giving good advice, I have written this sketch of my own history, to caution all honest, sober, discreet people against commencing a system of reform in their household. LET THEM BEWARE OF THE FIRST MURDER!

SIX WEEKS IN THE MOON.

SIX WEEKS IN THE MOON.

From my earliest recollection I have felt a great disposition to travel, which I inherit from my mother, who had a special vocation for out-door business, and who never missed a camp-meeting, an execution, or a quilting-frolic. So strong was this impulse, which I may almost call instinctive, that I remember on one occasion, instead of going to school, which was close by, I wandered away to a horse-race, several miles distant; and, at another time, being sent on an errand to a neighboring grocery store, I strolled to a pond a long way off, where I amused myself with skating on a pair of ox-bones. In short, my mother was at last obliged to dress me in petticoats, to prevent my straying. This passion for wandering increased as I grew up to manhood, and became at length unconquerable, in consequence of the late facilities afforded to travellers, by the introduction of steam-boats and locomotives. For my part, I don't see how it is possible for any rational, intelligent person to stand still in this age of progress. Even my grandmother — who is now fourscore, and so afflicted with Neuralgia, as the doctors call it, that she lies in bed half the time when at home — goes every year to Wisconsin, to visit a second cousin; and my good mother often travels thirty miles, to drink tea and discuss women's rights.

On arriving at the age of twenty-one, and becoming my own master, with a competent fortune, I determined to indulge this natural propensity. But an unexpected obstacle presented itself at the outset. The great difficulty was to find a country that had not been as often overrun by travellers as Syria and Egypt by locusts. At one time I had prepared everything for California; but, being unluckily detained a fortnight by indisposition, I found, on my recovery, that, in the interim, three tours, five reconnoissances, and seven explorations had been published. I then made up my mind to take a trip to the land of Egypt, and visit the Red Sea, the Dead Sea, Mount Sinai, and the cataracts of the Nile. But, on talking over the subject with a knowing bookseller, to whom I applied to publish my anticipated travels, he pointed to a whole shelf of books of travels in Egypt, the Holy Land, Arabia Felix, and Arabia Deserta, which he assured me contained nothing but repetitions of each other. I don't wonder at this, since such is the bad credit of travellers, that nobody will believe them without an endorser. Thus, wherever I turned my face, I found some one had been before me, until I was fairly driven to Australia, New Zealand, Van Dieman's Land, and the Mulgrave Islands, for a new field of action. But here too I was forestalled, by the discovery of gold in Australia, and was just on the point of sitting down in despair and turning philanthropist, or "*canvassing*" for subscriptions to periodicals, both which give great opportunities for seeing the world, when, lolling on my piazza one evening, my attention was providentially directed to that blessed planet, the Moon, which was then shining full in my face. It at once occurred to me, that, though I had often seen what pretended to be descriptions of the Moon by lying travellers and planet-struck stargazers, no authentic account of the country or its inhabitants had ever been given to the world; for, as to the legends of my Lord Rosse and the rest of those impostors that pretend to know so much about these matters, I shall show in the sequel that they know no more about them than the Man in the Moon himself — nay, not one tenth part as much; for I have evidence that he is not such an ignoramus as most people believe.

I therefore resolved at once to make the tour of the Moon. But how to get there was the difficulty. Various plans occurred to me, but had to be discarded as impracticable. At length I determined to consult the Spirits of Knocking, who all come from the Moon. Accordingly, I visited a first-rate "medium," who, by dint of a considerable quantity of knocks, called up the spirit of Pythagoras, which, after making me swear to seven years' silence, communicated a process by which any man could ascend to, and descend from, the Moon, as easily as a ray of light. What this process is, I cannot disclose without breaking my faith with Pythagoras; and, if this were not the case, I should keep the secret, because I mean to reserve the Moon all to myself, as an inexhaustible mine, and am perfectly assured, that, if I once showed the way, the poor planet would be as much pestered with adventurers as the Isthmus of Panama, the upper Nile, or California.

Let it suffice, that I arrived safely in the Moon, on the first of April, 1852, but at what hour I cannot say, as time goes backwards in that planet, which is a great advantage to the people, who can thus undo what they have done, without the least difficulty. While seeking for lodgings, the people gathered round in crowds, laughing most vociferously to see me walking forwards instead of backwards, as I found was the universal custom here. This, they assured me, was what they called "Progress"—in other words, growing wise by Experience, the safest of all guides, who always looks behind him, as every-body knows.

Having brought letters of introduction from Pythagoras, and a learned judge who is well known in the Moon, I was soon on the best terms with the literary and scientific portion of the community, one of whom carried me to pay my respects to the Man in the Moon, who, though not the actual legitimate sovereign, was a sort of Joe Smith or Brigham Young, and governed the people by inspiration. I found him a venerable old man, with a long beard, who, though bowed down by age, had yet a certain lustrous twinkling of the eyes that spoke volumes. He received me with great courtesy, and we had a long conversation on various subjects, in the course of which I discovered he was by no means either a madman or a simpleton, as has been represented. Indeed, he complained to me of the great injustice that had been done him in this respect, and condescended to give me a sketch of his life, of which I shall offer only a few leading particulars.

He traced all the misfortunes of his career to being wiser than his neighbors, and always in advance of the rest of mankind, the consequence of which was, that everybody called him mad, because he saw things they could not see, and foretold what never came to pass, owing to the obstinate, wayward stupidity of his fellow-creatures, who delighted in arresting events that ought to have happened, according to all reasonable calculation. It was always a great object of his ambition, to understand matters incomprehensible to all others; to achieve undertakings that others pronounced impossible; and to develop mysteries which had turned the brains of all those who had meddled with them. He assured me he had discovered the principle of perpetual motion, though he could never bring it into practical application; that he had actually taken the great Beast in Revelation by the horns; was acquainted with the occult mysteries of Spiritual Knockings, which he had taught several of his disciples, who had a predisposition to become "mediums;" and had mastered the process of making gold, which, however, he now never put in practice, since the discoveries in California and Australia had so diminished the value of that metal, that it cost more to make it than it was worth. These studies, which had hitherto addled other men's brains, he assured me, were mere sport to him. "But, alas!" said the old gentleman, "I at length found there were deeper mysteries, more profound depths of speculation, than these. I undertook to search for the wisdom of Congress, and that did my business." He complained bitterly of the injustice done to himself and his people, first, by the common saying, "I know no more than the man in the Moon," and secondly, by calling a species of madmen Lunatics, for it was plain to the meanest understanding, that the **people of the** Moon, inheriting the lost wits of all mankind, must of necessity be the wisest in the world. **He also spoke** with great **indignation** of the **enormous** fallacies **set** afloat by the astronomers, concerning the Moon, which he affirmed had no more to **do** with the tides, the changes of weather, **the wits** of men, or the shrinking of corned beef, than any **of** the planets. I was surprised at his knowing **so much** about the earth, until **he** told me he got all the news from people who were every day banished from that quarter, for being wiser than their neighbours.

Having received a passport from the good old man, with full permission to travel where I pleased, accompanied by **a** caution against the common infirmity of travellers, which **I** have observed most implicitly, I mounted a Spiritual Telegraph, **(a** great improvement on that of Mr. Morse), and **was** precipitated through the entire planet with such prodigious velocity, that, when I had completed my flight, I found I knew no more of the country than an English traveller who has made a tour of the United States. I therefore determined to go over the ground more leisurely, and adopt the mode of pedestrianism universally practised here, as I mentioned before. **I** can assure my readers it is not without its advantages, at least in point of safety, since **it is** notorious that a great portion of the dangers, insults, and aggressions we encounter **in** this world approach us from the **rear.**

As I proceeded, **I** found the people separated into distinct classes, the first in rank of which were the Spiritual Knockers, who, by virtue of their communion with superior beings, carried their heads above their fellow-mortals, who kept only the lowest kind of company. I asked one of them, very civilly, what was the use of this kind of spiritual agency, and he answered me rather contemptuously — " Use, sir ? I have already learned by direct communication with Sir Isaac Newton, that, since he became an inhabitant of the world of spirits, he has discovered that his system of gravity is only fit to be laughed at; and have been assured by Franklin that the moving principle of thought, impulse, and action, in all animals, rational as well as irrational, is electricity. Use, sir ? I should like to know how I could have discovered all this without communication with the spirits ? " I spoke of this as being only a revival of the visions of Swedenborg, which put him in a great passion. " Swedenborg ! " exclaimed he. " Pooh ! he only went half way ; but we go the whole hog, as the spirits say in these parts."

The most numerous, as well as the most zealous of the Knockers, were spinsters of a certain age, who seemed inclined to make themselves amends for the absence of flesh and blood beaux, by midnight flirtations with spiritual ones. There were, also, some desperate widows, and not a few persons whom I should have mistaken for reverend divines, had they not been so sweet upon the ladies, who seemed to take them for spiritual beings, for they did not at all mind being alone with them at midnight in bedchambers, in the investigation of these profound mysteries. The great bulk, however, of this sect consisted of people a little deficient in the furniture of the upper story. I expressed some commiseration for these to a sober, discreet person, who was a looker-on as well as myself, but he coolly replied, " It is of very little consequence, for if they had not run mad about spiritual knockings, they would have gone crazy about something else equally absurd and ridiculous." One of the " mediums" asked me if I would not like to have a talk with my great-great-grandfather, but as he happened to have been *Sus.-per-col.*, and no great credit to the family, I declined making his acquaintance.

Travelling onward, I arrived at a great city, where the inhabitants had made such rapid progress towards the perfection of everything, that they were compelled to go backwards in order to accommodate themselves to the pace of their neighbours. One of the most distinguished of the savans was a famous geologist, who had become so familiar with the materials of which the world is composed, that he undertook to make one to suit himself, and avoid all the errors in the construction of the old one. Being the great lion of the place, I paid him a visit, and found him hard at work, but he confessed that thus far he had made but a poor business of it. " It is strange," said he; " I have got all the materials, but, somehow or other, I can't put them together. I find it is not so easy to make a world as I thought." The next visit I paid was to a man who had the reputation of being a great seaman, though his experience had been principally on land and in his closet, as I was told. I found him busy in constructing a theory of winds and currents, by which he assured me the time and dangers in navigating vessels would be greatly diminished, if not altogether annulled. He pointed out to me on the chart the course which the winds and currents ought to go, if they respected his theory. "If," said he, "I could only get that obstinate old fogy, Experience, to be a little accommodating, I should establish my system beyond controversy; but, the mischief is, he won't pay the least attention to me; and, what is still more provoking, the winds and currents are, if possible, yet more impracticable; they are as obstinate as mules; and every navigator who, at my request, particularly noted these matters, assures me they seem to delight in running counter to my directions. But never mind; the learned, who study these matters in their closets and understand them much better than these illiterate tarpaulins, have all complimented me on my hypothesis, and, what is still better, almost all the members of Congress have become my converts."

"What!" exclaimed I, "have you a Congress in the Moon?"

"To be sure we have," replied he. "It is composed of men who have inherited the greatest possible portion of the lost wits of your planet, and who, I am happy to say, pay more regard to my theories than to the experience of all the officers of our navy put together. They are all men of Progress, and, between ourselves, sometimes are in such a hurry that they tread on their own noses."

This city abounded in lecturers on every conceivable subject. There was a lecturer on political economy, whom I found discussing a project for getting immense treasure from all sorts of people, and enriching them by taking it away. There was another, lecturing from a sand-hill to a great crowd, on socialism. In order to exemplify his theory, he heaped up great numbers of little sand-hills, all exactly of a size; but, unfortunately, as fast as he did this, a puff of wind disturbed the equilibrium of his system, and he was obliged to begin again. There was a female lecturer, who, by virtue of having a considerable beard, had set up as a champion of the rights of women. She was backed by a parson, who quoted Scripture to show that the Bible was behind the spirit of the age; and I could not help thinking that this union of the gown and the petticoat foreboded an awful catastrophe to the breeches.

These anticipations were speedily realized; for my next plunge was into the midst of a Female Republic, established on the principle of the rights of women. As I approached this regenerated region, I heard a great buzzing in the air, something like that we observe on approaching a bee-hive. This, I found on my arrival, proceeded from the legislative hall, where the female deputies had met, to discuss the fashions of caps and nether garments becoming their elevated position. They were all talking at once; for even the speakeress had her tongue constantly in motion, crying, "Order, ladies, order." But nobody seemed to hear her, or at least nobody minded her, and there was a perfect Babel. Finally, the previous question was called for, which threw several members into hysterics, and the house separated without adjournment. I was told that they had been in session several weeks, but no question had as yet been put; and one of the first practical difficulties experienced in this new system of petticoat government was found to be the utter impossibility of bringing a debate to a conclusion. At the hotel where I put up, I found the landlord rocking the cradle, and his wife dealing out mint-juleps to a parcel of Rights-of-Women devotees, who were smoking and chewing tobacco, and swearing like troopers. I had hitherto been an enthusiastic admirer of the sex, insomuch that I cannot recollect the time, since I arrived at years of discretion, in which I was not desperately in love; and to such a pitch did I carry this devotion that I have been three times cast in heavy damages, for breach of promises which I never made. But ever since I witnessed the scene just described, I never think of a pretty woman without feeling a little qualmish, as it were. Indeed I found the general complaint of the married women was, that their husbands no longer loved them; and of the married men, that their wives were always making love to them, thus infringing on their ancient inalienable rights. Certain it is, I never witnessed such a state of things, and was glad to get out of this Female Republic, especially after a strapping damsel had made a demonstration towards me that I thought very suspicious. Leaving this last stage of Lunar Progress backwards, I next came to another large town, where I found all the people walking rapidly around in a circle. Behold, on arriving at the point whence they started, they turned round and went back again. I inquired of one, who was in a great perspiration with his exertions, what he was doing. "What am I doing?" answered he, in high dudgeon, — "don't you see I am making Progress?" And away he went, whirling about like a dervis, or a lady waltzing.

In this city was a famous University, reckoned to be the most erudite in the Moon, because, though all the students carried a little learning with them there, few of them brought any away. Though no great scholar myself, I am a devoted admirer of learning, and, having procured a letter of introduction to the Professor of Transcendentalism, paid him a visit. He was very polite, and gave me a particular account of the system of education and discipline practised in the University. He informed me the basis of the system was utility, and that nothing was taught but what tended to that primary object.

The first class consisted of little children, of from five to seven years old, whom the teachers were stuffing with knowledge, as we serve turkeys, by thrusting it down their throats. I asked the Professor if they were not sometimes troubled with indigestion, and he told me, that, whenever this was the case, they stuffed them a little more, on the principle that the hair of a dog is good for his bite. They were taught geology, chemistry, astronomy, geography, and various other sciences, all at the same time, by questions and answers; and I noticed that, though the organ of memory was prodigiously developed, those of the other faculties had become almost invisible. They were not allowed to play at all, the professors being of opinion that it produced dissipation of mind, and drew their attention from their studies. Most of them looked rather pale and sickly, but the Professor observed, that, as knowledge was power, physical weakness was of little consequence. He requested me to experiment on them, and I found they could meet almost every question, the answer to which they had learned from books. I remember I asked one about the river Mississippi, and he told me it was a river in North America, which rose in the Gulf of

Mexico, and discharged its waters into Cedar Lake. I undertook to put him right, but the Professor interposed, and informed me that, according to the theory of the Moonites, all rivers began where they ended, and ended where they began.

From this class we proceeded to others, until we came to that consisting of those who were preparing to take their degrees. I found them engaged in various occupations, calculated, as the Professor said, to make them useful citizens. Some of these appeared to me to be rather strangely employed. I remember there was one who was washing a blackamoor white, by rubbing him with an abolition lecture. Another was planting potatoes in dry straw, and the Professor assured me, that he would not only have a great crop, but could at the same time roast his potatoes by setting fire to the straw. Another was catching beetles, and suffocating them in a little tin box, which, he said, was a great step in philanthropy, as this was a much easier mode of killing them than sticking pins. Another was extracting water from pumice-stones; another, milking goats in a sieve; another, shearing donkeys, and converting their hair into fine fleeces of wool; another, ploughing with a compass, in order to make straight furrows; and another, measuring how far a flea could jump. There were many others very busily occupied in various equally-useful pursuits, but I omit them for fear of being tedious.

We next visited the library, which, the Professor assured me, contained a vast many books to be found in no other collection. There were certainly many that I never heard of before, and I took a memorandum of a few of them, with the hope that they may be one day republished by some of our enterprising booksellers, especially as they will pay no copyright. The following list will suggest the general character of these volumes:

The World of Spirits, by A Teetotaller.
Speculations on Indivisible Atoms, by a Purblind Philosopher.
Nebulæana; or, the Planets in Embryo.
The Philosophy of Bacon, exemplified in Smoking Hams.
The Transmigration of Souls proved by the Change of Tadpoles into Bull-Frogs.
How Oysters may be made to climb up to the Tops of Mountains.
Dissertation on Chaos, showing how the World was made by Coral Insects, and rose from the Bottom of the Sea.
The Bottle-Conjurer, or Chemist's Manual.
Pathology of Sneezing.
Trip to Parnassus, or, Rules for Criticising Poetry on Mechanical Principles.
The Scrub-Race of Politicians.
The System of Progressing Backwards.
Gooseology, or, the Art of Standing on One Leg.
On the Feasibility of establishing a Universal Language of Signs, whereby Dumb Men would be on a Par with the Rest of their Fellow-Creatures.
Dissertation, proving that all Men's Virtues proceed from their Faults, and all their Faults from their Virtues.
The Cobweb of Metaphysicians.
Ichthyophagy, or, the Mysteries of the Loaves and Fishes.

Plan for supplying Rivers with Water, by Means of Hydraulic Rams.

Plan for reforming Scolding Wives, by making all Married Men deaf.

A Dissertation on the Causes why Old Men lose the Hair of their Heads, while their Beards continue to grow and flourish.

Remarkable Case of Professor Windygust, who, having all his Life been accustomed to swallowing Wind-mills, was at length choked by a Lump of Soft Butter he found at the Mouth of a Hot Oven.

This is only a small sample of the scarce and valuable books and manuscripts contained in this unique library. Many of the latter, as the Professor assured me, were rescued from the flames, during the wanton destruction of the Alexandrian Library.

The Professor then took me to the Hall of Disputation, where the faculty were debating interesting questions of science and philosophy. Among the rest, I remember one that was very learnedly discussed. It was, whether goat's hair was wool or not; and I was astonished to find what interesting results were involved in the question. Another was, which of the legs of a goose was his right one. The great difficulty in deciding the point was, that one of the disputants placed himself at the head, the other at the tail, of the goose. Hence, what appeared to one the right leg seemed to the other the left. I know not to what length the argument would have been carried, for both parties were getting rather warm, had not the moderator suggested that each of the disputants should imagine himself a goose, and then there would be no difficulty in ascertaining which was his right leg. This simple expedient settled the point to the satisfaction of all parties, and it was decided that the debate should be published in the Transactions of the Philosophical Society.

I was about to bid farewell to my friend the Professor, and return thanks for his attentions, when I received a telegraphic despatch, informing me that I had been "cornered" in a speculation in Canton stock, entered into previous to the commencement of my tour. This rendered my immediate presence necessary below stairs, and I accordingly made tracks towards home, leaving a great part of the moon unexplored. But I faithfully promise the reader, that, if I once get out of this "corner," without being a lame duck, he shall one day see the remainder of my travels.

A MOOD OF NATURE AND OF MAN.

A MOOD OF NATURE AND OF MAN.

I feel this morning a sort of humourous sadness; a sense of loneliness, and absence, and carelessness, that half amounts to a gentlemanlike melancholy. I believe I could entertain a score or two of blue devils; and be actually doleful, if I could only find a tolerable apology for gloom. Unluckily, I cannot light on a reasonable excuse to be unhappy; for I have got well of all my complaints, real and imaginary; have a fair supply of paper-money for my occasions; have buried my fears of French influence, ever since Napoleon began to grow fat;—and am a bachelor. Yet for all this, could I rail at the first-born of Egypt, and even find fault with the worthy lady at whose dwelling we now are, detained by a shower, although her face is the picture of good-humour, and her house the abode of good cheer. I intended to reason a little this morning on cause and effect—a new subject!—but I reasoned, as people sometimes get up of a morning, wrong end foremost. I then joked the waiter, but got worsted, which only made me more dismal than before. This state of mind, under the influence of which the heart falls into a heavy depression, without any particular cause that we know of, is sometimes ascribed to a presentiment of approaching evil — a warning coming from some mysterious source with which we are altogether unacquainted. But this is a superstitious idea, and consequently discarded by philosophers, who, in general, attribute it to an absence of real sources of misery, which leaves a vacuum for imaginary ones to creep in and make a great bustle. They say the best and only radical cure for this mental disorder is substantial care and actual trouble; and, accordingly, agree in recommending matrimony as a sovereign remedy; that being the great evil which renders all others insignificant. But, instead of flying to this desperate specific, I will try what occupation of mind will do in the way of relief.

In truth, the solitary nook into which I am just now thrown bears an aspect so interesting, that it is calculated to call up the most touchingly-pleasing emotions, in the minds of those who love to indulge in the contemplation of beautiful scenes. We are the sons of earth, and the indissoluble kinship between nature and man is demonstrated by our sense of her charms. I shall not soon forget last evening. It was such as can never be described: I will, therefore, not attempt it; but it was still as the sleep of innocence, pure as ether, and bright as immortality. It happened that I strolled out alone along the windings of a little stream about twenty yards wide, that skirts a narrow strip of green meadow, between the brook and the high mountain close at hand. You will confess my landscapes are well watered, for every one has a river. But such is the case in this region, where all the passes of the mountains are made by streams, that, in process of time, have laboured through, and left a space for a road on their banks. If nature will do these things, I can't help it — not I. In the course of the ramble the moon rose over the mountain to the eastward, which, being just by, seemed to bring her visage equally near; and the bright eyes of the stars began to glisten, as if weeping the dews of evening. I knew not the name of one single star. But what of that? It is not necessary to be an astronomer, to contemplate with exalted emotions the glories of the sky at night, and the countless wonders of the universe.

> "These earthly godfathers of Heaven's lights,
> That give a name to every fixed star,
> Have no more profit of their living nights,
> Than those that walk and wot not what they are."

Men may be too wise to wonder at anything; as they may be too ignorant to see anything without wondering. There is reason also to believe that astronomers may be sometimes so taken up with measuring the distances and magnitude of the stars, as to lose, in the intense minuteness of calculation, that noble expansion of feeling and intellect combined, which lifts from nature up to its great first cause. As respects myself, I know no more of these orbs than the man in the moon. I only contemplate them as unapproachable, inextinguishable fires, glittering afar off, in those azure fields whose beauty and splendour have pointed them out as the abode of the Divinity. As such, they form bright links in the chain of thought that leads directly to a contemplation of the Maker of heaven and earth. Nature is, indeed, the only temple worthy of the Deity. There is a mute eloquence in her smile; a majestic severity in her frown; a divine spell in her harmony; a speechless energy in her silence; a voice in her thunders, that no reflecting being can resist. It is in such scenes and seasons, that the heart is most deeply smitten with the power and goodness of Providence, and that the soul demonstrates its capacity for maintaining an existence independent of matter, by abstracting itself from the body, and expatiating alone in the boundless regions of the past and the future.

As I continued strolling forward, there gradually came a perfect calm — and even the aspen-tree whispered no more. But it was not the death-like calm of a winter's night, when the whistling wind grows quiet, and the frosts begin in silence to forge fetters for the running brooks and the gentle current of life that flows through the veins of the forest. The voice of man and beast was indeed unheard; but the river murmured, and the insects chirped in the mild summer evening. There is something sepulchral in the stillness of a winter night; but in the genial seasons of the year, though the night is the emblem of repose, it is the repose of the couch, not of the tomb. Nature still breathes in the buzz of insects, the whisperings of the forest, and the babbling of the brooks. We know she will awake in the morning, with her smiles, her bloom, her zephyrs and warbling birds. "In such a night as this," if a man loves any human being in this wide world, he will find it out, for around that being will his thoughts first centre. If he has in store any sweet, or bitter, or bitter-sweet recollections, which are deadened in the rush of business, they will come without being called. If, in his boyish years, he wrestled, and rambled, and wrangled with, yet loved, some chubby boy, he will remember the days of his childhood, its companions, cares, and pleasures. If, in his prime of romance, he used to walk of evenings with some blue-eyed, musing, melancholy maid, whom the ever-rolling wave of life dashed away from him for ever — he will recall her voice, her eye, and her form. If any heavy and severe disaster has fallen on his riper manhood, and turned the future into a gloomy and unpromising wilderness; he will feel it bitterly at such a time. Or if it chance that he is grown an old man, who has lived to see all that owned his blood, or shared his affections, struck down to the earth like dead leaves in autumn; in such a night, he will call their dear shades around, and wish himself a shadow.

THE END.

Cambridge: Press of John Wilson & Son.

www.ingramcontent.com/pod-product-compliance
Lightning Source LLC
Chambersburg PA
CBHW020537300426
44111CB00008B/705